FRINGE FLORIDA

UNIVERSITY PRESS OF FLORIDA

Florida A&M University, Tallahassee
Florida Atlantic University, Boca Raton
Florida Gulf Coast University, Ft. Myers
Florida International University, Miami
Florida State University, Tallahassee
New College of Florida, Sarasota
University of Central Florida, Orlando
University of Florida, Gainesville
University of North Florida, Jacksonville
University of South Florida, Tampa
University of West Florida, Pensacola

# FRINGE FLORIDA

University Press of Florida

Gainesville · Tallahassee · Tampa · Boca Raton

Pensacola · Orlando · Miami · Jacksonville · Ft. Myers · Sarasota

Travels among
Mud Boggers,
Furries, Ufologists,
Nudists, and
Other Lovers of
Unconventional
Lifestyles

LYNN WADDELL

**VIVA FLORIDA 500**
1513-2013

**A Florida Quincentennial Book**

Library of Congress Cataloging-in-Publication Data
Waddell, Lynn.
Fringe Florida : travels among mud boggers, furries, ufologists, nudists,
and other lovers of unconventional lifestyles / Lynn Waddell.
pages cm
Includes bibliographical references.
ISBN 978-0-8130-4493-4 (alk. paper)
1. Lifestyles—Florida. 2. Eccentrics and eccentricities—Florida.
3. Popular culture—Florida. 4. Florida—Social life and customs. I. Title.
HQ2044.U62F58 2013
306.09759—dc23    2013015095

University Press of Florida
15 Northwest 15th Street
Gainesville, FL 32611-2079
http://www.upf.com

To James, my partner in love and life,
and Mom, who never judged anyone but herself

CONTENTS

FRINGE FLORIDA

# Introduction

In 1998 I found myself standing fully clothed amid a herd of one hundred sweaty, shirtless and, in too many cases, bottomless men at a dumpy nudist campground in the wilds of Pasco County. Many were videotaping every jiggle and crevice of the Miss Nude Florida contestant on a makeshift stage. What a shot she was giving them. There in the bright, hot Florida sun, skin gleaming with oil, the nubile woman doubled over, rear to the crowd, showing everything but her uterus.

I'm no prude. I was a casino-beat newspaper reporter in Las Vegas for five years. I was the script researcher for the motion-picture flop *Showgirls* and combed the seediest of strip clubs searching for a dancer who wanted to be on a casino stage. But I was a little stunned, not to mention creeped out, by the tongue-lolling amateur pornographers. I had naively thought this was a nudist community in the purist sense, which is why I showed up to write about the contest for Tampa's alternative newspaper, then called the *Weekly Planet*. On paper at least, I found the event absurdly ironic given that nudism is touted to be about accepting your body as it is, thin or fat, smooth or wrinkled. Not that

I had ever visited a nudist environ, but I had envisioned nudists more as scrawny men with graying hippie beards (of which there were some) and patchouli-lathered women with sagging breasts (of which there were none), kind of a throwback to the 1960s communes, the type of people who would neither enter a beautiful-body contest nor, if they did, win one.

Yet I was here, less than an hour from Disney World's Cinderella Castle and family-friendly beaches where children ride SpongeBob SquarePants® boogie boards, watching young women giving vaginal displays in broad daylight to a horde of horny nude men. Vegas suddenly seemed tame.

Such were my early days in exploring the subcultures, the fringe, of Florida. I spent three years writing for that alternative paper, interviewing everyone from a madam to a retired circus clown. In the ten years that followed, I freelanced, which means, if one is to survive, taking on diverse assignments. I retraced the paths of 9-11 terrorists for *Newsweek*, chased hurricanes for the *New York Times*, and yes, wrote buttery travel stories for state tourism guides. Along the way I delighted in meeting oddball characters—a biker/hoarder with sixty thousand comic books crammed into his tiny house, the Little League mom who brings pet monkeys to her son's games, the retiree who drives his Corvette eighty miles once a week to dance around in women's lingerie at an Ybor City nightclub. I came to realize Florida's uniqueness has less to do with its theme parks and beaches and more to do with the unconventional lifestyles of those who live here.

The idea for this book came from the accumulation of my experiences. Beyond sensational daily headlines, I want to introduce you to unique lifestyles and guide you through places and events that you will never read about in *Travel & Leisure*.

My use of the term "fringe" is not pejorative. These outside-the-norm lifestyles are the decoration of Florida. On a map, the state even looks like a fat piece of fringe dangling from the United States, dividing the Gulf of Mexico and the Atlantic Ocean, and unraveling into the Caribbean.

I spent more than two years traversing America's slice of fringe for this book. I interviewed sideshow folks, people with pet lions, and Spiritualists who communicate with the dead. I rode through Florida muck on a 13-foot-tall swamp buggy and attended taboo events the descriptions of which will no doubt make my parents cringe. I also read almost every book and article I could find on the subjects in this book. Given the underground nature of some, I mined unconventional resources such as chat rooms and online forums, many of which required me to register. My e-mail spam filters went into overdrive.

The result of my reporting and research is this collection of ten vignettes, snapshots of the state's more iconic fringe lifestyles. They span a variety of subjects. Not every chapter's subject is sexual; in fact, most are G-rated. There is even one on Florida's unusual religious tourist attractions.

Given the wealth of fringe in Florida, this book is certainly not a compendium of all. There are countless other subcultures and new ones spawning all the time. By necessity, I established some parameters to determine what to include, or rather what to omit. Each subculture described in this book is distinct in some significant way from its cousins in other states. The lifestyles either originated in Florida or dwarf ones elsewhere in size or prominence. For instance, San Francisco and Boston are hot spots for fetishists who dress up like horses, but Florida is home to the International Pony Play Championships.

Although the chapters touch on seemingly disparate topics, the Floridians throughout this book have much in common. In some cases their interests cross and even morph. They fully immerse in their lifestyle and are not mere hobbyists. Most weren't born in Florida and didn't pursue their fringe with gusto, if at all, until after moving to the Sunshine State.

This brings up the question I've asked and have been asked throughout this project: Why Florida? Why do inhibitions seem to disappear at the state line?

The simplest answer is the state's sunny and mild year-round weather invites it. After all, it's pretty hard to be a full-time nudist or year-round biker in snowy Montana.

The full answer, though, is much more complex and elusive. Florida's diverse population, tourism propaganda, and the predisposition of its residents may all play roles.

Consider that more than two-thirds of Floridians weren't born here. We came by U-Haul trucks, arriving packed like Life Savers on transatlantic jumbo jets, riding flimsy wooden rafts across the powerful Gulf Stream, and sneaking across the Mexican border in the dark of night.

We hail from Yankeeville, the Heartland, the Bible Belt, south of the border and the equator, the Far East, the Wild West, and about every country you can and can't pronounce.

Many move to Florida hoping to start a new life and become whatever they thought they couldn't be in the cloudier place they are from. Such dreams are fed by media and tourism hucksters who for nearly a century have portrayed the state as a magical paradise. Today Florida is the world's top tourism destination. More than 87 million people visit each year to play, and another 19 million live here to do the same.

Most transplants were seduced by Florida tourism promotions before settling here, myself included. Television images of Florida's white sand beaches and Cypress Gardens water-skiers planted a kernel in my mind that the state was one big playground. That anything was possible.

Like many, I got my first taste of that paradise on a childhood vacation, the longest my family of five had ever ventured. Loaded in a Ford tank, we wheeled down from north Alabama to Panama City Beach, what many call the Redneck Riviera, a term I still embrace like a drunk uncle.

I had never seen the ocean before, and I rode the waves on a blow-up raft until my fingers pickled. Lathered in coconut-scented Hawaiian Tropic, I got the worst sunburn of my life. I built sandcastles with new friends. My typically straight-laced dad's spirits rose with every swig of a Budweiser, which he occasionally put down to play with us kids in the Gulf. My mom actually put on a bathing suit for maybe the second time in her life.

I learned to swim that summer in the pool of a motel with multicolored doors across the street from the Miracle Mile Amusement Park with a roller coaster that I thought was a hundred stories high. You could say that vacation eventually led me here. Years later, burned out from chasing daily news deadlines, I joined the ranks of hundreds of thousands who move here each year to start a new life.

Though I'm not a biker, furry, nudist, sideshow performer, or any of the other lifestyles touched on in this book, I'm a voyeur of the unusual, which is a category of fringe in itself. This brings me to the most elusive factor in "Why Florida?" Did Florida make me fringe, or was I drawn here because I already was a little gonzo? I say the latter, but many I spoke with couldn't answer that question about themselves, much less speculate about their fellow fringers. To a fringe voyeur, this conundrum only adds to Florida's mystique. I have no plans to move.

Being a Florida native, my husband, James, can't help but have a little fringe in his veins, too, although he is more reserved than I. He is a multimedia designer, a blend of artist and techno geek, and was my sidekick, sometimes begrudgingly, on some explorations for this book.

While he had trepidations about what I might experience, I began the project with some fear that I would find little that would surprise me. I was wrong. Though rarely shocked, I discovered how much I didn't know about my sunny state and, more important, about humanity in general. However weird or different a person's lifestyle may seem, whatever furry costume they wear, exotic pet they bed with, spirit they worship, or skin they expose, these activities do not wholly define them. Things are not always as they appear. People who dare to pursue an offbeat passion can be quite conventional in other aspects of their lives. I greatly thank all those in this book who expanded this insight. I applaud them for embracing the fringe. And I thank the universe for Florida, a state where fantasies can come true.

# CHAPTER 1

# Menagerie of Fla-zoons

On a sweltering summer afternoon at a Largo community baseball park, a Little League mom fusses over infants inside two fancy strollers complete with miniature parasols. A ten-year-old boy nervously steps up to bat, his oversized helmet floating on his head. His stout dad behind the fences barks for him to step closer to the plate, while his mom in the stands yells for him to move back.

I've joined a friend to watch her son play ball. It seems to be a typically American Little League scene, but in Florida, you don't have to dig deep to reach Middle Earth.

"Did you see the capuchins?" My friend asks excitedly.

I dazedly scan the stands, half-expecting to see a family circus act. I have no idea what she's talking about.

"The monkeys! They're right over there." She points to the baby strollers.

My friend is thrilled because she's crazy about monkeys, not because it's in any way unusual for someone to bring their exotic pets to the games. She's brought the family lemur to more than one.

Today Otis, her ring-tailed pet, is hanging out on a carpeted kitty-cat tree inside a bedroom closet that she converted into his cage. She took apart the accordion doors, stretched wire across the bare frame, and painted the inside walls Madagascar-forest green.

My Lemur Mom friend bought Otis from a neighbor who breeds prosimians in his small backyard. He claims to have sold some to actress Kirstie Alley, who has a house in Clearwater. Lemur Mom got a discount because she and the kids sometimes help out her neighbor with his various animals. Once they snake-sat his boa constrictor.

"Wanna see 'em?" she asks about the capuchins. Before I can answer, she hightails it to the strollers. When she returns, she's cradling something wrapped in a baby blanket, Capuchin Mom on her heels. I'm still trying to digest that at least two out of about fifteen team moms not only own exotic primates, but also bring them to their sons' baseball games.

My friend pulls back the baby blanket, revealing a tiny creature. He blinks his big eyes and puts his spindly little fingers to his mouth. He's wearing diapers far too small for even a premature human baby.

Capuchin Mom has three human sons, too. She's quick to inform me that she's licensed to have the monkeys as well as a lemur she left at home, but is reluctant to tell me where she bought them or how much she paid. "Normally they are about eight thousand dollars or more, but I know the breeder and he gave me a deal," she says. She graduated to monkeys from the less-expensive lemurs because "they are more humanlike."

Capuchins are one of the hottest exotic pets at the moment. This one is just a few months old but will never weigh more than two and half pounds. The pads of his tiny fingers and toes are as soft as velvet. His face is a mask of light fuzz punctuated by dark eyebrows and set against a head of dark fur with a widow's peak and sideburns. Spanish explorers who discovered the monkeys in South American rainforests thought their markings made them look like the hooded monks of the Order of Friars Minor Capuchin. This infant capuchin is more likely to wear a robe than climb a tree.

"I have to get him back," Capuchin Mom says. "I don't want him to get sunburned."

When I later mention the odd Little League Monkey Mom encounter to my Florida-born friends, one says matter-of-factly, "I used to date a girl who had a monkey," as if owning a wild jungle animal is the most natural thing in the world.

Another laughs, remembering his son's exotic lizards, frogs, and constrictors that he, dear old Dad, often had to search for when they escaped into the neighborhood. "I finally just told a neighbor she could have the boa if she wanted it," he says. "I was tired of chasing it down."

Topping them both, a cohort describes going to parties at the home of a wealthy central Florida couple who served dinner overlooking a backyard filled with big cats, that is lions, tigers, and such—beasts that could eat you for dessert.

Monkeys, giant snakes, and big cats—why wouldn't these exotic animals seem as native as pelicans and alligators in Florida? Monkeys have been running loose all over central and south Florida for decades, swinging through trees at Silver River State Park, stealing oranges from Orlando backyards, and hustling tourists for fruit at a Motel 6 parking lot in Dania. A renegade rhesus macaque, a.k.a. the Mystery Monkey of Tampa Bay, had more than eighty-three thousand Facebook fans in 2012 and was pictured on a local digital billboard with the cheer, "Stay Free Mystery Monkey!"

When Miami gets a freeze, locals have to watch out for falling six-foot Mexican green iguanas that have gone into hibernation. The Everglades slithers with thousands of Burmese pythons that grow longer than a car and weigh as much as a grown man. Carnivorous Nile monitors, anacondas, piranha, monk parakeets, prairie dogs, and African rats as big as housecats—the list of exotic species spotted roaming Florida is as long as a lemur's tail.

And those are just the ones that were freed or escaped over the years. Thousands more live in captivity. They reside in theme parks, roadside animal attractions, breeding farms, research facilities, backyard zoos, refuges, gilded mansions, and mobile homes. Some twelve thousand shipments of them come into the Port of Miami every year. Many are passing through on their way to another state, but a good number stay and breed. The subtropical climate makes Florida a natural incubator.

Exotic animals help fuel the state economy. Florida's reptile trade alone is a $280 million industry, cornering 20 percent of the U.S. market, according to the U.S. Association of Reptile Keepers.

Florida has so many exotic wild animals—exhibited and personal pets—that state and federal agencies don't attempt to keep track of them all. "Closest I could estimate would be a lot," says Jenny Tinnell, a non-native animal biologist with the Florida Fish & Wildlife Conservation Commission (FFWCC). "Bottom line: We don't know that answer."

Officials also can't say how many people own exotic animals since not all require permits and some owners illegally keep them. The best indicator is that four thousand facilities are licensed to house a variety of the more dangerous and invasive animals. You don't need a permit for an Australian sugar glider, chinchilla, parrot, tarantula, hedgehog, a variety of lizards, and dozens of others small enough to hold in one hand; you can buy and sell them on Craig's List.

In short, Florida is one big menagerie. I'm speaking not only of the thousands of exotic animals but also of the Floridians who do almost anything to make them a part of their family. They are a human subspecies, a distinct mutation; I call them Fla-zoons, my play on the scientific term "neozoon," meaning introduced species. They range from a mall clerk who saves up for a sugar glider, to a neo-menagerist who trades in his life insurance policy for a white lion cub, to the hundreds of volunteers who shovel poop and clean cages just to get close to beasts that could bite off their face.

As survival of the fittest is a rule of nature, so it goes for the Fla-zoons. Some find they just can't deal with a snake once it grows past ten feet or a teething lemur that starts chewing on the mini-blinds and sometimes friends. In efforts to keep overwhelmed pet owners from releasing their exotic children into the Florida wilds, the state started holding Exotic Pet Amnesty Days in 2006. Unlicensed owners can anonymously hand over their wild critters with no fear of penalty.

One of these events is being held on a Saturday morning in a grassy lot owned by Busch Gardens® theme park in Tampa. The FFWCC is accepting orphaned exotic critters within earshot of the screams of riders on loop-de-loop roller coasters. Nearby, giraffes, elephants, and lions roam the park's meticulously landscaped Serengeti Plains. FFWCC and park workers, meanwhile, mill around a tent of exotic castoffs that already reeks of musk and animal poop.

At the intake table, Lynn, a solid woman in an oversized zookeeper shirt, holds a knotted pillowcase that droops like it's filled with twenty pounds of sand. She unties it and pulls out a thick 8-foot-long ball python, a constrictor with a dazzling pattern of brown and black scales. The wildlife worker behind the table doesn't flinch, processing the python like a donated cake at a bake sale.

Lynn's husband stands by holding a big, fat lizard across his chest as if it's a baby he's trying to burp. The patch on his zookeeper shirt identifies him as Gator Ron, which helps explain his limp. He has an alligator tooth embedded in his leg from a long-ago incident with one of his favored pets. ("It was my fault," he says, sounding like a battered spouse. "She didn't mean to hurt me.")

Despite his hobble, Ron's a young seventy with a Mr. Green Jeans personality and a Captain Kangaroo mustache. He says he loves Goliath, his Savannah monitor, but he just can't walk him much due to his limp. "He needs more exercise than I can give him. But he's really no trouble," he says, as he strokes the lizard's back. "He likes watching TV with me."

Savannah monitors come from the grasslands of Africa. This one has dusty-gray speckled scales with a blunt snout and a deep-blue, forked tongue. Goliath also has a white scar on his back that Ron suspects he got from a heat lamp while living with a previous owner. The nonpoisonous monitors can live to be twelve years old and have a reputation for being escape artists. Goliath doesn't look in any shape to be so crafty. In fact, he seems content in Ron's arms and cute in a snaggletooth-bulldog kind of way.

The monitor is handicapped, Ron explains to a wildlife worker. He can't move his back legs. "He was like that when I got him about a year ago. He gets around fine just dragging them."

The wildlife worker's brows wrinkle with concern. "I'm going to take him back and have the vet look at him." She disappears with the reptile into the large tent.

While Ron and Lynn anxiously wait, they share stories about their personal zoo in Brooksville. Lynn pulls out a granny-brag-book of pet photos: there's Princess, a 9-foot-long alligator from her reptile posse; an African pygmy goat; a housecat; a mutt; and their most adored pet, Charlie, a 260-pound Montana mountain lion. No snapshots of their grandchildren.

They spend sunup to sundown, seven days a week, 365 days a year caring for about seventy-five animals. They share a mobile home with bearded dragons, a ball python, red-ear slider tortoises, and a house cat. Their backyard is filled with dozens of chickens, a red bone hound, the goat, Charlie, and a fiberglass pool of alligators. They're on a first-name basis with state FFWCC officers, who often call on them to take in captured animals. Ron says, "We never have too much that we won't take in anything that has nowhere else to go."

Gator Ron tells Florida wildlife officials that Goliath, his savannah monitor, is just too much for him. His wife, Lynn, on the left, has already turned in a ball python.

Ron and Lynn Gard are technically "exhibitors." Their license allows them to keep the mountain lion, alligators, big snakes, and other dangerous animals at their house as long as they publicly exhibit them a few times a year. There are scores like the Gards. According to the U.S. Department of Agriculture, Florida has more animal exhibitors than any other state. That's about 475 and doesn't include zoos and circus acts, of which there are dozens. Granted, a handful of those USDA licenses are for dog acts and pony rides, but Florida still has about seventy-five more licensees than the next-most animal-crazed state: California, naturally.

Ron and Lynn can't afford the liability insurance to allow the public to tour their five-acre backyard zoo, so they load the critters into a van with "Gator Encounters" painted on the side and hit the road. Most Fridays they schlep a sideshow of gators to Howard's Flea Market in Homosassa. Lynn spreads artificial grass over a 6-foot table and then tops it with a live gator that's sometimes just as long. Their jaws are taped shut. Ron educates bystanders about the animals and lets the curious touch their soft bellies. A few even hold the smaller toothy reptiles for photos. "We've had grandmothers get their picture made with them," Ron says. "They can say, 'Hey, I got this in F-L-A!'"

Before Charlie grew too big to control, the mountain lion accompanied them to the flea market. "Sometimes he would take off, and I'd yell, 'Step on his leash!'" Ron says, putting his hand by his mouth, mimicking his call-of-the-wild to shoppers. "People there loved him and still ask about him. 'Hey, where's Charlie?' they say. But we can't take him no more. He's got the strength of ten men. Wherever he wants to go, you go with him."

For a while, the Gards also exhibited the world's ten deadliest snakes—an eastern diamondback rattlesnake, a black mamba, a king cobra, viper, anaconda and others filled with enough venom to drop a grown man. Ron seems befuddled by the show's lack of success: "Why people wouldn't give a dollar or two to look at the ten deadliest snakes in the world is weird to me."

At home they kept the snakes sealed off in a small bedroom and followed a strict protocol of never opening a cage solo. But even the best plans can fall prey to the unpredictability of a wild animal. Eventually it happened. One escaped.

Ron was dropping a mouse into the glass cage of his 8-foot black mamba when the snake slithered free. The black mamba is known as the "bottoms-up snake." Lore has it that if bitten, you only have time to down one drink before you die.

The situation was grim.

"I told her to shut the door," Ron says of Lynn. "We had put seals around the doors and windows because we knew we could never let one escape. If it got out of the room, it could get out of the trailer. Even if it killed both of us, at least it wouldn't get out and kill someone else."

There they were, stuck in a hot, stuffy room walled with poisonous snakes, trying to catch a loose one whose bite could kill them before they could guzzle a glass of water. He says, "I figured we were going to die that day."

Using a snake-handler's hook, Ron eventually caught the deadly serpent and returned it to the cage. After that, Ron decided to get rid of the snakes. "That one thing made us think that maybe it wasn't a good idea after all," Ron laughs. "It was getting way too dangerous, and we decided to get rid of them while we still had all our fingers."

They still have a nonpoisonous ball python and help any wild snakes they find stretched across a road. Ron will pull over and wait with the engine running while Lynn jumps out, snatches up the reptile by its tail, and slings it as far away from the road as possible. She climbs back in, and they go on their merry way. He says, "We just can't bear to let one get run over by a car."

Gator Ron didn't always have a soft spot for serpents or such a fanatical love for any wild animal. His attitude changed when his family vacationed at a rustic log cabin in the Smoky Mountains. His daughters, sleeping in the loft, were scared by noises coming from the attic. Upon investigating, Ron discovered a long, black snake. He dragged it outside and shot it dead with his .22 pistol. "I hated snakes then."

Later a nearby resident told Ron his kill was probably one of the black rat snakes that had been raising a family in the cabin's attic for almost twenty years. The snakes mate for life, he told Ron.

"Right then my whole life changed with reptiles," he says. "From then on, everything I did was for animals, especially reptiles. I was so upset with myself. It still bothers me." For a moment he looks as if he's about to cry.

By their own accounts, Gator Ron and Lynn have always been risk takers even though they didn't acquire a zoo of exotic animals until they moved to Florida. They used to race Volkswagen Beetles off-road. "She was the only woman to win driving backwards," Ron brags. Before retirement, Gator Ron worked primarily as a chef and they moved a lot. He jokes that they lived in 150 places all over the country. They raised five children. They were living in Miami when they made the leap to the scrub of Hernando County just so they could house more than exotic snakes. (By law, the state requires 2½ acres for alligators and 5 acres for big cats.) Land was certainly cheaper in the wilds of central Florida than in Miami.

They put in a fiberglass pool and started filling it with alligators. They built a cage and playpen for a big cat, and installed an intercom system between the house and zoo area for safety and convenience. Mind you, they live on Ron's Social Security and Lynn's wages from an office job.

Although they primarily rescue their pets, they bought Charlie from a breeder when he was only five days old. He's now seven years old. Ron says he's never tried to bite. "I bottle-fed him for six months. He thinks I'm his mother," Ron says. "Now that he's grown, I can go into his cage and lie on top of him and kiss him on the mouth." Lynn, who's retrieved more snapshots, pulls out a photo showing just that.

Charlie is Lynn's baby, too. She taught him to play an altered form of soccer with a heavy-duty rubber ball, the Kong toy of big cats. "He purrs," Ron says. "The other day I called down on the intercom and she was petting him and I could hear him purring. I told her I was getting jealous."

"Of him or her?" I ask.

"Both!" he says. They laugh.

Their mood darkens when the wildlife worker returns. The news isn't good. "A vet has looked him over, and his back is broken, which has left his back legs paralyzed," she says of the monitor. "He has broken legs and his lump may be cancer. He is going to need a lot of medical help. We just don't know . . ."

There's a long pause. No one wants to mention euthanizing Goliath, but it's obvious that may be the monitor's plight. Lynn looks nervous.

Ron pipes up, "It doesn't seem to bother him. He gets around fine. I can hardly keep up with him. I'll take him back if no one wants him."

"Let me talk to the vet again," the worker says, grimacing.

"If no one wants him, I'll keep him," Ron calls out again. "I want him to have a good home."

The worker forces a smile and disappears back into the jungle of collected pets.

Underneath the tent, folding tables are stacked with cages and plastic containers holding iguanas, crested dragons, hedgehogs, tarantulas, colorful parrots, and an albino skunk. No primates or felines of any kind. Reptiles are the homeless pet du jour. Most are out back.

An African spurred tortoise the size of a giant beach ball futilely attempts a jail break. Estimated to weigh between 100 and 150 pounds, the domed-shell tortoise is trapped inside a dry plastic fishpond. He incessantly tries to get a stubby foot over the edge, his claws scrapping against the wall of hard plastic. No one else seems to notice. He looks pissed.

FFWCC started the Animal Amnesty Days with constrictors in mind. Pythons, boa constrictors, and anacondas aren't venomous, although they can bite and have more than one hundred needle-sharp teeth. They kill by wrapping their sinuous, muscular, scaly bodies around their prey and squeezing the life out of them. Then they swallow their catch whole.

Wildlife agents began seeing Burmese pythons in the Everglades in the 1980s, although a breeding population wasn't confirmed until 2000. How many there are and how they got there are sources of fierce debate. Herpers blame Hurricane Andrew in 1992, which damaged snake breeders' warehouses and allowed dozens to escape. But when pressed, even they acknowledge that an occasional pet owner may have set theirs free when it got too big.

The python invasion didn't get much attention until 2003, when a tourist videotape of an alligator battling one hit the airwaves. Eventually the python slithered away, leaving at least a sliver of hope that alligators, as feared as they are by humans, might be able to protect Florida against the slithery invaders. Two years later another image killed any optimism. A python that apparently misjudged its capacity was found burst open with a dead 6-foot American alligator poking out of its gut. The photograph made world news and went viral over the Internet. Here was a 13-foot-long snake loose in the wild that could kill Florida's most feared natural predator. And it wasn't alone. A federal biologist estimated that there could be as many as one hundred thousand of these giant snakes multiplying and gobbling up native wildlife. The news created a panic, and not just because the snakes threatened one of the world's remaining ecological treasures. If these snakes could swallow 6-foot alligators, they could surely eat people.

Then it happened. Like a disturbing scene from a horror flick, a pet albino Burmese python escaped from her cage in the middle of the night, slithered into the crib of a two-year-old Bushnell girl, and squeezed the toddler to death. A medical examiner who testified in the manslaughter trial of the child's mother and her live-in boyfriend said that given the child's puncture wounds, the snake had tried to swallow her.

The mom and her boyfriend were sent away to prison for manslaughter, third-degree murder, and child neglect; the python now lives in an undisclosed Florida wildlife sanctuary.

The python panic rose to hysteria. The state banned Floridians from acquiring seven varieties of pythons, the anaconda, and Nile monitors as pets. Then the federal government banned the importation and interstate sales of Burmese pythons, yellow anacondas, and two other pythons. Preexisting pet owners can keep their snakes as long as they pay one hundred dollars to register them and inject them with identifying microchips.

The FFWCC considers education and these amnesty days as the best defenses against a wider infestation of exotic animals in the wild. So far, they are right about one thing: A lot of snake owners want to get rid of them. Herpers started showing up with their reptiles about a half hour before the event opened. Two plastic ponds are filled to the brim with knotted pillowcases of snakes, an undulating patchwork of designs and colors. Glass aquariums, cages, and big plastic storage containers hold even bigger snakes such as Aretha the Retic—a reticulated python that's as long as a minivan.

Burmese pythons supposedly are easygoing, but the name Miss Hiss is loaded with dread, if not nightmares. She's 14 feet long and weighs more than 100 pounds. Her intake form also notes that "she might be aggressive" and is especially nasty when hungry. Sounds like a winner.

As the intake of animals winds down, men, women, and children trickle in and just stand around, waiting. Turns out the state isn't keeping the animals. "Oh, no, they are all hopefully going home with someone today," a state wildlife worker tells me. Registering the shock on my face, she adds, "We don't have a place to house them."

The event is sort of a swap-and-shop. Some pet owners drop off, and others take a few home. Or in the case of Gator Ron, swap out.

Ron is hoping to pick up some baby alligators. His have grown too big to hold for photo ops. He's strategically hanging out at the intake table.

Lucky for him, a young man walks up with three baby alligators. Each is about 2 feet long with its snout wrapped shut. "Let's just say a friend caught them when they had just hatched out," the young man tells a wildlife worker.

Ron quickly shuffles over using his wooden cane and lets a wildlife worker know that he wants them.

The crowd in front of the tent thickens. Men, women, and children shift in anticipation. A gray-haired science teacher is looking for a corn snake for the classroom terrarium. A mom wearing a Jacksonville Herpetological Society T-shirt says she's open to anything that she doesn't have to feed a live rat. Her blond-haired sons—four, seven, and ten—are antsy. They had just ridden three-and-one-half hours from Jacksonville.

The family already shares their home with two geckos, two tortoises, two frogs, aquariums of fish, and enough serpents to cast a horror flick. "I live with forty snakes in my house," Shannon jokes: "We don't have much company."

Shannon's a rescuer, a Florence Nightingale of animals. She used to be terrified of snakes, and took in cats and birds. But her kids are allergic to pet dander, so by default she had to cozy up to herps. She now has one of her own. "We don't have any venomous ones, mostly rat snakes and constrictors," she says.

I ask her and her husband, Rick, if they are concerned about having constrictors around the kids in light of the Bushnell two-year-old's grizzly death. They bristle. "Those people shouldn't have had it," Shannon says. "Some people just shouldn't have them if they aren't going to take care of them. He [the snake owner] hadn't been feeding it, and it was starving!"

"They didn't have it locked up either," Rick says.

(The Bushnell couple admitted that their aquarium was topped only with a quilt.)

"We keep all of ours in cages," Shannon says, "and don't let them out unless we're playing with them."

"Exactly how do you play with a snake?" I ask.

"You can let one crawl up your arm and onto your shoulders. Some really like being held," Snake Mom says. "Like people, they have different personalities; some can be friendly and some don't like being messed with."

**Then There Was One**

By 1:30 p.m. about 110 animals have been turned in, mostly reptiles. More than forty people stand outside the tent like early birds at an estate sale. There are so many shoppers that FFWCC passes out numbers for a lottery because they can't all fit under the tent at once. A worker shouts out the first round, and the lucky ones giddily file inside. They browse. They study snakes, lizards, and tortoises up, down, all around. They ask questions.

"Can I see this one?" Snake Mom asks a worker as she holds up a bulky knotted pillowcase tagged as a ball python. The worker hesitates, saying they don't have time to pull out all the snakes. The perky mom melts his resistance with a smile. He pulls out the snake. Shannon leans over, squinches her nose, shakes her head no, and moves on to the lizards.

People can adopt only one animal per round. Some go through four times.

The testy giant African tortoise is going home with a young guy in flip-flops and a ska band T-shirt. He says he plans to take the tortoise back to his home in Holiday and use it in an animal act that he does at a local American Legion and anywhere else that will pay him. That's if he can fit the 100-pound-plus tortoise and pond into his compact car.

A Busch Gardens worker helps him lug it through the parking lot, while Mr. Tortoise continues to try to get his short foot over the edge of the plastic pond. They sit him down beside the car, and the new tortoise owner clears the backseat. Meanwhile, another couple walks up with a smaller African tortoise. They say they came just to observe, but they enjoy showing off their tortoise, which is outpacing them. "He could walk a mile," the man says, following his pet. "Sometimes I walk him through the neighborhood and he can wear me out."

With the backseat empty and the front seats pushed forward to the max, the new tortoise owner and the wildlife worker try to squeeze the pond into the backseat as Mr. Tortoise becomes more frantic in his escape attempts. They attack the backseat straight on, but the pond is just too wide. They tilt it this way and that. In sweaty exasperation, they set the pond and tortoise down on the grass. The owner looks back and forth between the backseat and the reptile. He's determined to take it. The tortoise is worth about $1,200, and he's just gotten it for free. In one motion, he grabs the tortoise on both sides of its thick shell, lifts, and sits it on the velour car seat. Mr. Tortoise, clearly puzzled by his new surroundings, for once doesn't move. They bend the pond, fit it through the doorway and somehow manage to slide it under Mr. Tortoise. The pond fills the back, crushing against the front seats. An angry Mr. Tortoise returns to escape attempts. The new owner and his wife jump in the front, their knees against the dash. They set out on the hour-long drive home—no doubt to the sound of claws frantically scratching to escape.

Back at the tent, the crowd has thinned, but plenty of snakes remain. Wildlife workers are encouraging shoppers to pick out two and three at a time. A couple of men in home-eviction service T-shirts study

Aretha the Retic and Miss Hiss, snakes large enough to clear a house of any squatters. Anthony, the boss, already owns about twenty snakes.

Since Floridians can no longer buy many of the constrictors as pets, Amnesty Days are about the only legal way they can get one. Anthony's been working the Amnesty Day circuit, adopting snakes, birds, and chinchillas. Like Ron and Lynn Gard, he turned in two snakes. "I've handled snakes most all my life, but those African rock pythons were just too mean," he says.

Undaunted by Miss Hiss's rap sheet, Anthony dons leather gloves and begins uncoiling her from her pet carrier. True to her name, she hisses, flicking her long ribbon of a tongue. His home-eviction employee and a Busch Gardens worker move closer to help. The snake seems endless. By the time she's fully out of her cage, Anthony has threaded her behind his neck, and it takes both him and his employee to carry her over for a microchip injection.

Wearing the snake behind his neck and across his body like a sash, Anthony hurries her to his pickup, while his employee follows along carrying the snake's tail end. They store her in a built-in snake box and then secure the rest of Anthony's cache from the day: three other pythons, a couple of boa constrictors, and a yellow-naped Amazon parrot, which usually sell for more than a thousand dollars at pet stores. All in all, a pretty good catch for the day if you happen to like big snakes and talking birds.

A Polk County father-and-son team adopt Aretha the Retic. Her glass terrarium barely fits horizontally in their pickup.

The Jacksonville herper family ends up with two bearded dragons, a California corn snake, and a tarantula. The boys seem pleased, the oldest petting the overgrown lizard as it cleaves to his shirt. The dad walks around grinning with the other lizard on his chest.

Gator Ron is tickled to have the baby gators. The monitor? He's going to Gatorland in Orlando. All but one sickly python goes home with someone. Fish & Wildlife celebrate the day as a huge success.

## Want a Gator with That Fill-Up?

Given that two-thirds of Floridians weren't born in the state, many Fla-zoons are also alien to Florida. They were brave enough to leave their native environment and settle on the fringe of America, a land of hurricanes, sinkholes, and people different from themselves. They are risk takers by nature. And the native Floridians? They descended from people who were perhaps even more so. Pioneering the swampy state before air-conditioning and mosquito control took a strong constitution. Trying to tame a wild animal that can take your head off in a single bite or strangle you in the middle of the night is a risky proposition.

No doubt, the state's tourism industry also influences the Fla-zoon mind-set. Ever since tourists have had cars, exotic animals have helped lure them to Florida. Early tourism pioneers used creatures from afar to create an illusion that Florida was a magical, exotic wonderland full of colorful, wild, yet friendly animals. With the right touch, they could even be tamed.

In the early 1920s, Carl Fisher, the father of Miami Beach, brought in elephants to help sell his newly developed coastline as the Riviera of America. His favorite, Rosie, was photographed giving children rides to an Easter egg hunt, dancing with a flapper, and even caddying for President Warren Harding. The images made newspapers around the country.

By the 1930s, the common man was able to walk among the macaques at Monkey Jungle. Soon afterward, other stand-alone animal attractions such as Clyde Beatty's Jungle Zoo, Parrot Jungle Island, and the Miami Serpentarium dazzled the public with animal acts and the handling of creatures that could kill near instantly with one bite.

Roadside zoos became as much a part of the Florida tourist experience as riding a wave. You could see monkeys jockey greyhounds, parrots perform card tricks, and an Asian elephant water-ski. Florida's natural wonders—Ty-D-Bol blue springs and orchid-filled botanical gardens—became more surreal with captive wild beasts from the other side the globe. Operators of gas stations and tourist huts along routes to south Florida got in on the trade, advertising live alligators, monkeys, lions—any wild beast that tourists couldn't see at home. Travelers pulled over and had their picture taken with the animals as they filled up the family wagon.

As time went on, Florida became a residence where exotic was no longer exotic.

Meanwhile, cookie-cutter subdivisions began to spring up around backyard zoos, and public officials started getting complaints about the smelly and dangerous animals next door. Five-foot green iguanas began peeking through hedges in Miami. Seven-foot African Nile

Anthony Green of Tampa wrapped in his new pet, Miss Hiss, a 14-foot-long Burmese python.

monitors started feasting on housecats in Naples. Many residents began to think living in a menagerie wasn't all it was cracked up to be.

As a result, Florida now has the most comprehensive regulation of captive exotic wildlife of any state in the union. Perhaps the most notable restriction came in 1980, when the FFWCC said people could no longer keep as pets twenty-four of the most dangerous animals—lions, tigers, leopards, elephants, rhinos, baboons, orangutans, and generally mammals that you rarely see outside of zoos in most states. Preexisting pet owners could still keep their animals. The restrictions may have slowed backyard zoos, but it hasn't stopped the most fanatical from living with exotic animals. They just have to jump through more regulatory hoops and spend more money to do it.

Basically, the requirements are: You must have 5 acres, proper fencing, two experienced animal caretakers (one a licensee) who will vouch that you have one thousand hours of experience handling the animals, a disaster plan in the event of a hurricane, and a ten-thousand-dollar surety bond, which typically costs less than two hundred dollars. Licenses are either to sell, exhibit, or both. To be considered an exhibitor, you either have to open to the public or occasionally exhibit them on the road, say, at schools, birthday parties, or restaurant openings. Yes, I said restaurant openings: a chimp once mixed cocktails at the premiere of his owner's trendy Miami restaurant.

In 2011, the FFWCC issued 865 commercial licenses to people and businesses to keep one of the twenty-four species of dangerous zoo animals. Licensees range from Disney's Wild Kingdom to a retired circus performer who lives with his two longtime partners, African lions. Of the 865 licensees, only fourteen are accredited by Association of Zoos & Aquariums (AZA), the gold standard of captive animal husbandry.

The Everglades Outpost Wildlife Rescue falls somewhere in the middle. While not accredited by the AZA, the nonprofit works closely with the FFWCC. The Outpost often takes in unwanted or FFWCC-confiscated wild animals.

The 5-acre piece of jungle sits in the outback of Homestead along the main road to Everglades National Park. The land is flat and dotted with new and old homes and striped with rows of tomato plants. Farms of palms and papayas remind that you're in tropics. Even in October, the air is so muggy you can smell the fruit ripening.

A wooden parrot and hand-painted sign mark the Outpost's entrance across from a preserve of south Florida pinelands. Nearly two hundred animals, mostly caged reptiles, live amid the trees, palms, and landscaped foliage.

Bob Freer and his wife, Barbara Tansey, also live onsite. Bob is a licensed trapper, which in south Florida means he's the guy you call to fish an alligator out of your pool or remove a 26-foot python from underneath your house. He also wrestles alligators just up the road at the Everglades Reptile Farm. He got his first one at five when his dad stopped to get gas at a Tampa station that was giving away the baby reptiles with every fill-up. He's been caring for wild animals in one way or another ever since.

Bob and Barbara opened Everglades Outpost back in 1994 primarily as a rehab for Florida's native critters, nursing them back to health and then returning them to the wild. Not long after opening, the Outpost started getting requests to take in exotic pets. Like Ron Gard, Bob just couldn't say no.

An outgoing, burly man with a graying mustache and jazz chop, Bob's uniform is a safari hat and a T-shirt with cut-out sleeves. He's gearing up to hunt pythons in the Everglades and graciously passes me off to a longtime committed volunteer. Like most Florida exotic animal sanctuaries, the Everglades Outpost relies heavily on volunteers to help care for its wild residents. Terine is a fixture there. She enthusiastically welcomes the chance to show off her exotic friends.

Terine is a petite, wiry Latina with a black mullet that hugs her head like a helmet—bangs and sideburns in front and longer curls dusting the collar in back. She's dressed in hiking boots, cargo shorts, and a T-shirt with a dreamy image of a mountain lion. A pendant of a gold lion's head hangs from her neck, and a tiger and a leopard are tattooed on her legs, all the markings of a big-cat person, a Fla-zoon felidae.

"These animals aren't pets," Terine says as we start down the shaded trail between the tall fenced pens of various pets—hyenas, owls, parrots, donkeys, miniature horses, and various monkeys. "People tried to make them pets, but they are wild animals! People get them when they were cute and little, but when they get bigger and start to bite, they want to get rid of them."

She points to the caged ring-tailed lemur that is foaming at the mouth. "His owner had his teeth removed because she said he was biting too much. That's what they do! They bite! Especially when they are teething," Terine says. "Look at him. Now he has to gum his food." She sighs.

Terine says one overwhelmed monkey owner called demanding that the Outpost take her pet, complaining it was biting and being generally unruly. Before Terine could get the OK from Bob, the owner left the monkey in the Outpost parking lot, and scrammed without even telling the refuge it was there. "She had the nerve to call us back a few weeks later and ask if we had trained it yet."

A shed snakeskin hangs on a hibiscus bush outside the reptile house. The sign over the door says, "Snakes of the World." Inside, the walls are lined with glass enclosures filled with about every snake known to man, including some of the deadliest—rattlers, anacondas, mambas, and king cobras. Refuge herpetologist Albert Killian is uncharacteristically absent. He does the snake shows and is a legend in the herper world; he's been bitten by poisonous snakes so many times that the county venom response unit calls him a "frequent flier." Terine says this is only a small portion of his collection; he has more than three thousand snakes. The screws on the terrariums seem perilously loose. Our time inside is short.

Each animal at the Outpost has a unique Florida story. Buc, a grizzly bear, was confiscated from a backyard in Miami Beach. A cougar came from a cocaine dealer's crib. A camel was to be housed only temporarily while the owner built an enclosure. That was more than three years ago.

Deeper inside the sanctuary, Terine points out a couple of wolves in a large pen dotted with tree stumps and rocks. "I'm one of the only people who can get in there with them," Terine says and calls to them. They don't respond.

Helping out at the Outpost is more of an addiction than a hobby for Terine. She quit her job as a photographer for the Florida Marlins, a professional baseball team in Miami, to volunteer there full-time, she says. She tried volunteering at the area zoo, but it wouldn't allow her to get close to the animals. She drove down to Everglades Outpost.

"The first day I was here from ten to four pulling weeds and cleaning out cages. It was hot, and by four o'clock I was covered in fleas and crap. I was going to tell them it was just too much work. Then they asked if I could do them one more favor—Could I help walk the white tiger?"

She led the juvenile tiger around the compound and got her picture taken with it. "Then I said, 'This isn't so bad.'"

The Outpost asked her to work Thursdays through Sundays. She ultimately decided that wasn't enough. "I realized that I would never be as happy as I was working here. Where else can you go and in three months be able to get in the cage with wolves?"

For the past five years, she has volunteered seven days a week. "I can actually go into any one of the cages. I can feed all the animals. They know me, and I know them."

Money is tight. Terine scrapes by on a modest inheritance from her grandfather. She bubbles, "I'd rather be poor and happy than rich and unhappy."

Lions and tigers at the back of the refuge see us coming and pace behind towering chain-link fences. Seeing a live tiger up close used to be as rare and awe-inspiring as watching a volcano erupt, both dangerous natural beauties. But frankly there are so many of the big cats now in Florida that the thrill is gone.

A tiger in captivity eats about the equivalent of its weight each month, which means that by the time the massive feline is grown, it consumes 6,500 pounds of meat a year. You would think that kind of grocery list along with widely publicized cases of seemingly docile tigers mauling their longtime owners—Roy Horn of Siegfried & Roy, for instance—would weed out the pussycat neo-menagerists. Not so. A cub's cuteness can be very seductive, and there's an enormous black market of exotics. Some people actually try to get away with illegally keeping a wild pet as big and ferocious as a tiger without being detected. Then, of course, there are those who are just downright ignorant of the law.

The former owner of Rocky, a 550-pound Siberian-Bengal mix staring at us through the cage, is a prime example of the latter. Rocky was confiscated from a local stripper who was bold enough to tool around Miami with him as a six-month-old cub in an open-top convertible. "Fish and Wildlife had heard about a woman riding around with a tiger in her car, and they just happened to see her one day," Terine says. "She told them she was going to use him in her act." Wildlife officers brought the cub to the Outpost. Terine admonishes, "She said she would come visit him, but she never has."

Not all big-cat lovers have the fortitude to grow old with a tiger or the time to volunteer at a sanctuary, but Florida's wannabe neo-menagerists can be just as committed in their fandom. Consider the infamous Bobo-Tarzan incident: The 600-pound Siberian-Bengal mix was the pet of a former Spanish Tarzan actor, who apparently had trouble escaping his role. (He also played a biker who mutates into a monster turkey and goes after drug dealers in the 1972 B-movie *Blood Freak*.) Steve Sipek was able to keep big cats because he owned them before the state outlawed them as pets. Up until 2012, he lived, swam, and slept with them at his Loxahatchee compound. He views himself as having a special gift, a "sixth sense," that allows him to communicate with the cats, he told ABC News. Call him a tiger whisperer.

His abilities failed him in 2004 when Bobo escaped and roamed his south Florida neighborhood for more than twenty-four hours. Neighbors were terrified, but the bigger outcry came after a wildlife officer shot and killed Bobo. The officer said the cat growled and lunged at him. Tarzan didn't believe it and called the shooting a murder. Hordes of tiger fans agreed and mourned Bobo outside Tarzan's gate. They left a shrine of signs, wooden crosses, flowers, and giant posters of the cat. They held candlelight vigils. They attended Bobo's burial service, which was complete with a priest, guest book, and a hearse. Later a fan compiled a YouTube.com memorial video, a Bobo photo montage set to Lionel Richey's "Just for You." The FFWCC got so many angry calls from outraged big-cat lovers that supervisors warned unarmed FFWCC biologists not to wear their uniforms in the field. The wildlife officer who shot Bobo in self-defense? He got death threats.

Seven years later, big-cat people still grieve for Bobo and berate the FFWCC on Internet message boards. Given the intensity of the lingering outrage, I dare not bring up Bobo to my Fla-zoon felidae guide.

"People just don't realize what they are getting themselves into," Terine laments again as we trace our path back to the entrance. "They may mean well, but they just don't stop and think. If they only just looked it up on the Internet and read just a little bit. A wild animal isn't like having a dog or a cat."

Most sanctuaries preach this same message. The sentiment, however earnest, often comes across like daredevil Evel Knievel's warning—"Don't try this at home, kids"—before he drove his rocket-cycle off the edge of Snake River Canyon.

Back where we started the tour, an adorable lion cub about the size and color of a large golden retriever bounces back and forth inside a small cage. He rears up on his hind legs and puts his front paws on the gate like a puppy in a pet store begging for attention. Terine laughs. "That's my Mus. He wants to play."

Terine, an Everglades Outpost Wildlife Rescue worker, warns against exotic animal ownership as she tries to control Mus, the young African lion that lives with her. Photo by James Harvey.

Mus (pronounced Moose and short for Musafa) lives with Terine. The black-maned lion cub isn't a rescue. A local breeder bought him from a Kansas breeder when the cub was only five weeks old. Terine is just caring for Mus until he's old enough to breed.

He comes to work with her and sleeps in her bed at night. She had a live-in boyfriend when she got Mus, but says, "He was jealous of Mus, so I got rid of him."

When Mus was smaller, he followed Terine around as she went about her chores at the refuge. At seven months, his paws are already bigger than a man's palm, so he stays inside a pen or on a leash.

Terine leads him out of the cage. He's full of personality and seems to smile at me. I admit that the urge to pet him is strong because he acts more like a puppy than a ferocious lion. Terine sits on top of a wooden picnic table and poses with him for some photos. She leans down and kisses him on the mouth. When she diverts her attention, he bats at her playfully with his mitt. She pushes it away while continuing to talk; he doesn't give up. Mus probably already weighs as much as Terine. When she leads him around in the grass and stops for a second, he tugs, jerking her to the side with each pull.

Mus is a feline celebrity. He's been on *Jimmy Kimmel Live* and NBC's *Today Show*. On one trip, a network put him and Terine up in a suite at the luxurious Ritz Carlton in New York. The hotel treated Mus like royalty, and he had his own bed. Terine walked him in the posh hotel's designated doggie area and laughs that it freaked out some chihuahua owners.

This raises some fundamental hygiene questions: Where does Mus go to the bathroom?

As a small cub he used her cat's litter box, but now he goes outside like her dog, she says.

Mus is male, and by instinct mature male felines spray urine to mark their territory. Lions are super-soakers; they can spray urine up to 10 feet away and are notorious for aiming at people. Terine says Mus doesn't spray, and she doesn't think he will because he hasn't been around a male feline that does. "I think it's a learned behavior."

I make a mental note to check back with her on that in a year.

After leaving the Outpost with the image of Terine kissing Mus etched in my memory, I think of Florida big-cat rescuer Carole Baskin, and her former self, Carole Lewis.

## Cat Fights

More than a decade ago Carole shared her bed with a wild feline. She has since transformed into Florida's fiercest critic of the exotic-pet trade. The Tampa breeding facility and refuge she cofounded in the mid-1990s is now Big Cat Rescue (BCR), a "no-touch" retirement home for about 115 big cats and a few other exotics. She argues that playing with cubs gives people the idea that they can be pets and perpetuates captive breeding of the cats when there aren't enough decent facilities to keep them now. "We have to turn away more than fifty a month," she says. Several of Florida's roadside zoo and backyard sanctuary operators also breed and sell big cats to help support their operation, or, they say, to "preserve the species." All of which makes Carole extend her claws. "It's just obscene to consider your facility a sanctuary when you are breeding animals that have nowhere to go."

Carole's dream is that big cats will one day exist only in the wild, not in sanctuaries like hers, not even in big accredited zoos. Her methods can be prickly. She's penned venomous articles and blogs online about many of Florida's backyard zoos and sanctuaries, characterizing them as thinly veiled personal menageries with operators who delude themselves into thinking they are martyrs.

She's posted critical USDA inspection reports of other big-cat parks and refuges. She mailed 1,500 letters to the neighbors of licensees, notifying them of dangerous wildlife living next door and upcoming public hearings about new regulations. She's lobbied Washington and Tallahassee for stricter laws on captive wild animals, shared her views with national publications, and enraged other exotic-animal owners in Florida and beyond.

"She's the most hated person in Florida among exotics owners," says one Florida big-cat exhibitor, summing up what I've heard from several others.

Big-cat people can be a little catty with one another, or play rough, especially when their pride is threatened. Many, like Carole, are multimedia savvy; cat fights often take place in a virtual arena.

An anonymous critic devotes an entire blog, "Big Cat Rescue Lies," to pointing out exaggerations in BCR's cat stories, along with characterizing Carole as a "sociopath."

Ticked off by Carole's criticism of white-tiger breeders in a *Newsweek* article, the director of Feline Conservation Federation, which caters to pet owners and breeders, posted a scathing opus: "Rebuttal to Carole Baskin's Campaign of Hatred."

Her most colorful critic is Oklahoma exotic-animal-park-operator Joe Exotic, whom Carole has vigorously lobbied to shut down. His YouTube.com series rants about everything from where Carole got her cats to the size of her ass. He's posted more than seventy lengthy expletive-filled diatribes, a few with his talking mouth and bulging eyes morphed onto the face of a baby. Yes, a grown man's teeth in the mouth of a babe saying Carole's claims are "a big old thing of crawdad bullshit."

Carole's well aware that she has armies of enemies. The tires on BCR's vans have been slashed more than once; she's asked security to escort her out of FFWCC meetings. One refuge owner she targeted, a man from Seminole who rides around with his pet tiger in the back of his pickup, regularly protests at her glitzy Fur Ball fund-raisers. Carole says hostility peaked when she lobbied to require owners of the twenty-four most dangerous exotics to get a ten-thousand-dollar surety bond. The bill was especially controversial because it also outlawed pythons as pets. "People would come up screaming at me and threatening me, especially the snake people. They're whack jobs." Many of her detractors, naturally, make the same assessment of her.

Invariably, their main criticism is that she's a hypocrite. They point out that she has a sanctuary and that she and her late husband once bred and sold wild cats. They emphasize that many of the animals she claims that she "rescued" were once her pets. All true.

Carole insists that was only the case in the 1990s, when she was married to Don Lewis, a man whose mysterious disappearance has also been juicy fodder for her foes. Wildman Joe Exotic even offers a ten-thousand-dollar reward for information about Don's disappearance.

I first met Carole in 1999 while writing a story for a local alternative newspaper about her eccentric missing husband. A shapely woman with big, blue eyes, she met me in leopard print leggings and invited me into her small, hodgepodge home that also served as the sanctuary office. Her personal space was limited to a cluttered bedroom with a tiger print spread on a bed she had shared with a bobcat.

Don made his millions dealing in tax-deed property and from selling RVs and treasures he plucked from dumpsters. He was a trader to the core; everything was a commodity including, sometimes, their big cats. Carole says they didn't set out to be big-cat owners. They went to an animal auction to buy llamas and were horrified to see a young bobcat on a leash. They bought it, and Don loved it as his pet. Later at an auction in Minnesota, they bought fifty-six baby bobcats that she says were destined for a fur farm. "We bought them all to keep them from being killed," she says. She admits they sold them as pets. "We didn't know how stupid it was. We made an awful lot of mistakes over the years. The only people who could offer advice were the breeders."

They raised the cats on 40 acres down a dirt road in what was then a semi-rural area on the fringe of Tampa. They lived in a small, older house surrounded by cat cages and called it Wildlife on Easy Street.

During those years, Carole says she awakened to the ugliness of the exotic pet trade and the problems of keeping them as pets. (Finding a piece of raw meat in your bed can do that.) Like parents often do with children, Carole and Don argued over their animals. She wanted bigger cages; he argued they were fine. Don wanted to move the animals to their property in Costa Rica; she wanted to keep them in Tampa.

Then one day, Don vanished. Carole says he went to look at an ultra-light plane at a nearby airstrip and never returned. A sheriff's investigation ensued. Searches were conducted. Carole was interviewed. One of Don's children accused her of feeding him to the cats. Don's long-time secretary insinuated the same, adding that Don was planning to divorce Carole. Without a body, the investigation hit a dead end. What happened to the cat man remains a mystery.

Carole says that after Don's disappearance, she stopped breeding exotics and started taking in unwanted ones: a crippled tiger confiscated from a drug dealer's basement, retired circus performers, former pets that grew too big for owners to handle. Her missing husband's $6 million estate was stuck in probate for six years. She sold her jewelry and her car to keep the sanctuary going. She allowed tours for ten-dollar donations; volunteers built a small cottage amid the large cat pens and rented it out on weekend nights to tourists who wanted to wake to a lion's roar.

After Don was officially declared dead, Carole got the lion's share of the estate, which was mostly real estate investments. She's stopped renting out the onsite cottage, enlarged cages, and spruced up the sanctuary. She moved into a house away from the cat compound and eventually married a Harvard MBA who's apparently as much a cat fanatic as she; he wore a tiger-print toga to their beach wedding. He helped Carole restructure the nonprofit. They renamed it Big Cat Rescue because it sounded more professional, she says.

Though visitors can no longer stay overnight, for a donation they can take a guided tour of the 55-acre big-cat habitat. You can even get married there amid the pens of roaring cats on a faux beach. Just remember to keep the guests out of the lions' soaker range.

Carole says the donations go toward feeding the cats, which eat 1.2 million pounds of specialized food a year. The sanctuary has about one hundred volunteers and ten paid employees. Carole doesn't earn a salary from the sanctuary even though she devotes most of her time to big-cat projects. Her latest charge has been assembling an online pride of like-minded big-cat lovers she labels AdvoCats. When one of them

Carole Baskin, founder and chief executive officer of Big Cat Rescue, the Tampa woman that big-cat owners across America love to hate. Photo by Jamie Veronica. By permission of Carole Baskin.

learns about an offensive event or operation, Carole sends out the alert and the AdvoCats leap into action. They overwhelm with calls, e-mails, letters, and posts to the offender's Facebook page. If that fails, they contact anyone associated with the operators, such as all their Facebook friends. Perhaps not surprisingly, their social media prowess has been effective. AdvoCats successfully pressured a bar owner not to use a tiger cub for a promotional event. More than nine hundred AdvoCats complained to PetSmart for allowing Dade City's Wild Things to bring a white tiger cub into a store near Tampa. Carole says the corporation reminded managers that exotic animals are forbidden in its stores.

Carole is waiting on a list of state licensees to check if they have bought the insurance she lobbied FFWCC to require. "I'll bet when they send it back to me there will be an awful lot of people that haven't gotten it," she says. Yes, Carole still wears leopard print.

## A Real Live Monkey!

A year has passed. The Little Leaguers are now a hand taller and only a hop from puberty. In an instant they go from hanging on the bullpen fence and singing silly cheers to keenly taking their positions on the field and not only paying attention to the pitch, but appearing ready for whatever ball may come their way.

Monkey Mom and family are at their traditional spot between the concession stand and the bleachers, a place where everyone passes, a crossroads. A capuchin in a striped infant snapsuit clings to her neck. There's a new addition to the family: a tiny bundle hidden in a baby blanket is nestled in her lap.

Little brothers and sisters occasionally stop to look at the capuchin but don't linger. They've seen him before. Team parents no longer give the monkey a second glance. Even Lemur Mom doesn't seem interested. She's overwhelmed with her own pet dilemma. Otis, their lemur, is teething and starting to chew up the furniture.

"I don't know what I'm going to do with him," she says. The kids have lost interest and won't be too upset if he gets a new home. But where will she take him? "I can't sell him because I don't have a license to sell. I just have the pet permit."

As she ruminates I go check out Monkey Mom's newest child.

The bundle in the blanket is an infant spider monkey; they can grow up to 14 pounds and 2 feet tall, not including their prehensile tail. They're chatty with high-pitched attention-seeking screeches and barks. Their calls sound like a gurgling chicken. This tiny guy hasn't started talking yet.

Monkey Mom says she brings her furry ones to games to acclimate them to different people. Even seemingly tamed wild animals require frequent human interaction to prevent them from reverting back to their natural fear of people. Lest he forget she's his adopted mom, she plans to bottle-feed him for the rest of his life. "You have to, to keep that bond."

One of her human sons runs up, and the monkey leaps from Mom's lap to his chest. The boy laughs as the furry creature runs around his shoulders. A couple of kids stop to watch. A passing pudgy ballplayer in an Auburn Tigers jersey stares back at the capuchin as his mother drags him along to the bleachers.

The Tigers are new to the league, new to the faithful presence of monkeys at their games. The kid who discovered it dashes up into the stands, shouting out to his teammates: "Did you see the monkey?" "There's a monkey down there! A real, live monkey!"

He doesn't have to say much more before half the team stampedes down the bleachers, their cleats clanking against the metal. One of their parents shouts for them to not get too close. An Auburn team dad grumbles to another parent, "Yeah, some woman over there brought a monkey to the game."

The kids don't brake until they are about 3 feet from Monkey Mom, and then it's as if they have hit an invisible wall; they bump into one another, nearly falling down. Spread out in a semi-circle like TV reporters at a press conference, they gawk and whisper in each other's ears, but don't dare inch closer.

Monkey Mom looks horrified. She holds tight to her capuchin, while her mother, Monkey Grandma, keeps the baby spider monkey hidden by a blanket. She avoids eye contact with the boys and talks to her friend. Obviously she wants the little Auburn Tigers to move along. It's unclear whether she fears the monkey might hurt the kids or worries that the squirming boys will stress out her pet.

The boys finally return to their seats at the insistence of one of their parents. Monkey Mom relaxes and contentedly returns to watching her son play ball while the capuchin dressed like a baby hops back and forth across laps and shoulders. One big happy family.

# CHAPTER 2

# The King of Trampa

From the outside, you wouldn't guess that Joe Redner's Mons Venus strip club is as synonymous with Tampa as its world-famous cigars. It looks more like a grungy topless joint you might see beside a truck stop off a lonely interstate ramp. Built in the 1960s, the plain building is no larger than a modest home with a flat roof, rock siding, and flashes of purple trim. Squeezed between a full-service car wash and Joe's Pizza, which Redner also owns, the all-nude dance club is easily overlooked on this congested section of Dale Mabry Highway. The roadside marquee is modest by strip-club standards; a small, digital board claims, "Home of the Most Beautiful Women in the World!!!" and a backlight sign bears the word "NUDE" and the club's name, "Mons Venus," a euphemism for part of a woman's vulva.

At 9:00 p.m. on the muggy eve of Memorial Day, the club is still dead enough to find a front parking space beside a Porsche. A couple of men in their thirties having a smoke underneath the front awning share Mons lore. "You want to know how famous Mons is?" asks Kristopher, who in glasses and a button-down seems an authority on the club. "I got into a cab in Hong Kong a few years ago and the cab driver asked me where I was from. When I told him Tampa, Florida, he said, 'Oh, Mons Venus!'"

Of course, Tampa cab drivers are even more familiar with the club. They claim that Mons and Bern's Steak House are the most common destinations of fares they pick up at Tampa International Airport. About 85 percent of Mons patrons are from out of town, largely conventioneers, businesspeople, tourists, and sport fans. The home stadium of the Tampa Bay Buccaneers and the New York Yankees spring training field are within walking distance. Sometimes after games, the crowd around the Mons stage is four or five deep. Joe Redner has estimated that in some years, more than a quarter of a million people walked through Mons's doors.

Florida certainly has bigger and fancier places to see skin. Based on various strip-club databases and registries, the Sunshine State has more topless and nude strip joints than any other state, which is understandable considering it attracts the most tourists. South Florida's venues are some of the loosest and largest all-nude clubs in America. Customers are allowed to get not only a nude lap dance but also a shot of alcohol along with it—a hedonistic mix prohibited in California, New York State, and most cities, including Las Vegas and Tampa.

Rapper Lil Wayne sings about making it rain at Miami's swanky King of Diamonds (K.O.D.) in "Hustle Hard," and he held his star-studded homecoming there in 2010 after he was released from prison. A one-stop hip-hop he-man cavern, the K.O.D. is as big as a Wal-Mart Superstore with a basketball court, barbershop, shoeshine service, restaurant, spa services, and tanning salon, which is a little perplexing since the clientele is largely African American.

Then there's more rural Pasco County, long home to the nation's largest concentration of nudist communities and resorts. Pasco gets Tampa's spillover of residents and all-nude strip clubs. And Pasco clubs can sell alcohol.

Despite Mons's lack of a bar, it ranks as the best in the entire U.S. of A. among the one hundred thousand strip-club connoisseurs who subscribe to the Ultimate Strip Club List, a Las Vegas–based website that serves as a Tripadvisor® for lap dance junkies. Members laud it for the "major contact" with dancers and the "hot girls." Mons ranked third among 2,800 strip clubs worldwide, losing out to two Tijuana clubs that are also brothels.

Many locals know the club more for its opinionated owner, Joe Redner, who's forever in the headlines battling social mores and running for political office. He's been arrested more times than he can count (he estimates about 150) and canonized in the documentary *Strip Club King: The Joe Redner Story*.

He's Tampa's most despised and most admired iconoclast. Church folks view him as the devil incarnate, while strip-club lovers consider him a god. Some local politicians complain that he exploits the First Amendment for personal gain. Many others, including some who'd rather get indigestion than a Mons lap dance, applaud him for slapping conventional norms on the ass and battling a government they view as heavy-handed.

"Joe's a local folk hero," says Kristopher, who, as it turns out, is an editor at a national trade publication for strip-club owners. (Yes, it's based in Tampa Bay.) He adds, "Some people call Joe the local Larry Flynt."

In 2010, readers of *Creative Loafing*, Tampa's alternative newspaper, voted Joe as Tampa Bay's "Best Troublemaker." That's a little misleading. Joe would give you his last fruit smoothie. But if you took it from him, he'd step on your broken toe and broadcast to the world that you're a bastard thief and your breath stinks. Then he'd likely take you to court and win your last dime. In the face of adversity, his scrappiness and chutzpah cannot be exaggerated.

When Bob Buckhorn, then–city councilman and the latest Tampa mayor, led a charge to outlaw lap dancing, Joe replied on a portable sign in front of the Mons: "Bob Buckhorn is an asshole." After someone complained about the profanity of the word "asshole," he changed it to "dildo." During one of his many battles with his nemesis Ronda Storms, a local politician and fundamentalist Christian, he posted: "Ronda Storms, Censor This You Retarded Fat Fascist Pig." A recitation of Joe's hostile signs could fill pages.

His nasty verbal comebacks could fill a book. The chair-tossing incident on a local public-access show made national news and went viral on YouTube.com. The confrontation started when a Republican Internet talk-show host called Joe a liar. Joe called him fat. The political pundit got hot. Joe said, matter-of-factly: "You called me a liar. I'm not a liar.

The Mon Venus marquee is a beacon for many Tampa Bay visitors.

I called you fat. You are fat." The pudgy pundit stomped off the set cursing. Joe couldn't resist calling him "fat boy" one more time. The pundit threw a chair at Joe and hit him in the head. Joe just laughed. After all, he's faced much worse.

Joe got death threats, he says, when mobsters tried to muscle their way into his earlier strip club. He says he told them he would die before letting them control him. The threats stopped.

No one is too sacred for Joe's barbs. Once after a church group carrying wooden crosses protested outside the Mons, Joe showed up outside their chapel the next Sunday with about forty of his friends, dancers, and their children. The angry strip-club band waved signs and shouted that parishioners were anti-Christ. The church group hasn't been back to the Mons.

Over the years Joe has increasingly taken on other causes, using his mouth and his wallet to fight what he thinks is unjust. He counterprotested the members of Westboro Baptist Church—a congregation notorious for picketing soldiers' funerals due to the military's tolerance of homosexuality—when they demonstrated outside a Tampa rock concert. Joe called them hypocrites and shouted through his bullhorn that their minister was gay.

When the Hillsborough County Commission passed an ordinance against any acknowledgment of Gay Pride Month, Joe declared himself gay and sued on grounds that it violated his First Amendment rights. WFTS Tampa ABC Action News anchor Brendan McLaughlin later asked Joe if he truly was gay, and Joe responded: "I'm gay, I'm black, I'm an Indian, a Jew. I'm everyone and anyone who has ever been oppressed for anything other than their bad character."

By the time Joe donated use of his city park to Occupy Tampa protesters in 2011, he was solidly one of the area's fiercest social activists. Admirers clamored to his Facebook page to post tributes. "The establishment sees Joe Redner as a nuisance," wrote Cary Strukel. "I see Joe Redner as a self-made man who is willing to stand up for the rights of those who are not even willing to stand up for their own rights!"

Joe isn't at Mons tonight, but has given me full access to the club and dancers with the exception of their dressing room—which is fine by me since it's on a live pay-per-view website. I have no desire to be an extra in the fantasy of some man sitting at his computer in Topeka.

We're scheduled to meet next week at Joe's nearby office. I've interviewed him on the street several times over the years, but have never been inside the Mons, something I feel guilty about since I'm an area reporter with a background on the subject. I researched for the movie *Showgirls* in the early 1990s and interviewed dancers in most every nude and topless club in Las Vegas. I'm long beyond squeamish.

Given my insight into the mechanics of the flesh industry, Joe's success is a mystery. He can't sell alcohol and only makes money off the door. Nonalcoholic nude clubs I've visited skidded by selling ten-dollar sodas and offering questionable backroom encounters with dancers who wore evening gloves to cover the needle marks on their arms. By all accounts that's not the Mons modus operandi, and none of the Mons dancers I've met fit that image. Sure, some of Mons's success can be attributed to its mystique. There's a novelty in saying you've been to a club from the national headlines. But what keeps customers coming back, or even risking their lives to get here?

Down the street a kitschy alien spaceship flashes like a beacon atop 2001 Nude Odyssey, one of Mons's competitors. A couple of college-age guys leaving a hotel bar a few doors down don't even glance at it. They dart out across the busy highway, laughing as passing drivers blow their horns. One in an SMU ball cap briefly loses his flip-flop and narrowly avoids becoming roadkill.

Does the Mons offer big-screen NFL replays and an unlimited supply of opium as well as nude women who will rub breasts and butts all over you?

I'm about to find out. Well, as much as a straight woman can.

Inside the mirrored foyer, the door girl texts on her cell phone between bites of a to-go salad. She stops cyber chatting long enough to take the SMU fans' money and waves them through. The cover is twenty dollars, and if you look past her you can get a peek at why you're paying it. On stage, a woman's bare booty jiggles like Jell-O on a bumpy road.

Beyond the threshold, Mons is a voyeur's dream designed with the practicality of a Golden Corral. Mirrored walls and ceiling tiles allow customers to see dancers from almost every angle. A disco ball hangs from the ceiling, one of the few modest attempts at decoration. Multicolored spotlights frame the stage.

Reflective of Joe's matter-of-fact personality, the club makes no pretenses about what it's selling. Plain and simply, Mons is a lap dance factory. Continuous black leatherette couches that look like bench seats for a 50-yard-wide Impala snake through the room. There are few tables. No TVs, no cozy booths, and no private VIP rooms, which are staples at most strip clubs.

Not that there's a need for separate rooms at this point. Only forty customers are scattered about, including a handful of women with boyfriends or husbands.

Being the only unescorted female, I draw curious glances from a couple of geeky guys in glasses with shirts buttoned to their clavicles. I take the nearest seat and cease to exist. A clothed middle-aged woman is no competition for a three-ring circus of bare nubile flesh.

On the octagonal stage, a woman scales the stripper pole like an army cadet climbs a rope. She descends slowly, holding on by only her inner thighs. Her long, wavy brown hair cascades toward the floor.

She poses like a swan in flight, her body horizontal to the stage, back arched, neck stretched, and legs parted like scissors. The acrobatics are so artistic I forget she's wearing nothing more than 8-inch platforms. Based on their expressions, the people sitting around the stage haven't.

On the back of the stage, a skinny blonde wearing only a cowboy hat forces her small breasts together to accept dollar bills from a couple in their late fifties. Along the front, a dancer in a string bikini top performs contortionist feats for a couple of guys in designer shirts. In an amazing display of elasticity, she crosses her calves behind her neck exposing her hairless vagina inches from their faces. For added effect she rolls over and slaps her bare ass. They tuck bills under her garter.

None of the dancers look over twenty-five or wear larger than size 6 jeans. Without exception they have the thin, toned bodies of cheerleaders and the flexibility of a Slinky. No hint of cellulite, no saggy breasts, or implanted basketball-size hooters. Just a range of firm B to D cups. I don't know whether to be impressed or depressed.

Unlike most strip clubs that reek of cigarette smoke, spilled beer, and things you don't want to think about, the air is clear enough to get a whiff of passing dancers' perfume. Most of them wear little more than that. String bikinis, shorts that look like panties, push-up lacy bras, tight midriffs that expose the underside of bare breasts, short skirts exposing rears. On stage or during a lap dance it all strips off. That is, except for the 8-inch platforms that invariably give the dancers a slight zombie gait.

A curvaceous waitress in a tight T-shirt and jeans serves me a soda that costs only two dollars. The club's most expensive drink is four dollars—Red Bull, for those times when a cavalcade of bare vaginas isn't enough to keep you awake, or rather, sober you up. Seriously. Mary, the night manager, says drunken patrons have passed out in the club.

The waitress says most customers arrive drunk. "There's a bar across the street, a topless bar on the other side of the car wash, then there's their cars," she says, indicating where they imbibe. When I explain why I'm here, she smiles. "I guess you don't want any singles," she says, handing back my change. It doesn't register that she would otherwise assume I am there to stuff dollar bills down a woman's garter. That realization comes later, on the darker side of the room.

The acrobatic pole dancer, Frenchy, agrees to talk for no charge, which has more to do with Mary's introduction than the dancer's generosity. Talk typically isn't free in the Mons, even to other women.

Frenchy's now wearing a flimsy black dress that barely covers her rump. Offstage, she looks much younger and radiates an innocence and naiveté. She's twenty with a girl-next-door beauty. Her skin is as smooth as pudding, and her genuine smile easily gives way to giggles. She looks more like a schoolgirl trying to sneak into a Miami disco than a woman who rubs her naked body on men for cash.

This is Frenchy's first night at the Mons. She and her friend just moved from New Jersey and auditioned this afternoon. She's been dancing since she graduated from high school, where she had in fact been a cheerleader.

"What brought you to Tampa?" I ask, shouting to be heard over a hip-hop song.

"I flew," she shouts back with dead seriousness.

"No, why did you come here, to Tampa?"

"There's no money in New Jersey. It's dead," she says.

I ask if they chose Tampa because of its reputation for strip clubs, and Mons because of its worldwide fame. She's oblivious to both. They picked the city because they had a place to crash, a girlfriend's apartment, and Mons because their friend suggested they could earn good money here. "We looked at the website," Frenchy says, "and it looked good." Bottom line: Dancers don't care about strip-club ratings. Show them the green.

Frenchy has been working an hour and a half. Traffic is slower than she expected, but she's made $150, which doesn't seem to excite her until I point out that's more than a dollar a minute. She earned it from lap dances, which is how Mons dancers typically make 80 percent of their take-home; the other 20 percent comes from stage tips.

A lap dance is in progress on the couch along the wall. Keeping one platform on the floor, a petite blonde rubs her breasts all over the placid face of a blubbery man in Bermuda shorts with white socks nearly to his knees. He's about five times her width and slides his hands down her back to her behind. Nude Barbie grinding Santa. A sign above them reads lap dances are $20 to $30, prices negotiable.

A two-way contact lap dance is about the closest thing you can get to having sex without penetration or hand stimulation. If you believe the stories of some strip connoisseurs who claim to wear condoms underneath their clothes, they are not always without happy endings. Although there's no nipple-sucking in sight, it's allowed if dancers are willing.

A lap dance lasts one song, about three minutes, and it's not uncommon for men to drop upwards of four hundred dollars a night for fifteen or twenty dances. Mary's seen men spend thousands of dollars in one night. Sometimes they later complain and bad-mouth a dancer online to strip-club groupies. Mary merely calls it "separation-from-money anxiety."

Explicit fondling is one of Mons's claims to fame and infamy. In many American cities, including Las Vegas, customers legally aren't allowed to touch dancers above the thigh. Many locales even prohibit nude and topless performers from dancing within 6 feet of customers, essentially banning lap dances. Such is the case in Tampa.

I've actually just witnessed an illegal act. The police could rush in any minute and haul Barbie and Santa off to jail. Such things have happened, but not in a decade.

## Ninjas and the Super Bowl

Tampa's adoption of the 6-foot rule in 1999 attracted more public outcry than any other action in the city's recent history. No issue has highlighted the city's dichotomy of goody-goodies and the lovers of sleaze quite so well. You have to know the story to fully appreciate Joe Redner's fame and the city's bipolar nature. Tampa isn't completely Sodom or Gomorrah.

During the lap dance war, city council meetings turned into fiery five- and ten-hour debates. Crowds swelled with hundreds of exotic dancers with their kids in tow, fire-and-brimstone preachers, church ladies wearing "ban lap dance" stickers, grizzled cab drivers, suited lawyers, a radio shock jock, a hive of reporters, and a few ordinary citizens.

Yours truly, covering the spectacle for the local alternative newspaper, sat through all fifteen hours plus the lead-up, taking notes on the disrobed democracy. An eighty-one-year-old lady called dancers "sinners." A tearful Mons stripper wheeled her quadriplegic brother to the podium. "I need constant care, and cannot feed or bathe myself without the care that she is providing me," he said.

The final vote drew so many people that the meeting had to be held in a Tampa Convention Center ballroom that seated five hundred. Even still, there was an overflow, and three hundred were relegated to watching the debate in another room on closed-circuit TV.

Leading the charge for the morality brigade was Councilman Bob

Buckhorn. With his eye on the mayoral throne, Buckhorn had already gone after massage parlors and alcohol-free raves. Joe was the strip-club king, though he looked more like a typical businessman. He wore his hair short, his face clean-shaven, and dressed in a sports coat and slacks.

The two men were established adversaries. Joe had recently run against Buckhorn for the city council seat and lost miserably. This time Joe's empire was on the line, and he spared no expense to fight back. He brought his high-priced lawyer and hired economists and statisticians. Uncharacteristically quiet at the meetings, Joe let them make his case that strip clubs don't promote crime and help bring millions of dollars into the city.

Ostensibly, Joe's clubs (he had three at the time) weren't the impetus for the ordinance. The Tampa Police Department had just completed a two-year undercover investigation of some seedy strip clubs, massage parlors, and lingerie-modeling joints. Officers said they witnessed oral sex and hand-jobs inside the businesses and dancers prostituting themselves for rendezvous outside the clubs. The city's smoking gun was a composite video of bawdy stage performances shot by undercover vice cops, featuring girl-on-girl sex acts and one particularly absurd contest involving a remote control toy truck with a dildo the size of a forearm mounted on its front. Customers paid five dollars to attempt to ram the roving phallus into the vaginas of dancers lying spread-legged on the floor. Invariably the fake penis bounced off the dancers' crotches. Vice cops made no arrests during their long investigation, though they captured many gratuitous close-ups of bare breasts and vaginas. City leaders considered the video too raunchy to air at the family-filled council meeting. I viewed it in the city attorney's office.

Although the pro–lap dance crowd outnumbered its opponents by more than two to one, the council unanimously passed the ordinance. Mayor Dick Greco, a former Mons customer, signed it into law before daybreak.

National media lapped up the salacious story. Anderson Cooper, then with ABC's 20/20, did a lengthy piece interviewing Joe and some Mons dancers. Comedy Channel's *Daily Show with Jon Stewart* mocked the ordinance and Bob Buckhorn. The show's Vance DeGeneres demonstrated the effect of the ban. A Mons dancer fondled him using a 6-foot-pole tipped with a plastic hand.

On the conventional front, Joe and other club owners sued the city, arguing that the lap dance is protected as free speech under the First Amendment. Joe publicly needled city leaders to come after him. Sounding like a Wild West gunslinger, he told Tampa's WTVT Fox News, "I'm not going to stop anything until the mayor comes in and shoots me."

In his typical fashion, Joe shared his rage with drivers along Dale Mabry Highway by posting sign messages such as, "Mayor Greco and His Looney Tune Police Dept Are a Joke." He posted council members' phone numbers. City Hall was overwhelmed with calls from irate critics, some living outside the state.

Seven months after the ordinance passed, Joe got his wish. Police started raiding clubs all over Tampa, including the Mons.

Kristopher, a University of Central Florida student at the time, was at the Mons with school buddies during one of the busts. "I was just standing there and this cop carrying an automatic assault rifle, in full-on combat gear, runs right by me . . . It was such a bizarre juxtaposition. You had these nude women and these men dressed like ninjas." The police grabbed up those in the act of a lap dance—women and their customers—and loaded them into a paddy wagon. "Then they were just gone, and everything goes back like it never happened," Kristopher says. He and his friends headed back to Orlando. "What a killjoy. I didn't feel like getting a lap dance anymore."

By the time Super Bowl XXXV came to Tampa in 2001, the ninjas had arrested more than two hundred Mons lap dancers and their customers, including National Hockey League players Ted Donato and Tyler Bouck of the Dallas Stars, who were in town for a game. Afterward in a preemptive move, the National Football League sent letters to professional football players warning them to keep their carousing in check while in town for the match-up between the Baltimore Ravens and the New York Giants. Tampa Police slacked off the week of the big game, but the threat of arrests kept many away. It didn't help Mons that television crews camped outside all weekend hoping to capture a scandalous raid.

Strip-club operators caught a break shortly after that when Hillsborough County Judge Elvin Martinez ruled that the ordinance indeed violated free speech and couldn't be fairly enforced. Joe also wore down the city by insisting on a separate hearing for each of the two hundred plus dancers charged. The court system was overloaded, putting prosecutors in a politically delicate situation of prosecuting the dancers at the expense of letting off violent criminals. Joe says he negotiated a better deal for the dancers, and their penalties were no harsher than a ticket for jaywalking.

Since that summer, Tampa police haven't arrested anyone for dancing too close, although the law remains on the books. Bob Buckhorn, who was out of office long enough for people to forget or overlook his failed decency crusade, was eventually elected mayor of Tampa.

## Lap Dance Alley

No one inside the Mons tonight seems the least bit worried they might be hauled off to jail. The club fills by the minute. There are no empty chairs around the stage. A group of young men and women who look hardly old enough to vote sheepishly take seats along the wall. One watches wide-eyed as a nude dancer rubs all over a man sitting less than 3 feet away. Rather than being impressed, the young woman looks like she's going to throw up.

One of the geeks ventures to the darkest side of the room, where the armless couches are back-to-back. One side faces the stage and the other, a mirrored wall with little room to pass without tripping over a lap dancer's foot.

A well-dressed couple in their thirties sit facing the stage and sip O'Doul's. They silently watch the half-nude dancer's act as if it were a Broadway show. The geek sits in the shadows directly behind them. In short order, an older, heavily made-up dancer stationed there gives him a boob facial.

Men on each side of him are getting full-friction dances, too. This is lap dance alley.

Others seated about are checking me out, no doubt wondering what this woman is doing there all alone, standing and watching men get lap dances. I quickly perch on the closest seat, just two spaces down from the O'Doul's couple. Soon I hear soft "oohs" and "yeahs" from behind and feel the tickle of someone else's hair against my shoulder. In my haste to blend, I inadvertently sat behind a man who's getting a lap dance by Cousin Itt.

Ms. O'Doul's keeps glancing at the dance behind me. I peek at the geek's dance behind her. Inevitably ours eyes meet. In panic, we spin our faces back to the stage.

Fortunately, the walls are mirrored. They reveal that the man behind me is getting a lap dance by not one, but two dark-haired women. Stacked like Pringles in his lap, it's hard to tell where one body begins and ends. They are a dark mass of hair and torso with six legs, a human spider.

No wonder Ms. O'Doul's keeps spying on them.

On stage, a tigress puts on a novel show. With her back to the men at her feet, she hikes up her shredded dress and exposes her bare, round rump. Then she performs a feat you might expect to see in Tijuana. No, ping-pong balls aren't involved, although she could probably play the game with her ass. She flexes her glutes to the beat of the music, alternating butt cheeks.

As the song changes, she removes her wisp of a dress. The bodies of lap dance alley part. Behind me the females of the ménage à trois chat like friends who just finished yoga class. The woman on top wasn't a Mons dancer, but the man's wife or girlfriend.

As the couple leaves, their dancer pulls on a short T-shirt and walks around to my side. Maybe she thinks I'm waiting in line. Maybe it is a line, and I just don't know it. But here it comes.

"Honey, would you like a dance?"

"No, I'm just researching. I'm a writer."

She laughs, backs away, and says, "I get it." Does she? Or is she just aware of how little writers earn? Either way, having been hustled by a stripper for the first time in my life, I feel a little exploited.

She moves on to the O'Doul's couple. "Would you like a dance?" she asks and takes the woman's chunky hand. The two women disappear into the shadows of lap dance alley. Skinny Mr. O'Doul's stays behind and sneaks glances.

Are the female customers a sign of widespread sexual liberation or simply an indication that Tampa attracts more female libertines? After talking with the couple who earlier poked bills into the cowgirl's cleavage, I suspect the latter.

Jack and Sandy, who prefer pseudonyms, are part of a threesome who share a condominium at Paradise Lakes, a Pasco County nudist community. Sandy's a nurse; Jack's a retired cop from Michigan. Martha, his wife, also retired, couldn't come with them tonight. Clarifying their living arrangements, Sandy says that she and Martha have separate bedrooms and Jack goes back and forth. "I'm bisexual," she adds. "Though not so much anymore since I got with Jack."

Jack rolls his eyes.

They aren't scoping for a fourth companion, although they haven't ruled out getting a lap dance. "We were just bored and had nothing else to do," Sandy says, proving that even polygamy can get stale. "We've never been here before so we decided to come down and check it out."

"I heard about it when I lived up in Michigan. But it's just one of those famous things that when you live near it you rarely get around to checking out," Jack says as if the strip club is a national landmark. Of course, he has also been distracted, what with sharing the beds of two women at a nudist resort that just hosted the Miss G-String International contest.

Little surprises Mary when it comes to customers' sexual preferences. Back when a mother, in her forties, and her daughter danced at the Mons, a couple of men regularly bought lap dances with both at once, inferring incestuous fantasies. "There are some sick puppies that come in here sometimes," Mary says.

Wearing jeans, an oversized T-shirt, and little makeup, Mary looks more like a friendly Home Depot garden employee than a strip-club manager. She has bangs and a loose ponytail that's dark with a few strands of gray. She's worked for Joe for twenty years. She's been a waitress, a door girl, and now a manager, but never a dancer. "Sometimes I think I should have been because I would have made more money," she jokes. In seriousness, she adds. "I couldn't do it. I don't judge the girls who do, but it's not me. I'm more private about that stuff, and I couldn't stand people touching me."

The stage is briefly empty, and Mary calls out over the microphone for a dancer to take the stage. She sighs in exasperation. "We tell them over and over that they will get more dances if people see them onstage."

Mary likens her job to being mom to five hundred teenage girls. "They have so much drama in their lives. A lot of the girls come here open and fresh, and some go from that frame of mind to being sucked into this fucked-up drama with the other girls," she says.

Although the club is nonalcoholic, dancers can stash drinks in the dressing-room refrigerator. If one gets drunk, Mary makes them sit in their car until they are sober enough to drive home or come back to the stage.

Naturally, the club has a no-drug policy, but invariably some dancers develop a habit. "Joe has put girls through rehab," Mary says. "He will help those who are willing to help themselves. Ones that don't, he lets them go."

She says before the Great Recession, Joe kept a therapist on retainer for dancers and offered health insurance to full-time employees. "Joe's an exceptional boss," Mary says. "He's only here a few hours a day, but he's always here. He lives close. I can call him on his cell and he'll show up in minutes."

Joe pioneered a rather laissez-faire approach to managing dancers. His dancers are free agents, essentially operating as vendors in his mall of flesh. He doesn't pay them, and they don't share their earnings with him. They only tip other employees—the waitresses, door girl, manager, and bouncers. At night, dancers are expected to tip out thirty-six dollars, which is less than half the rate of most other clubs.

In addition to their tip-out to other employees, dancers feed the jukebox. They prefer that to tipping a DJ because it saves them money since DJs typically demand 10 percent of a dancer's tips. Plus, DJs bring their own drama, Mary says. "A lot of times DJs play favorites, try to get the girls to pay him more, and all kinds of stuff. Some are real slimeballs."

Mons dancers set their own hours, allowing them to attend class or raise families and still earn as much as six figures a year. Most don't work there longer than seven years, Mary says. "More than not, they see it as their ladder to something else. A lot go to college. Some leave and then come back because they want to make extra money. They may want to buy a house or pay for their kid's school."

Standing nearby, Alana, a twenty-three-year-old dancer whose white, lacy pull-up bra glows against her chocolate skin, says she's working her way through design school. She likes working at the Mons because unlike a local topless club where she worked, she doesn't have to perform in a private VIP room and is not expected to do more than dance. She says, "That other place was basically a whorehouse."

With money so good and the hours so loose, Mary says that Joe has no problem getting *Playboy* centerfold–quality dancers like Alana. She notes that he prefers petite women and insists that they stay trim. "Beauty is in the eye of the beholder and some men complain that they would like a girl with more meat, more curves, but this is what Joe likes," she says with a sigh. "Like that girl," she says pointing to a dancer on the stage who weighs no more than 125 pounds. "She's pushing it but she has nice curves."

Feeling thoroughly dejected with my physical state, I call it a night even though closing isn't until 5:00 a.m. As I squeeze past a horde of incoming customers, Mary calls out: "You know you can't write about this without getting a lap dance. You're going to have to come back. And bring your husband!"

I laugh. That's not going to happen.

## Crack Whore Stories

Mons may garner the most glory, but it is but a small, though highly touted, piece of Trampa. The area has forty-three topless and nude clubs. The phone book and adult business directories list more than 120 other erotic businesses within Tampa's city limits. Name a medium of sexual pleasure and Tampa has it, homegrown. The city is heavily spiced with pornographers of film and books, XXX theaters, swingers' bars, fetish clubs, massage parlors, lingerie modeling, and adult bookstores.

Then there are the unlicensed outcall services and advertised paid escorts. Tampa's prostitutes don't just work the streets, hotels, and tourist haunts; they get on jets and fly to meet Johns across the country. One madam tells me she based her operation in Tampa Bay because of the beaches and the convenience to Tampa International Airport.

Paul Allen, publisher of *NightMoves,* Tampa Bay's leading adult-entertainment guide, naturally relishes the flourishing local flesh industry. "It isn't quite the holy land, but it's a very adult-friendly atmosphere," Paul told the *St. Petersburg Times'* Christopher Goffard in 2002. "We've got beautiful girls, beautiful weather. We've got the best attorneys we'll ever need. And guys like Joe Redner have laid the groundwork."

Paul says that three of the four largest booking agencies for strippers are based in the area. The porn industry? Well, Paul's more than a cheerleader. He founded Tampa's NightMoves Adult Awards and week-long convention that annually draws national XXX-stars such as Angelina Valentine, Alexis Texas, and Ron Jeremy and filmmakers such as Adam Glasser, a.k.a. Seymore Butts.

It was Butts's extracurricular videotaping during the 1998 event that put Tampa on the porn map and nearly caused city leaders to spontaneously combust. The porn title alone may have caused aneurisms: *Tampa Tushy Fest Part I.*

Butts shot his girl-on-girl fisting porno (that's fist inserted in vagina) in a hotel room on Dale Mabry, not far from the Mons. Released during the lap dance war, the film won the "Best All-Girl Sex Scene" video award at the 2000 AVN Awards in Las Vegas. Butts was later arrested on obscenity charges in California because of the film, giving him and Tampa all the more notoriety.

Around the same time, female roommates in a west Tampa home were showering and having sex on a live pay-per-view website called Voyeur Dorm. The city aggressively tried to shut it down and took the case all the way to the U.S. Supreme Court, where it lost. The first of its kind, the case set a national precedent and made nightly network newscasts, shining an even brighter red light on Tampa. Then, adding even more wattage, U.S. attorneys prosecuted the infamous Max Hardcore in downtown Tampa. His sexually sadistic films weren't filmed in Tampa, but one of his thousands of mail-order customers lived there. Since obscenity is based on the community standards of the jury, Hardcore's conviction speaks volumes about the vulgarity of his films. Even Joe grimaces at their mention.

These are just the raunchy films that made mainstream news. Countless other Tampa pornographers operate in the shadows, some topping Seymore Butts's crudeness. Videographer Dirty-D and his porn actress girlfriend live on upscale Davis Island. He puts out a sordid series of porn with names like *Tampa Bukkake* (a woman being ejaculated on by a horde of men), and *Glory Hole Girlz* (women performing fellatio on penises stuck through a hole in a wall), and his ever-popular *Crack Whore Confessions* (train-wreck stories of low-end prostitutes, which he claims are authentic).

Although busted by the Florida Department of Law Enforcement in 2010 for videotaping a seventeen-year-old, legally a minor, for the *Glory Hole* series, he continues to peddle his porn online. "Florida is great for what I do," Dirty-D says. "People are more open and the sunshine makes the bikinis smaller." He says he also has no problem finding local actors. He shoots videos at local XXX-rated theaters, adult bookstores, and in the Florida room of his home. He complains his neighbors call the cops if his car hangs an inch over the sidewalk.

## Skin Deep

It's important to note that Tampa battled a skuzzy reputation long before Joe opened its first all-nude strip club. Joe is more of a grandfather to the modern era of tawdriness. In fact, *Life* magazine tagged the city the "Hell Hole of the Gulf Coast" in 1935.

Tampa political corruption was so out of hand that year that the National Guard was called in to prevent armed factions from gunning down one another. Tampa was like a lawless frontier town with fraudulent elections, warring bands, brothels, and open gambling halls. The city cracked down on prostitution at the behest of the Army Air Corps when it opened MacDill Field (now part of MacDill Air Force Base) and forced the trade underground. The title lingered due to midcentury violence between local mobsters and the Italian Mafia. During the "Era of Blood," there were gangland shootings on Tampa street corners in broad daylight, scenes right out of the *Godfather*.

By the time the turf war ended, Santo Trafficante Jr. had taken over the family business. He would go on to reputedly be one of the American Mafia's most powerful dons overseeing La Cosa Nostra casinos in Cuba and leading a covert U.S. assassination attempt of Fidel Castro. He was never convicted or served a day in jail. He allegedly controlled Tampa's underworld until his death in 1983, seven years after Joe opened his first club.

Evangelicals have deep roots in Tampa as well. At the same time the city was considered a hell on earth, University of South Florida historian Gary Mormino notes, it had an abundance of street preachers who attempted to save the wicked from flames in the afterlife. Rev. Billy Graham, famed spiritual advisor to presidents, got his start preaching to bums, prostitutes, and derelicts on Tampa's downtown streets. Graham studied nearby at the Florida Bible Institute. A historical marker on Franklin Street memorializes his ministry.

Many a street preacher has attempted to save Joe's soul, but none as persistently as Larry Keffer. He frequently appeared outside Mons with a tiny flock, signs promising hell to sinners, and a bullhorn powerful enough to project his fire-and-brimstone message to Mars. Keffer called passing dancers "harlots," customers "masturbators," and Joe a "wicked Sodomite." Joe was known to storm out with his own bullhorn and heckle Keffer and his flock. Once, when Joe was really worked up, he shouted: "You just want to suck my dick, don't you? . . . You're a closet queen! You can't fool God!" The spectacle made for darkly entertaining streetside theater and became its own mini tourist attraction; sometimes, motorists stopped to take pictures.

The Joe I meet in his office is infinitely tamer. He offers tea or bottled water and, as always, is disarmingly candid. Physically, Joe's not an imposing figure. At seventy-one, he's lean to the point of being wiry, toned from daily gym workouts, and as spry as men half his age. A vegan, he lives on raw vegetables and fruit smoothies, lunching at nearby Sweet Tomatoes. Only the deep crevasses on his angular face betray past forays in the fast lane. Frameless glasses disappear between his thick, dark eyebrows and hollow checks; his lips are thin. A thick gold chain around his neck gleams against his olive complexion. Dressed with a hip nonchalance, he's wearing cargo shorts, a black V-neck T-shirt, and a baseball cap advertising his son's next-door brewery. A salt-and-pepper ponytail hangs past his shoulders. He looks like a well-to-do old hippie, which in many ways he is.

He talks about his philosophy of the big life questions as if we're sitting around a campfire staring at the stars. "There always has to be a beginning and ending to everything. I used to think that, because that's what I was taught," he says referring to his upbringing in a Protestant church. He leans back in his leather executive chair and stretches his ponytail straight up, running his hands over it unconsciously as if pulling thoughts from his brain. "Now I think we don't have the ability to know what that concept is. There's no beginning or no end. We don't have the ability of understanding. Everything could not have appeared out of nothing. It's not a legitimate concept. I don't know what it is, but what I do know is that no one else does either. There's not a God."

Running a flesh business and being vilified by the morality police for more than thirty years can understandably lead a man to a Nietzschean philosophy of life, one where God is dead and the superman creates his own moral standards.

Yes, this man who's made millions from all-nude lap dance factories is quite principled, although his is a modified Golden Rule. "It's not the government's moral code. It's my own, and it's much better than theirs. I don't lie, cheat, or steal. My moral code is not about how adults have sex. As long as I'm doing what I think is right, I'm not going to let anybody tell me what to do. Not the government or the mob."

Joe believes that he and anyone else has the right to upend social norms as long as no one else is hurt. If it merely irritates other people, well, that's part of the fun.

On the surface it might seem that Joe has adopted a convenient philosophy, one that allows him to run a taboo business with a clear conscience. Hang with him long enough and it's clear his convictions run much deeper. He's a maverick to the core.

You get a sense of this just by studying his headquarters. He converted an old warehouse into a hip space leaving the high ceiling and ductwork exposed and painting the walls warm colors. Quite an improvement over the Mons and slightly bohemian. Newspaper clippings, antiwar and environmental ads, mockeries of former President George W. Bush and his nemesis, Ronda Storms, campaign posters, protest signs, and *Doonesbury* cartoons cover his office walls.

A large poster of Joe wrapped in and chained to an American flag hangs in the shadows behind a big-screen TV. He used the image in his campaign literature, though given his ponytail, high cheekbones, and dark complexion, the poster more resembles the propaganda of the American Indian movement.

A sign propped against the wall quotes a 1969 U.S. Supreme Court decision: "Freedom of expression would not truly exist if the right could be exercised only in an area that a benevolent government has provided as a safe haven for crackpots." Joe notes that he carried it when he protested Free Speech Zones, during a Tampa appearance by President George W. Bush in 2002. Naturally, Joe did this outside the designated protest area. He was arrested, but charges were later dropped. He sued, claiming designated protest zones violate the right to free speech. He shakes his head in disappointment. He lost that battle.

Surprisingly, a mayoral campaign sign for his staunch opponent in the lap dance war is tacked to his wall. Joe says he voted for Bob Buckhorn in the final election. "I'm not going to vote for or against somebody just because of how they are going to deal with my adult business. I'm going to back the person I think would be best for the city of Tampa. They kind of go hand in hand because if they are the kind of person I think they are, they really aren't going to mess with an adult business unless they are a nuisance. And I'm not a nuisance."

He adds that prior to the election, Buckhorn privately indicated that he wasn't going to go after the strip clubs again. "I don't worry about

Joe Redner, Mon Venus
owner and perennial political candidate, shown inside
his club. Photo by Chris
O'Meara. By permission of
Associated Press, New York,
NY.

Buckhorn," Joe says. "I think he has grown up. It was a real, real embarrassment for them, that 6-foot-rule. Of course, I might be wrong. If I am? I've still got some other tricks I haven't pulled out."

No doubt.

Referring to his various news clippings, Joe says he spends a good part of his day reading news stories and editorials. "I'm not interested in fishing and all the things that most people want to do when they've got enough money where they can do that stuff," he says. "So, I have nothing to do but gather information."

Joe is fidgety and sometimes rudderless in conversation, often forgetting what he was just saying. His self-diagnosis is "attention deficient hyperactive disorder," which he can't fully remember the term for. "If I get off-track I can think and think and think, and I can't get back to where I was. It's always been that way . . . I'm almost immediately bored with anything. Once I've done it, I need something else to stimulate me."

He attributes this to why he's been such a philanderer, though admitting that running strip clubs hasn't helped. He's had two failed marriages and has run through so many girlfriends that he's given up on relationships. He dated some of his dancers, but in the distant past, he emphasizes. "I'm seventy-one," he reminds. "There are other things on my mind. It's not like it used to be."

He still appreciates a beautiful woman's touch. "I go in and get a back rub, feet rub, lotion," he says of visits to the Mons. "I swear to you, I never ask anybody to do anything. They know they don't have to do that. They know they aren't going to be treated any differently because they do or don't do it. They like me. I like them. And they like me because I like them. I don't mean sexually. We like each other. We respect each other, treat one another with dignity."

Joe lives alone in a house under 1,200 square feet just a couple of blocks from the Mons. He has five children by three women, a slew of grandchildren, and several great-grandchildren. Framed baby pictures are scattered around his office.

Like most Floridians, he's not originally from the Sunshine State. He was born in Summit, New Jersey, in 1940. His dad left when he was just a baby, and his mother moved with him and his older brother to Tampa in 1949. Joe was shy, had trouble learning in school. His mom, a waitress, wanted her sons to know God, the Bible, and Jesus. She insisted that they go to a Christian church of their choosing. Joe settled on a Methodist church within walking distance and took communion around age ten. He was disappointed when it didn't give him instant enlightenment. "He put this thing in my mouth, I sit there, and they all join in this prayer. It didn't change a goddamn thing."

Joe started drinking at sixteen, quit school in the tenth grade, and for the next sixteen years drifted from one job and woman to another. He married a local girl who got a job stripping in Peoria, Illinois. Joe worked the door. They had two kids. Joe took a job with a Tampa carnival operator coaxing fairgoers to play game-toss for plush toys. He stuck with it for five years. Divorced and back in Tampa, he bounced through occupations. He laid terrazzo floors, sold furniture, made tin cans in a factory. In between jobs he hustled pool in downtown Tampa dive bars and shacked up with a woman who had his third child.

In the early 1970s, he was doing some carpentry work at one of his favorite bars when owner Pat Matassini offered him the manager's job at the Deep South, a rough-and-tumble go-go club that Matassini owned with Bobby Rodriguez. The Deep South was a dive with one small pedestal for dancers who wore pasties and G-strings. Joe built more platforms and added dancers. Within eight months, business doubled. Life was good. An alcoholic, Joe was managing a bar, and better yet, he was surrounded by scantily clad women who weren't averse to hanging out with him after-hours. Religion? The Bible? Forget it.

One night about 3:00 a.m. on his way home from the club, Joe heard something on the radio that would change his life and ultimately the face of Tampa. The U.S. Supreme Court had ruled that a Jacksonville drive-in theater could show movies with brief glimpses of nudity. The highest court deemed it free speech protected under the First Amendment. Joe thinks, "Dance is speech—ballet, the Indian war dances, dances in Africa. Nudity is content of that speech, therefore it's gotta be protected by the First Amendment. Christ, let's see if they really mean that."

Joe couldn't convince the Deep South owners to go all-nude. There was no law in Tampa against it, but no one had ever dared try. It was sure to bring heat. Matassini, Deep South's co-owner, was already facing a federal conviction for counterfeiting.

Joe didn't give up. He became partners with a bail bondsman who owned a dying beer joint. They reopened it as the Night Gallery in 1976, making it Tampa's first all-nude strip club. As Joe says, "That's when the crap hit the fan."

What followed sounds like an X-rated Looney Tunes series.

Within a week, Tampa vice cops began hauling Joe's dancers to jail. Just as he would later do, Joe posted antagonistic signs out front such as: "Come and watch your local vice squad at work." Joe explains, "I wanted to draw customers to what they were doing. I would just devise ways of combating them. People got interested in it because they wanted to see what would happen next."

Joe's partner, the bondsman, stationed at the jail. He bailed out dancers as fast as they came in so they could get back to work. Even so, the raids left the club temporarily without dancers. Joe caught on to the cops' modus operandi; the undercover officer would watch through a rotation of dancers and then arrest them all. "Once I figured out their M.O. I would just rotate three girls, and keep six to the side. When they would arrest those three and take them downtown, I would put up the next three. They would go downtown. By this point the first ones would be bonding out. It worked out perfectly. By the time they arrested the last three, the first three were back."

"This would happen three or four times a day except on Sundays and Mondays because the vice squad didn't work on Sundays and Mondays." He laughs. "They are such funny people. They just can't think outside the box. Today it's the same."

Joe and his partner were making so much money at the Night Gallery that his former boss Bobby Rodriguez financially backed him in a larger all-nude club on Tampa Bay that they named the Tanga Lounge. The club became so legendary that when it was damaged by fire, the sportswriters who followed the Detroit Lions held a moment of silence.

Police raided the Tanga, too. But Joe says they were forced to change their tactics after they had used every undercover officer, thus making them immediately recognizable.

The cops became more direct. Joe went covert. "When they saw I had that figured out and it was just a waste of time, five or six of them would rush in at once," Joe recalls. Officers showed up throughout the day to snatch a nude dancer off the stage and whisk her to jail.

Joe says he devised a guerilla wiring system to warn dancers of approaching police. He ran a line underneath the carpet from the stage to a button outside the front door. When the doorman saw the police coming he would push the button and the light over the stage would come on. The nude dancer would hide and one wearing a bikini would quickly take her place. "The police would rush in and the girl would be dressed," he says. "They'd come back a few hours later. They'd rush in again and the girl would be dressed."

This ruse worked until one of the dancers ratted to police about the button. "The next time they came I'm standing outside," Joe says. "The cop looked at me and rushed up and said, 'step on that button and I'm going to shoot you.' 'I said, 'you idiot.' I pushed on the button and that was the end of that."

Joe was arrested thirty-six times that first year, though he was never convicted. There was so much money rolling in that the hassle of arrest was worth it. And he even enjoyed the drama. "People go to movies for action. I was living it," he recalled years later to *Tampa Tribune* reporter Ellen Gedalius.

Meanwhile, more than a dozen other all-nude clubs opened. City leaders were frantic to come up with a way to outlaw nudity that would hold up in court. By the time a 1978 U.S. Supreme Court ruling delivered local governments an option, Tampa had twenty-two all-nude clubs.

The high court ruling allowed the city to ban the sale of liquor in businesses with nudity. Most clubs went back to having the dancers wear G-strings and pasties. One chose to show dancers nude on film and clothed on stage. Joe took a risk and kept all-nude dancers. He charged for mixers, gave away liquor, and allowed BYOB. The city quickly put the kibosh on all of that. To make up for the loss in alcohol sales, Joe increased his entry fee from one dollar to five. "Actually what I thought was going to happen, didn't," he says. "I didn't get more people, but I made more money because I charged more." Such is the allure of a totally nude woman, especially one willing to touch you and let you touch her.

"When they took away my liquor license, the lap dance just kind of happened. The girls would be dancing in front of the customer and they would be touching them." Joe is careful not to say the obvious: Without alcohol sales, dancers had to offer an additional incentive to keep customers coming back. Joe says he doesn't require dancers to allow touching. "My only rule is they have to get naked on stage, and they can't be touched between their legs. Otherwise the customer can touch anywhere the girl will agree to be touched, on the breasts wherever. It's fine with me. I studied the statutes. Anything beyond that is a felony. So I took it up to the limit of the state statutes."

Emboldened by his success at the Tanga, Joe virtually flipped off

City Hall by opening another all-nude club and naming it City Council Follies. The Follies couldn't sell booze, but customers only had to walk across the parking lot to get a drink at Joe's Tanga Lounge, where dancers wore string bikinis.

## Virtues of Jail

Joe's battles with the city are well-documented, but he's rarely spoken publicly about how he managed to keep out the mob, which had its fingers in all types of Tampa cash businesses when he started. It's a touchy question and the only one he hesitates to answer. "It didn't happen right away," Joe says of the mob's overtures. "Well, I say that, but let me tell you the guy that had the jukebox in the Night Gallery; I think he was mobbed up. Frank Diecidue (pronounced De-ce-du). People say 'the mob,'" Joe says, fingering quotation marks. "I don't really know. Actually I had a big problem with him because he didn't service the jukebox and I told him if he didn't, I would put him out. He didn't, so I did, I threw him out. And then they threatened to kill me."

He rushes on with his tale, as if the death threat was no more than a bluff of a schoolyard bully. "I put someone else in there, and then they decided not to go after to me, but they threatened him. He pulled the jukebox out." Joe laughs. "They scared him."

After that, Joe says, someone arranged a meeting, and Frank Diecidue promised to do a better job. "We resolved the problem," he says, not elaborating. "I didn't care as long as he serviced the jukebox properly. So, he did, and we got along just fine."

Given that nobody broke Joe's legs, you might think that the jukebox operator was a minor-league thug. Later I discover from Scott Dietache, author of multiple books on the Tampa Mafia, that the feds coined Diecidue a made-man in the Trafficante crime family, an underboss to Santo Trafficante Jr. himself. His jukebox business closed in the mid-1980s. Although Joe's laughing about the death threats thirty years later, upon reflection, I question if he was then.

Later, other reputed mobsters wanted to operate valet parking at the Mons. Joe recalls telling them: "No, it's not going to happen . . . You're going to have to kill me first." Mons has never had valet parking.

Joe suggests mobsters have always backed off because they saw him as a kindred spirit. "I think they respected me because I was fighting the government, and I was just fighting and fighting and fighting. I think they saw that, and they kind of liked it."

He adds: "I guess having [Diecidue's] jukebox in there was kind of a protection for me from the others while he was there."

When Joe opened Mons Venus, it actually was an upgrade from the building's previous tenant. The Huddle House Inn—opened by hometown celebrity Rick Cassaris who was a running back for the Chicago Bears—had evolved into a house of ill repute. Its horseshoe-shaped booths were numbered and equipped with telephones. Prostitutes would sit in a booth and Johns would dial up ones they liked. The city was shutting it down, and the owner was desperate to sell. Joe bought the building in 1982, ripped out the booths, and opened what would become the world-famous Mons Venus.

With the Mons and the Tanga bringing in thousands per week, the high-school dropout and former carnie was living large. He started looking more like a strip-club owner, sporting a thick gold chain, pinky ring, and a Burt Reynolds mustache. He bought a five-bedroom house on the Hillsborough River and 26-foot luxury cruiser. There was weed, cocaine, and all the stereotypical trappings of a nightclub lifestyle. He was caught snorting at a Tampa Bay Buccaneers game in 1983. Not long after that felony arrest, he decided to get healthy. His alcoholism was so bad his skin was yellow and his hangovers put him in bed for two weeks at a time. He claims he gave up all his poisons at once, including booze and cigarettes. (He later confessed that he had continued smoking pot until he was diagnosed with lung cancer.)

Sober, his world got bigger. He and his full-time lawyer, Luke Lirot, started a public-access show called *Voice of Freedom*. Although billed as a place to debate free-speech issues, Joe used it to blast opponents of adult entertainment. He relished debating callers, exchanging insults, and cussing with abandon, confrontations that would never be allowed on network television.

Throughout the 1980s and into the 1990s, he expanded his strip-club enterprises, opening clubs in Ybor City, Clearwater, St. Petersburg, and Homosassa and battling local governments in court. *St. Petersburg Times* writer Jeff Klinkenberg reported in 1991 that Joe had at least thirty-one cases pending in county, state, and federal courts. Although unsuccessful in many, he won more than $600,000 in judgments the following year.

The bulk of the damages were paid by the City of Homosassa, where he had attempted to operate another nude club. He spent two months in jail there for operating the club against a court order. He used the time to get his GED diploma and study law.

## Legacy of Skin

Since the end of the lap dance war, the Mons isn't even Joe's primary source of income, although he says it's a nice chunk of it. He doesn't plan on selling the Mons. "There's no retirement. My life is doing this."

The bulk of his income these days comes from real estate investments. He's a landlord of more than a dozen homes and several commercial properties, including an old Ybor City building retrofitted with the latest green technology and a massive office building he rents to the IRS, an irony that he relishes. He has a film-production studio and is invested in his son's brewery.

He sold his other strip-club properties. He got a sweet $7 million for the former City Council Follies and two adjoining properties after beating the Florida Department of Transportation in court in 2005. The state had originally offered $3.4 million. It was the largest eminent-domain settlement for an adult business property in Florida's history.

What does someone do with all that money? Joe has given chunks of it away. He financed a new city park in a rundown neighborhood and gave generously to children's charities.

Joe has let his hair grow and restarted his weekly public-access show, now espousing broader political views. He argues for a cleaner environment, development that pays for itself, high-speed rail, and healthier school lunches. He rants that Wall Street stole American's home equity. He rails against Florida Republican Governor Rick Scott.

Despite his populist appeal, public office eludes him. Joe has run for office nine times and counting.

His best showing was in a 2007 city council primary. He beat out four candidates to make the runoff. He lost to the incumbent, garnering only 44 percent of the vote.

He laments that many people see him only as the nude-lap-dance king and says the local media perpetuates it. "They just don't listen to me. My campaign slogan was 'My name is Joe Redner and I'm NOT FOR SALE.' I never once saw that in print . . . The press does not print what I say. They just do not."

Granted it was hard for voters to forget that he's made a living off nude women who give boob facials to strangers when he offered free Mons admission to anyone wearing "I Voted" stickers.

He also can't help but antagonize conservatives on the campaign trail. Even though he's an avowed atheist, Joe said a prayer at a 2011 candidates' forum held in a Baptist church. It just wasn't one that would win him votes with that crowd. He thanked God for the California judge who overturned a law against gay marriage. "Doing things like that, you can't win an election," he says with a sigh. "You've got to kiss some people's ass."

Joe says he now focuses on helping get others elected. But his eyes sparkle at the suggestion that voters might be willing to elect him given the outcry for widespread governmental reform.

If for no other reason, Joe may run again because he hungers to be heard. Public-access TV just isn't a large enough stage. "When you're running for office you get to go to these forums and say what you've got to say and people listen. They're not hearing but they're listening, so if you say something outrageous . . ."

He lets his words trail into quiet introspection. What legacy will he leave behind?

The Mons, the Mons. The stage he created may not be for his feet, but it is never far from his thoughts.

"Mons brings in so much money to Tampa that it's unbelievable," he says, beaming about his brainchild. "It has a more positive economic impact than the Bucs because Mons brings money in from outside the area."

I share with him Kristopher's Hong Kong cab experience. He grins, but is not surprised. Joe has a cabbie story of his own.

"I was in New York about fifteen years ago. I was staying at the Marriott Marquis on Times Square. I went downstairs, got in a cab, and said 'take me to one of your local strip clubs.'"

"We're on the way and he said, 'Where are you from?'"

"I said 'Tampa.'"

"He said, 'You're not going to like this place.'"

"I said, 'Why not?'"

"He said, 'There's nothing in New York City like Mons Venus.'"

"I said, 'I own the Mons Venus!'"

"He didn't believe me!"

# CHAPTER 3

# Sisters of Steel

Coastal Highway A1A rumbles with the sound of twin engines. Bike Week, the world's largest motorcycle event, is at full throttle. Nearly a half million motorcycle lovers have converged on the central east coast of Florida to check out bikes and show off theirs. The majority are men who spend a good deal of time downing beers and gawking at woman in wet T-shirts and assless chaps.

A motorcycle posse of middle-age men in standard biker uniform—black leather jackets and vests, boots, and reflective shades—pulls out two by two from a pasture campground. A farmer, no doubt, has found bikers more lucrative tenants than cows for the week.

I glimpse patches on the backs of the men's vests. Before I can make out the club names, they zoom past on rumbling Harleys toward the epicenter of mayhem—Daytona Beach's Main Street—and leave behind a cloudy trail of exhaust and testosterone.

Could they be one-percenters (1%ers), as outlaw bikers call themselves? Or are they merely posers? This being Florida, it could go either way.

You see, in the male biker world there are clubs of weekend motorcycle enthusiasts with spit-shined $20,000 motors, sometimes referred to as Plastics (bikers who bought the look with one swipe of a credit card) or RUBs (rich urban bikers). There are daredevil professional racers with corporate sponsors. There are "Power Rangers," whose clothing and helmets match their Japanese sports bikes. And then there are the true rebels—the 1%ers. This nihilistic minority proudly lives on the fringe and relishes in shredding societal norms.

One-percenter clubs embraced the term long ago after a newspaper reported that 99 percent of motorcyclists are law-abiding, while 1 percent are deviants, outlaws. They are the Hell's Angels, the Outlaws, the Mongols, and other clubs of assorted vicious names indicating they are badass bad. They inspired the Marlon Brando black-and-white classic *The Wild Ones* and modern Technicolor fictions such as the AMC cable series *Sons of Anarchy*. Daytona Bike Week is their mecca, and Florida, a favored home address.

I'm heading in the opposite direction of the questionable male biker herd, bound for an annual gathering of the Leather & Lace Motorcycle Club, a group of women bikers. But I'm not sure the scene will be any tamer than the machismo one in Daytona.

Lace's founder and president, Jennifer "Jenn" Chaffin, has danced in and around the gritty 1%er world since she was sixteen. Her first husband was chapter boss of the local Warlocks Motorcycle Club, an MC. He was assassinated in their garage by members of a rival motorcycle club in 1991.

Her second husband is the chapter boss of the local Mongols, an MC that the U.S. Justice Department considers so dangerous that it tried to ban their name and emblem—a stoned-looking Asian man in biker uniform kicked back on a chopper. His head is shaven with a spit of a topknot as to remotely resemble Genghis Khan's warriors, who wore helmets plumed with horsetail hair.

I discovered Jenn and her club on the National Geographic Channel. The documentary *Biker Chicks* portrayed them as thrill-seeking women who ride in the shadows of a dangerous world of crusty biker gangs that treat women like property and pee on new members' patched vests as part of the initiation ritual.

Jenn laughed about that fabled ritual when I reached her by phone. "I don't know where they got that." Her voice is like a smoldering campfire, smoky and steady. She talked candidly about her club and her late husband's murder. She chuckled about how her late husband's 1%er brothers picked on her when she rode with them, situations that would make most people, male or female, weep in self-pity or crack with anger.

Despite Jenn's candor, I still didn't understand why women would subject themselves to the sexist world of hard-core motorcycle clubs, much less a woman who had lost her first husband to its brutality. I wanted to learn more.

She invited me to join her and about fifty Lace members who are camping at her house during Bike Week. She added that only officers are allowed to sleep inside the house. In other words, I'll have to sleep in the yard with the other members and the yet-to-be-initiated, the prospects.

I packed my sleeping bag and made a hotel reservation just in case there was a random police raid.


## Tending Farms and Killing Fish

Jenn lives about 30 miles south of Daytona Beach in the Intracoastal hamlet of Edgewater, a small town fueled by boatbuilding and retirees. Her subdivision is middle-class circa 1970s with streets named after native flora such as Orange Tree and Needle Palm. Her ranch-style home sits on a half-acre lot dotted with palm trees. Purple and red plastic flowers fill the window boxes. A large screened pool hugs the side of the house.

Any other time of year, her place wouldn't stand out. This week you can't miss it. Her front yard is lost to tents, RVs, bike trailers, and a blue Port-a-Potty. A shiny rainbow of muscle bikes, mostly Harleys, arches the circular drive. The motors wait like prized steeds at a hitching post, resting, but ready to bolt.

The afternoon is quiet. Two Doberman pinscher pups hop around in a portable pen. A burly, bearded man wrapped in quilts sleeps on the floor of an open bike trailer. A couple of women in black leather jackets hover by a smoldering fire pit sucking on cigarettes. The "sisters," as club members call one another, are resting up for their annual Moonshine Wednesday party.

The sign posted on the front door spells out Jenn's rules:

NO drugs.

No smoking inside the house.

No parking motorcycles on the grass.

No stray animals, 2-legged or 4-legged. This means that if anyone "meets" someone while they are out they may NOT bring them back to the house.

Evidently things aren't always this sedate.

A leather-vested, lanky sister with a bandanna wrapped around her head answers the door seeming puzzled that anyone would bother to ring. "A journalist? Come in. I'll get Jenn," she says and leads me past the formal living room where an artificial Christmas tree still stands. It is March.

We follow the smell of roasting beef and potatoes to the eat-in kitchen, the pulse of the home. A half-dozen middle-aged women sit

Leather & Lace sisters are always ready to ride.

around a heavy dining table quietly pecking at their laptop computers as if they are devising a plan to solve world hunger. No one's drinking beer, smoking pot, or partying in any form. If it weren't for a couple of club leather vests, they could be mistaken for a ladies' Bible study group.

The kitchen is homey, in a matronly biker way. Tiny ceramic bikes line whatnot shelves; a motorcycle mobile dangles from the ceiling; yellowed newspaper clippings about the club hang on the wall like a child's school artwork.

Jenn saunters in and greets me as if I'm the cable guy, friendly, but not gushy. That's not her style.

Jenn's in her fifties, a grandmother. She's wearing slouchy black knit pants and a denim shirt. Her long, ash-blond hair is as straight as straw, her nose is broad, and her eyes are the color of a clear Florida sky. She speaks with the nonchalance of a hippie, but has the magnetism of a queen.

She says the club just finished its business meeting as if to explain why the women are busy at their laptops. Dinner will be in a couple of hours, kicking off the Moonshine party, which doesn't actually involve White Lightning but homemade Kahlua and vodka Jell-O shots.

Jenn's not one for idle chitchat, and after causally announcing who I am to the other women, who barely look up, she heads back outside and leaves me standing alone by the Crock-Pots.

An enthusiastic young newbie from Colorado Springs bounces in and assumes I'm a club member. Before I can explain otherwise, she hugs me and says, "It's so nice to meet another new sister!" She is not any less thrilled when I awkwardly explain that I'm a journalist.

Someone at the table finally speaks, She Bear, identified as such by the name patch on her leather vest.

"I keep killing my fish," she says without lifting her eyes from the animated world on her laptop.

Turns out the women are playing Facebook games. They're tending one another's crops on FarmVille, sharing menus in Café World, and feeding each other's virtual pets.

A sister returns from a bedroom wearing glittery red slippers and announces, "I had to take off my bra. It was killing me."

Another with a heavy New York accent shows off her new lipstick, which she claims stays on for days. "But I think it might be too red," she says and purses her lips for all to see. "Whattaya think?"

"Maybe wear it more at night," another responds.

A graying sister from Missouri ducks out to check on her international award-winning Persian cat and kittens that are curled up in her RV.

Jenn floats back in and announces that a certain sister is taking a nap and suggests they write something on her forehead. Another remarks about the woman's size. Jenn decides maybe it's not such a good idea.


## "We're Not 1%ers!"

When Jenn formed her club in 1983, most women were stuck riding pillion, clinging to the backs of men. Despite how mainstream motorcycling is today, women riders are still a minority. The American Motorcycle Council reports that women accounted for less than a quarter of American motorcyclists in 2008. That's up from one-eighth in 1990.

Lace claims to be the world's largest women's MC, although there's not a lot of competition for that title. The largest women's group, the Motor Maids, calls itself a motorcycle organization rather than a motorcycle club, an MC. As I delve further into the fringe, I come to realize this is an important distinction.

Jenn says she formed Lace to help raise money for children's charities while doing what she loved most, "being in the wind." Married to a 1%er, she understood their hierarchy. She liked the familial bonds, the clothing, the structure, and, of course, the rambling group rides. She even liked 1%er's rebellious spirit, but not the violence that sometimes comes with it.

Loyalty is the highest code to 1%ers. They pledge to place their biker brothers above all others, including their families and most certainly the law. That's not to say that every 1%er runs guns, sells drugs, beats money out of business owners or commits any other nefarious act. The 1%er clubs also pride themselves on raising money for charities, typically ones for children. Many hold respectable jobs, and some even send their kids to private schools. But the Justice Department labels them "Outlaw Motorcycle Gangs" and says they vow loyalty to clubs that are nothing less than organized crime. Law enforcement is always on their heels, and they are forever portrayed in the media as rogue gangs of sociopaths, sometimes justifiably.

Lace exists in a nebulous world between the recreational riders and outlaw bikers. It is in essence a hybrid, the fringe of the fringe.

Sisters bond like blood, supporting one another through the toughest of times, something they say the 1%ers only claim to do. They help raise one another's children. They mail chocolates and bright-yellow socks to cheer a sister with a broken heart. Sisters might not kill for one another, but when one needed a kidney, several offered theirs.

Jenn says the Lace sisters' only illegal act was riding their bikes on a sidewalk.

Although the women's club activities seem rather innocuous, calling your biker group an MC requires navigating more than roads and wearing leather. To ride peacefully, motorcycle clubs, male and female, must honor protocols of 1%ers even when it comes to naming conventions and fashion. Lace pushes those boundaries.

The women dare to wear their club identification patch, which MCs call "colors," in a similar fashion to 1%ers. Granted, Lace's colors aren't likely to be confused with 1%ers'. No grim reapers or slutty wenches, rather two female angels, a brunette and a blonde. Black and hot pink are their colors, which Jenn says, like their name, represent "inner strength" and "femininity."

Also like the 1%ers, Lace initiates have to prospect for years. They do chores, work fund-raisers and must attend meetings to prove themselves worthy of the final patch, a symbol of full membership.

The club doesn't allow wimpy mopeds or skinny-tire street bikes. Sisters must ride muscle bikes with engines of at least 550 cubic centimeters. Harleys are preferred. Like men's clubs, Lace has a sergeant-at-arms. Sisters refer to Jenn as "the boss."

Lace sisters make it clear that they aren't affiliated with any male club, 1%er or not. Some sisters are a little sensitive about the subject. When asked the club's relationship with the Warlocks and Mongols, Niki Schmidt, a sister from North Carolina, exclaims, "We're not 1%ers. They're criminals!"

Granted, after learning more about the members' backgrounds it's easier to understand why they find comparisons insulting. They are as diverse in age and profession as the vegetable garden beside Jenn's pool. Their ranks include a Maine marine biologist, a Daytona Beach chiropractor, a New York doctoral candidate, a Pennsylvania vet assistant, a Colorado accountant, a Florida circus chef, waitresses, bartenders, and housewives. Many are mothers. Most are married or have

Leather & Lace MC founder and president Jennifer Chaffin takes a break from overseeing her club's weeklong gathering to show her bike.

serious boyfriends. The founding chapter is based in Florida, but the club has members in more than thirty states and other chapters in Pennsylvania, California, the Carolinas, Alabama, and as far away as the United Kingdom and Australia.

Even though they are scattered, Lace sisters stay tight by talking once a week in an online chat room. Each chapter hosts charity biker rides, yard sales, and biker balls throughout the year. They walk together at breast cancer awareness events. At 10:00 a.m. on the third Saturday of every September, each Lace member is required to start her bike and ride 100 miles, solo or with others, to connect in spirit with her Lace sisters.

They have two annual clubwide gatherings. They take care of business during their annual meeting at Jenn's, which they refer to as nationals. Their summer meeting is more for play, and they take road trips outside of Florida. They have ridden from Florida to New Mexico. Once they rode to Missouri and put flags on the graves of veterans.

Being all about encouraging financial independence, they formed an investment club. They are entrepreneurial. They have their own clothing line, cookbooks, and board game honoring noted female bikers—Boots, Scoots and Roots!

Jenn's home is the headquarters of their business enterprise, Lace Sales. A commercial embroidery machine with big spools of thread fills a table in her den. Lace makes custom biker patches for women's and men's clubs. It designs T-shirts and vinyl banners for women riders, charities, and Little League teams.

The club sells wares online and out of a small storage building with matching window boxes beside Jenn's house. During nationals, the store is open in case members want to pick up some additional Lace flair, say a beach towel embroidered with the club's angels logo, rhinestony biker appliqués, or glass Christmas ornaments embossed with "Leather & Lace." Racks are filled with club-member-designed biker T-shirts that would have made feminist Betty Friedan proud, even though she wasn't a motorcyclist. Messages such as "Fear the Pink" champion breast cancer awareness, and "I Beat the Reaper" celebrates the survivors. The shop covers feminine desires from tot to adult, including toy water pistols and women's intimacy kits "for her personal pleasure."

Outside by the fire pit, Jenn's precocious granddaughter hits me up to buy a five-dollar tin of popcorn. "It's for Future Lace," she tells me. "Next I'll be in Teen Lace!" The club schools two age groups of daughters and nieces in the ways of business. To that end, the club loaned the Future Lace girls three hundred dollars for a popcorn machine, charged them 2 percent interest. The Lace sisters taught the girls to calculate how many bags they needed to sell in order to pay the loan back. The girls paid off their debt and started making a profit.

The sisters also give the older girls tips on how to deal with men. "They learn a lot about relationships with guys," Jenn says. "Like how not to put up with things and how to be your own person."

Lace sisters live what they preach. But unlike the white-gloved Motor Maids who pride themselves on ladylike behavior, Lace sisters like to throw sexism right back in men's faces. They make a sport out of coaxing men in bars and at parties to give up their boxer shorts. It's a twist on a crude male ritual of keeping women's underwear as trophies. Jenn estimates she has more than thirty pairs.

During a prior Bike Week, nine sisters stood outside the Boot Hill Saloon, a notorious Daytona Beach biker bar, and graded passing men on their looks, posting their scores on a chalkboard. "A few of the men who got low grades left in a huff," the *Daytona Beach News-Journal* reported at the time. Jenn recalls some the men's girlfriends liked the ratings even less. "They would say, 'He's a ten.' We'd say, 'No, girlfriend. He's a three.'"

At the time, Jenn told the Daytona reporter that "Riding is one of the last frontiers for them, and we're stepping into it." Clearly, motorcycling wasn't the boundary they were breaking.

Perhaps not surprisingly, many Lace sisters got into motorcycling following a divorce. Over pot roast and drinks at the Moonshine Wednesday party, the sisters share stories of why they love riding on two wheels. "I think because it's liberating," says Blythe Joslin, as a sister passes with a tray of pudding shots.

Blythe is a stout Alabama woman with wild, shoulder-length salt-and-pepper hair and a strong jawline softened by plump cheeks. She had always been too scared to try riding a motorcycle. Then, after her third marriage, she met Country, a wiry, bearded bike mechanic with forever a cigarette in his hand and a grin on his face. She rode on the back of his bike until his son started coming along. Then she was stuck following them in a car.

"I told myself there's not that much to riding a bike," Blythe says matter-of-factly. "I'd ridden horses a long time. So I went out and bought a bike."

She found out it wasn't so easy when she was riding in the rain by herself and dropped her Harley Softail. "It happens to everyone at some point and you have to be able to get it up by yourself. And it weighs about eight hundred pounds!" She raises her knee, then stomps down on an imaginary foot pedal to demonstrate how she did it.

Once Blythe got down the basics, she found a Zen-like peace in motorcycling. "It puts everything in perspective. When I'm on my bike, I'm not worrying about bills, my job, the kids. I'm not afraid. I've done a lot of things in my life. If I die tomorrow, I'm fine with that."

For all their independence, Lace still plays by the rules of the male clubs, even though they sometimes gripe about it.

Much of the tension is over something as seemingly superficial as colors—the club patches. Next to their bikes, club colors are 1%ers' most prized possessions. In the early days, they cut their patches into three pieces to distinguish their club from more ordinary, law-abiding ones. The top patch, which in biker speak is called the "top rocker," bears the club's name. The middle patch is the club's symbol—be it a skull and crossbones or two angels. The bottom rocker bears the chapter location.

Jim Dillman, who tracks outlaw biker clubs for the Florida Intelligence Unit and the Collier County Sheriff's Office, says 1%ers feel they own the three-piece patch. They don't want every ordinary, law-abiding MC wearing three-patch colors. That would dilute the hell-raising significance of theirs. Furthermore, 1%er clubs have gone to war with one another over who has rights to wear a location name. "People have gotten killed over the bottom rocker," Jim says in reference to a biker shootout in a Nevada casino that started because a club wore its colors in what another considered their territory.

Around the time Lace formed, 1%ers weren't keen on women riding their own bikes, Jim says. Most women in the outlaw biker world wore patches that said they were property of a club member. "I don't think all 1%ers are chauvinists now," Jim says, "but at one point it was pretty much if you weren't a white male, you could forget about it."

So, when Lace sisters became a three-patch club, it caused quite a stir in the 1%er world. The fact that the club was Jenn's, a woman whom outlaw bikers knew through her late husband, Bear, Jim says, probably made it worse.

Jenn says that 1%ers let her know they weren't happy about it. "They said, 'Wait a minute. Do you know what you are doing, little girl?'" Jenn played girly back, albeit with nerves of steel. She told them, "It looks better. It's a fashion statement, and you know I'm all about fashion."

Out of respect for the men's clubs, Jenn says, Lace didn't put chapter locations on its bottom rocker. Rather the patch simply says, "Sisterhood." She doesn't see that as much of a concession given that Lace sisters are scattered and many are nomads, meaning they don't have local or state chapters.

The issue of patches is still touchy, as it is for any MC that dares to wear three. It makes traveling as a club particularly onerous, as 1%er protocol demands they notify every ruling club along their route that they will be passing through.

Leather & Lace member Blythe Joslin, the club's web designer and national board member.

The territorial rule might seem arcane and the implied threat, melo-dramatic, especially when you consider that Lace focuses on raising money for breast cancer and teaching its kids how to run a popcorn business. Lace sisters found out how maniacal 1%ers are about that control when they took a road trip outside of Florida.

Lace sister Gail recalls the incident over Kahlua pudding shots. Due to a miscommunication, she and other sisters found themselves in a bar with 1%ers who didn't know Lace would be in their town. "We were only in the bar for a few minutes when these guys came in and closed the doors. They wanted to know what we were doing there," says Gail, who isn't someone you'd expect to down beers with outlaw bik-ers. She's working on a doctorate degree in emotional intelligence and owns a horse-supply business in Stanfordville, New York. She's careful to phrase her reaction to the incident, as if 1%ers might take offense to her depiction. "It was kind of interesting. We were in their territory."

## Outlaw Nation

Florida is a two-wheel state. One in twenty-five adult residents sports a bike, making it second only to California in motorcycle saturation. Weather, naturally, plays a big role in the state's popularity with bikers. Florida riders don't have to worry about getting caught in snowstorms and can ride year-round. Legally, they don't even have to wear helmets, or "brain buckets," as many bikers call them.

Florida also has hundreds of miles of coastal highways offering views of light sandy beaches and rolling turquoise seas. Inland, well, much of inland Florida is rural with long, flat two-lane roads stringing together small towns with mom-and-pop grills and hole-in-the-wall bars welcoming bikers.

Florida's large tourism engine also lures bikers with festivals throughout the year. In addition to Bike Week, the biggies are Biketoberfest and the Leesburg Bikefest, which draws a quarter million bikers. Even the carnie community of Gibsonton throws a biker extravaganza complete with high-wire acts, which don't involve motorcycles.

Florida is flooded with motorcycle organizations and club chapters. Recovering drug addicts, policemen, firemen, war veterans, lesbians, Christians, nudists, Scientologists—every subculture you can think of has an organized motorcycle club. On any given weekend there's a biker poker run going on somewhere in Florida.

Real estate being second only to tourism in Florida, developers happily cater to the lucrative biker market. One planned motorcycle community in central Florida advertises "Live Where You Ride" and offers customizable garages for motorcycles. Its motto: "We're building freedom."

But Florida isn't just a big motorcycling state. It's a gun-toting 1%er nation.

One-percenter bikers have laid claim to Florida since the end of World War II. When the largest 1%er clubs later divvied up national territory, the Hell's Angels got California, the Banditos got Texas, and the Outlaws MC scored Florida. "Everything else in the country was kind of open for everybody else," says Jim, the intelligence investigator. "That makes Florida a very significant state."

The FBI, Bureau of Alcohol, Tobacco, Firearms and Explosives (ATF), and local law enforcement agencies have entire units devoted to infiltrating and tracking the moves of 1%ers in Florida. They estimate that hundreds of 1%ers and their affiliates call Florida home. "It's constantly evolving," says Jim, who works closely with the FBI. "Someone asks me who's fighting who, and I have to ask what day it is."

Although each chapter of the Outlaws MC may have only a couple dozen members, Jim says they still dominate the growing number of smaller 1%er clubs. Swallowing prejudice, in recent years Florida clubs have formed alliances with younger, minority clubs that ride Japanese street bikes, commonly referred to as crotch rockets. This is a significant change, he says, given that 1%er clubs for the most part are exclusively white and have a reputation of bigotry. "Colors are everything to these guys," Jim says. "But in the long run, the color that matters most is green."

Every few years, the feds and local cops swoop in like the winds of a hurricane and carry a posse of Florida's 1%ers to jail on charges of everything from drug trafficking to gunrunning. In the years between raids, they attempt to infiltrate club ranks or surveil them like commandos, sometimes from just across the street.

At Bike Week 2010 they are more overt.

In the twilight of dawn, a huge RV emblazoned with "Daytona Beach Police Department" rolls into an older sketchy neighborhood and parks across the street from the Outlaws MC clubhouse. Dozens of members from around the nation are bunking inside a dingy white house surrounded by a chain-link fence.

About a dozen cops gather at the mobile command post for briefings. The bikers send their lawyer over with hot doughnuts. The cops respond by issuing tickets to bikes parked illegally on the sidewalk.

Throughout the day, the show of intense machismo escalates. Tattooed bikers with potbellies, beards that could hide food for weeks, and vests patched with the Outlaws' trademark skull and crossed pistons sit on the front porch glaring across the street. Uniformed police glare back.

"We just want to send them a message," Police Chief Mike Chitwood tells the *Daytona Beach News-Journal*. "We'll be holding our briefings there for Districts 1 and 2, and the command post will be there for an indefinite period of time."

Indefinite becomes one day. Several neighbors complain to local television and newspaper reporters—not about the bikers, but the cops.

One neighbor tells Orlando's WOFL-TV news that the Outlaws cleaned up the neighborhood. "There was prostitution, crime, broken car windows . . . These guys are the best thing that ever happened to this town."

The mobile command center pulls out the next afternoon.

### Motorcycle Mayhem with American Express® Cachet

Farther south on A1A, Lace sisters are busy doing chores. Jenn runs a tight household. With more than fifty people consuming every square inch of her home and lawn for a week, no one except officers gets the luxury of slacking.

"I have yard duty," says an eighteen-year-old who came along with her mother in hopes of getting a Florida tan. Upon arrival all members, except the officers, had to sign up for a housekeeping job—either cooking or cleaning the yard, house, or bathrooms.

Between chores, bike safety and CPR classes, investment club meetings, shopping, media interviews, and nighttime parties around campfires, some of the sisters get talked into leading newbies up the beach to see the mad scene in Daytona Beach.

Bike Week is of little interest to the longtime club members these days. Jenn holds nationals during Bike Week so that members' male companions, the club's "Big Brothers," have something to do.

Bike Week veterans grumble when I mention Main Street. "We've taken a few new sisters up there to see it because you need to see it once. But we hate going. Once you've done it, you don't need to see it again."

They complain the event has become overly commercialized and overrun with posers and weekend warriors. That wasn't always the case. The genesis goes back to 1937 when daredevils raced on the hard-packed sands of Daytona Beach, the guttural sound of their motorcycles choking out the hollow roar of the Atlantic surf. The tide dictated start times, and most racers were semi-pro at best. They sped 80 mph around a primitive 3.2-mile track that stretched 1.5 miles north along the flat, tan beach before banking between the dunes to finish down a narrow, raggedly paved stretch of Atlantic Avenue. Onlookers lined the unfenced course, often getting sprayed with sand from the passing full-throttle Harley-Davidson, Norton, and Indian motorcycles.

The Daytona 200, then coined the Handlebar Derby, became the premier motorcycle race in America. Riders set speed records. News photographs of bikers racing along the crashing waves sent a romantic image of motorcycling on Daytona Beach around the world—freedom and thrills in paradise.

When the annual race was put on hold during World War II due to the rationing of fuel, tires, and metal, something funny happened. The bikers continued to come. They cruised into Daytona Beach for four days every March, riding on the sand, checking out other bikes, and of course, partying until they couldn't stand. Bike Week was born.

After the war, the races returned, drawing increasingly rambunctious crowds and national media attention. In 1948 *Life* magazine reported that "for four days last month the resort city of Daytona Beach could hardly have been noisier—or in more danger—if it had been under bombardment." The magazine went on to note that the American Motorcycle Association was considering policing future races: "One duty will be to restrain sophomoric cyclists who amused themselves this year by tossing firecrackers into the crowd."

Racing aficionados still consider the Daytona 200 the most grueling motorcycle race in America even though it's been held on asphalt at the Daytona International Speedway since 1961. The partying in bars and on the beach long ago eclipsed the race in popularity. The majority of motorcyclists who come to Bike Week these days don't even go to the race.

Bike Week's geography changed, too. Due to Daytona Beach residents' complaints about noise and traffic, the city imposed restrictions, sending the more raucous to the outskirts. The event now spans 30 miles north and south of Daytona, from Ormond Beach to Edgewater and another 30 miles inland to Orlando. Even so, most bikers manage to make at least one trip to the center of the mayhem.

## It's Not Going to Lick Itself

On a cool March morning, bikers cruise Main Street to show off their steel horses and leer at the half-naked women who are there either for thrills or by profession.

The core eight-block stretch is already lined with parked motorcycles of every make, color, and style—cruisers, softails, touring bikes, speed bikes, and a curious handful of mopeds. There are *Easy Rider* choppers with handles so high that riders could throw out their shoulders reaching up to them. Others stretch as long as a car. Bikes are wrapped in bandito belts of ammo. Some look like space capsules. A number of tricked-out trikes (three-wheeled bikes) pull trailers, begging the question, Why not get a truck? Gas tanks, fenders, and trunks are airbrushed with lightning bolts, topless big-breasted women, helicopters, and the Last Supper.

Owners in leather jackets who reek of designer cologne stand near their pimped-out rides, swigging beer or in the case of the Jesus clique of two, passing out small New Testaments. A steady stream rolls down the street in both directions underneath welcoming city banners. One three-wheeled trike pulls a cart of German shepherds wearing goggles; in another, there's a matching airbrushed casket. Herds of leather-clad men with middle-aged women in chaps riding behind them inch between the red lights, seeing and being seen. Engine rumbles add to the cacophony of rock, country, and rap music blasting from open-air bars with names like Dirty Harry's and Froggy's.

There are no club colors in sight since bars along Main Street now ban them. An occasional biker suspiciously wears his vest turned inside out.

Young barmaids bear the chill in low-cut midriffs and shorts that look more like panties. As rock blares over the speakers they grind, jiggle, and kick around a stripper pole that tops a sidewalk bar in hopes that out-of-town bikers will open their wallets for a brew and a big tip.

Bikers on foot scour the endless line of souvenir stands and stores. The design "Support Single Moms" with a silhouette of a naked woman at a stripper pole is ubiquitous, appearing on T-shirts, posters, and bathrobes. There are hundreds of patches with messages ranging from the tame "Harley-Davidson" to the crude "I Eat Pussy and I Stutter."

A couple of middle-aged men in jeans and Harley jackets stop to check out a wall of women's black booty shorts with sayings across the back such as "It's not going to lick itself," (perhaps a nod to women's growing strength in the biker world). The men look, laugh, but aren't buying.

Meanwhile, about 20 miles inland in the farming community of Samsula, women pull hair and pin one another in a rank pit of soured coleslaw. The winner gets five hundred dollars and the infamy of a title. More than one thousand beer-guzzling bikers and posers upwind cheer from behind a web wire fence. A stout contestant yanks the bathing suit top of her rival, exposing fake breasts. The hooting and hollering becomes almost deafening.

The women's coleslaw wrestling competition at Sopotnick's Cabbage Patch Bar has been a Bike Week tradition since 1985. Owner Ron Luzner started the contest to entertain the hard-core bikers who camped in the adjacent field. Other bars already used mud and whipped cream, so he chose coleslaw to reflect the club's name. Ron, also known as Mr. Polka Man, mixes 1,000 pounds of shredded cabbage and 5 gallons of Wesson oil for a day's meet.

The event has become such an attraction that some contestants dress up like Pocahontas and action heroes. Local mom Heather Spears, four-year reigning champion in 2010 and winner of pudding and creamed-corn wrestling at other Bike Week events, described the competition to the *Orlando Sentinel*: "It is rough. I've had crater marks on me from all the girls digging in their nails and tearing my shirt and skin off. It is slimy, too. This is just oil, and you just have to put your weight to one side and hold it. The more you do it, the better your technique becomes."

### Campfire Stories

Back at Jenn's, exposed flesh is mere talk for the half dozen Lace sisters and their friends huddled around a fire bowl in the backyard. None of the odd assortment has witnessed the coleslaw wrestling extravaganza, or at least will admit it.

A newbie, a Massachusetts credit union accountant in a Lands End–style jacket, had never met any of her Lace sisters until this week. Her tall, clean-cut boyfriend, John, rides with a mainstream club.

Blythe and Country and their friends, another couple from Alabama who aren't affiliated with Lace—the grizzly bearded biker who had been napping earlier and his petite girlfriend—seem more familiar with the rowdier biker scene.

The napper is now in high gear, downing beers and entertaining the lot with one-liners in his hillbilly southern twang. Since I'm also from Alabama, we engage in a little state bonding, then talk books. "Who is your favorite writer?" he asks, leaving little time for an answer. "I love

Bikers are all about patches, and not just their club colors. Ones like these sold at Bike Week leave little unsaid.

to read. My favorite writer is Lewis Grizzard. He wrote some funny shit."

The group starts sharing memorable sights and experiences at past biker events, which naturally include women displaying flesh.

An older Leather & Lace sister standing by the fire quietly recalls seeing a flabby woman in a thong riding on the back of a bike at a Sturgis rally. The Bama biker twangs, "That sounds like two sheets of paper flapping in the wind."

The conversation turns to the Main Street scene of whale's tails (the back of thong panties exposed above low-riding jeans) and women in mere body paint for tops. John jokes in his rubbery Massachusetts accent, "I've thought about taking Viagra, putting on tight sweat pants and walking down Main Street."

Without hesitation, the Bama biker chimes in: "I'd have to wear a fuckin' sign that said, 'I've just taken Viagra' or nobody would know!"

All crack up. He continues. "I'm not kidding. It's like a button on a fur coat."

The newbie laughs, nervously.

Someone asks about thong pulls, a contest big in biker circles and advertised at numerous area bars during Bike Week. The visiting Alabama couple seems to intimately know the details and explains that the contest involves a woman wearing a thong that's attached by rope to two loaded carts. In their experience, the carts roll in opposite directions and the women whose thong rips off first wins. The thin Bama woman fesses up that she once won such a contest. Then adds that she cheated by cutting her thong so it would easily rip off and then split the hundred-dollar prize with the only other contestant. "Hey, that's fifty dollars for less than an hour's work," she says.

Typically, thong pulls at bars during Bike Week involve women dragging cases of beer in one direction until all but one, the winner, is still wearing her panties. In other words, the one with the strongest elastic wins. The bar contests require women to wear something underneath their thong, a double-thong ensemble; but safe to say, there's always a lot of ass showing at thong pulls and typically not the Playboy Bunny variety.

The sisters lining the patio bar are loosening up from swigs of tequila and the sweet Kahlua pudding shots. In their midst, a short, bouncy woman with a gray braid running halfway down her back and honest blue eyes holds court with her younger sisters. Lois Upson, a sixty-five-year-old administrator at Miami-Dade Water & Sewer, has been riding a motorbike since she was in elementary school. She was the only kid in high school, male or female, to arrive by motorcycle. Her father rode and sold bikes and boats in Miami. Her family has lived there for four generations, long enough for her to pronounce the city "Mi-amah" and ride a trail bike through swampy fields in the Everglades before they were protected.

While raising her children, Lois got away from biking trips. Then in 1987 her husband, also a rider, spotted an article about Leather & Lace in a biker magazine. Eager to check it out, she and a girlfriend biked up to Edgewater from Miami and joined the fledging club on a ride. "We went out at night with Bear [Jenn's late husband] and his friends, and they rode hard. They would go 60 to 70 mph on these dark, winding roads. It was so cool! We didn't have that in Mi-amah. We have square blocks and streetlights. We were all silly about it and screaming. We would go down the highways, and it was black in front of us. I was sure my eyelashes were frozen and my eyeballs would fall out because it was so cold and we were riding so fast." After one late-night impromptu ride, Lois stayed over and kept the others awake chattering. Jenn dubbed her "Ewok," after the fiery fur balls of the *Star Wars* Trilogy. The name stuck as her biker handle.

Ewok loved the challenge of hanging with the hard-riding 1%ers on the country roads. "One of the things Bear was proud of was that none of the ladies in Lace were sissies," Ewok recalls. "We felt real proud he would recognize that in us."

Riding with 1%ers had other advantages. "There was security in being with Bear and his brothers," Ewok explains. Contrary to the hype that all 1%ers treat women like dirt, Ewok says the Warlocks could be quite chivalrous. "They never took us any place that a lady shouldn't go. We were untouchable. None of them ever pursued any of us. Some of the single girls were a little disappointed. They were like, 'Gee, they always just take us home.'"

In the early days of the club, the sisters were less about business and more about riding and play. A trip to the store might turn into a 70-mile ride. They had weekend getaways, sunned in hotel pools and played with silly string. Once, at the Holiday Inn in Sebring, they crashed an outdoor wedding in biker style, wearing their leathers and making a scene. Jenn pushed Ewok into the hotel pool.

Not surprisingly, they weren't always welcomed. Niki recalls a stop in Yeehaw Junction, a crossroads about 30 miles inland from Vero Beach that is as lonely as it sounds. The sisters, leathered up and sporting their colors, pulled over at the only gas station. "It was hot as hell. We were dying," Niki says. "We got out the hose and started wetting each other down." The station owner ran inside and locked the doors. "He was scared!"

## Warlocks, Outlaws, and Harry "Taco"

During the 1980s, the perception that black-leather-clad bikers were dangerous wasn't so farfetched, especially on the desolate country back roads through sugar fields and cattle pastures between Miami, Orlando, and Tampa. Florida biker gangs had been breaking the law and raising hell for decades, but when a wave of recruits fresh from the bloody fields of Vietnam joined the ranks of 1%ers, they pursued new lines of business—pot, meth, cocaine, and heroin—all of which were flowing liberally in and out Florida. Hard-core 1%er clubs, in particular the Outlaws, strengthened their presence.

Under the leadership of International President Harry "Taco" Bowman, whose given name and nickname form a crude euphemism for a vagina, the Outlaws MC waged a full-on war against any club in Florida that threatened its illicit livelihood or even bruised Taco's tender ego. The Warlocks MC, a Florida-based club with about one hundred members, was a primary target. As a central Florida Warlocks leader, Jenn's late husband, Raymond "Bear" Chaffin, wore a bulls-eye.

Federal prosecutors in Taco's later trial claimed that the Outlaws and Warlocks were warring over the drug trade, that the Warlocks were selling drugs for the Hell's Angels, whom Outlaws loathe so much they wear a patch with an acronym to express their sentiment: "ADIOS," meaning "Angels Die in Outlaws States."

More than one former Outlaw has said the bloody rivalry ignited over something on its face far less sinister—the bottom rocker patch. The Warlocks dared to wear Florida chapter locations on theirs.

The Warlocks were also aggressively expanding. In fact, they were so eager to grow that they unwittingly recruited undercover federal agents who rode rented bikes. In an absurdly careless move, the Warlocks encouraged the undercover agents to start a new chapter in Fort Lauderdale. The U.S. Bureau of Alcohol, Tobacco and Firearms ran the 1%er chapter for more than a year, dubbing the investigation "Operation Easy Rider."

In 1991, the Florida biker war and the feds' undercover investigation culminated in death and massive arrests, touching even the Lace sisters.

Bear was alone in the garage working on Jenn's bike when an Outlaws prospect walked in and shot him execution-style, four times at the base of the skull. Bear and Jenn's twelve-year-old daughter discovered his body when she got home from school.

ATF agents, fearful that Bear's assassination would prompt a Warlocks-Outlaws bloodbath during the upcoming Bike Week, decided to end their elaborate two-year undercover investigation of the Warlocks. They planned their big bust at the one place they knew they could find the club members, Bear's funeral.

Local police warned Jenn not to bring the kids to the service, saying the Outlaws might launch another attack. Warlocks showed up armed. After the funeral, an army of feds and local police hemmed in everyone riding a motorcycle, including Lace sisters. Officers forced men and women to the ground for a search and confiscated machine guns, knives, and personal stashes of pot from the men. They hauled thirty-four Warlocks to jail. Many of the charges were later dropped.

Understandably, being herded and searched by a SWAT team traumatized some of the sisters. "None of us had any records. These guys are the bad boys!" Ewok says, as if talking to the police. "We're women. We don't do that kind of stuff! We do charities! We do yard sales! We do good things! We help people!"

The event highlighted the complexity of the sisters' relationship with 1%ers. They didn't approve of the gunrunning and bomb-making that the Warlocks were accused of, but on a personal level they liked some of them. "Even though you are with people who are 1%ers, many of the people in his little chapter were friends. At least I had met them a few times and I'd ridden with them," Ewok says.

The experience certainly colored their opinion of law enforcement. "To see how it went down after the funeral was so disheartening. How disrespectable of the police to do that at his funeral."

Federal focus on the Warlocks only emboldened Taco, the Saddam Hussein of bikerdom. Florida Outlaws members blew up rival club-houses, threw errant members off balconies, broke bones of non-1%er bikers they thought were too chummy with Hell's Angels, and even attempted to control Bike Week, which had long been neutral turf for 1%ers. Outlaws club members were gathering explosives to blow up the Warlocks' Brevard County clubhouse when the feds raided theirs and brought down indictments against more than two dozen members, including Taco.

Taco was on the lam for years, making it onto the FBI's Ten Most Wanted Fugitives list. He wasn't captured until 1998 and was tried in 2001 at the federal courthouse in downtown Tampa. Testimony sounded like something from a movie script. Security was tight. Federal snipers manned the rooftops of surrounding buildings. Taco was convicted of orchestrating the executions of a suspected snitch and Jenn's husband, "Bear" Chaffin, ordering clubhouse bombings and assaults, and various drug and firearm offenses. He's serving two life sentences at Coleman federal prison. He keeps in touch with friends and foes by mailing an annual Christmas letter reciting what he's been up to the past year, as if he has a rich life in prison.

During his first few years in jail, he included Jenn on his mailing list. "I sent them back saying, 'you have the wrong address,'" Jenn says of his Christmas cards. "I thought about suing him for wrongful death."

## An Old Lady Becomes Boss

Jenn's snapshots show she was quite a head-turner when she met Bear at a self-serve car wash in Daytona Beach back in 1976. At sixteen, she had flowing blond hair, an hourglass figure, and a white smile that set off her beach-bunny tan. She and her mom were vacationing from Wisconsin.

Bear, riding a chopper, was a tall, lanky twenty-nine-year-old with shaggy brown hair that swept across his forehead. Despite being fourteen years her senior, she says, Bear was a little shy. She jokes that she had to ask him out. They were married a few weeks later after her mother signed a consent form—she was too young to marry without one in Florida. Soon after, Bear joined the Warlocks MC and she became his Old Lady, riding on the back of his Harley and wearing the patch "Property of Bear."

Club business kept Bear on the road. He was sometimes away for six weeks at a time, leaving Jenn at home to raise their two daughters. "He supported his club. That's just the way it works," Jenn told *National Geographic*.

Jenn wanted to share Bear's love of motorcycling on her own terms, on her own bike. He rebuilt her a Harley for her nineteenth birthday. She rode it around town on errands. "I remember seeing her once coming back from the grocery store with her two girls, one in front and one in back, with a rope around them so they couldn't fall off. It was the funniest sight," recalls Candy, a Port Orange nurse who has been a member of the club since its early days.

Riding with Bear's Warlock brethren wasn't always fun. "They didn't want me riding with them," Jenn says. "Back then it wasn't a cool thing to do. For the most part they were Neanderthals, always trying to convince me that I wasn't smart enough, that I wasn't coordinated enough to ride. Fortunately I had a husband who was comfortable in his own skin."

Bear's biker brothers went along; he was the chapter boss. That didn't stop some of his club members from playing cruel and dangerous jokes on Jenn. "Sometimes it sucked hanging out with them. We would be riding and they would wave me on to pass, and I'd pull around and be looking at a semi. I'd just hug the center line and wave at the guy in the car I'm passing as I'm riding along next to him. What do you do? You can't move forward and you can't move backward—you just have to ride. It was scary at the time, but now it's kind of funny," she says.

Bear came up with the idea for Jenn to start her own club. He placed an ad in the back of a motorcycle magazine. She distributed fliers. Before long she started getting calls and letters from around the country from women like Ewok wanting to join, wanting to ride as equals at a time when most male riders would rather stay home than be seen riding beside them.

## Married to the Club

Jenn's Lace sisters helped her deal with Bear's loss, and they showed up in droves when she married John "Joker" Ely, another 1%er. John, a husky truck driver with an earful of piercings, is the local chapter boss of the Mongols MC.

Jenn says that after Bear's assassination, she swore she would never get involved with another 1%er. She didn't know John was a Mongol until after they got romantically involved. They met at a Lace event for kids. He had won a bunch of coupons and she bought them from him.

He started calling her about a year later. He lived in Atlanta as did Jenn's daughter. "She was going to get married and I had to run up there and stop that," Jenn says of her daughter. "We went out while I was there."

By the time Jenn found out that John was a Mongol, she was already hooked. They married about a year later.

To make it convenient for her sisters, Jenn scheduled the ceremony during Bike Week 2009. The sisters camped in the yard as usual.

The wedding quickly took on Hollywood proportions. *National Geographic* showed up with cameras. Adding to the drama, the U.S. Justice Department still had authority to confiscate any paraphernalia from John's motorcycle club. The right would later be overturned in court, but at that point federal agents could legally strip Mongols colors off members' backs. The wedding was held in a city park in daylight.

Since this was a wedding of two biker club presidents, wearing colors was considered essential. Plus, what self-respecting 1%er is going to let the law dictate what they can wear at their own wedding?

The Mongol brothers compromised. Groomsmen customized a dress coat for John with the cryptic code "MFFM Florida" standing for "Mongols Forever, Forever Mongols."

As dictated by Jenn, Lace gals wore their colors and lined up their bikes as a runway to the altar.

The ceremony was Cinderella meets Harley-Davidson. Jenn, with her hair swept up in ringlets, marched down the aisle of motorcycles wearing a tiara and white wedding gown with lace, seed-pearl beads, train—everything *Modern Bride* insists is necessary. John wore a black tuxedo, his receding hair swept back. Ewok performed the ceremony in a white top hat and white tails complete with a Leather & Lace patch stitched to the back. "I wanted to wear something outrageous," she later confesses.

The two exchanged vows underneath a white gazebo in front of nearly two hundred leather-clad bikers. Jenn's grandson, the ring bearer, delivered the wedding bands via a miniature Harley.

After the vows, territorial matrimonial lines were drawn. Lace sisters helped Jenn put on her vest over her wedding dress. John's Mongol brothers help him with the custom-coded jacket. The ritual symbolized that their respective clubs will always come first. In other words, if John and one of the Lace sisters are drowning, Jenn will rescue her biker sister first. And vice versa. Oh, the romance of a biker marriage.

A year into their union, Jenn tells me that John is still understanding and supportive of her and her club. Being a trucker, he's away from home a lot much like Bear was. Jenn says, "I kinda like it that way."

**Hear Her Roar**

John isn't around for the media spotlight this year. After an afternoon CPR class, Lace sisters are prepping for interviews. A crew from the cable show *Throttle Junkies* is coming by to shoot a segment on the club.

Jenn's wearing makeup, lipstick even, and is dressed in biker black from neck to toe. A flouncy hot-pink scarf wraps her neck and sets off the pink Leather & Lace logo on her vest. Her hair has soft waves that pass her shoulders. She is the embodiment of the club's theme, feminine, yet as strong as steel. Even her Harley has those qualities. The dual, flared chrome tailpipes scream masculinity. The hubs and gas tank are painted an iridescent purple so deep that it looks almost black. In the sunlight, the pink Leather & Lace logo bleeds to the surface.

Sisters wearing the patched vests hang out and puff near their bikes in anticipation of the cameras. The film crew is late, and the sisters are concerned there won't be enough daylight for them to be taped riding their bikes.

Talk turns to the mechanics of motorcycles, and Sassy from Orlando mentions she's having problems with hers. With Sassy's permission, Keri, a young fire department paramedic with a smooth, rosy complexion and a body that could take down a tree, comes to Sassy's aide. As the unofficial road captain, Keri later explains she is one of the few club members who have authority to ride another sister's bike (yet another biker code: Members don't sit on each other's motor).

The *Throttle Junkies* crew arrives in a huge van spewing cameramen and boom mic operators. A director trailed by a female assistant with a clipboard gives orders while the on-air talent stands by, seemingly along for the ride.

Light is growing scarce. They need to shoot Jenn and club members riding while they can, the director tells his crew. Jenn hops on the back of her bike. Gripping the handlebars, she cranks it. "Potato, potato, potato . . . potato, potato, potato." The deep guttural, gravelly pitch and irregular cadence that define Harleys ignites the group. The sisters scream and shout adding melody to the rhythm of the engine. "Yahoo!" "Alright!" hands clap, fists raise.

For a woman, little can compare to seeing, and almost as important, hearing, another female straddle an 800-pound mass of rubber, chrome, and steel and bring it to life with a roar. The feminist symbolism is empowering, and the engine's sound evokes a primal energy. Swept up by the force, I holler and cheer along with the sisters.

Cocked back on the seat with her heels pressed forward on the footrests, hands chin-high on the handlebars, Jenn seems to propel the machine forward with her presence alone. Once on the street, she opens it up. Long blond locks fly and the hot-pink scarf floats behind as Jenn disappears in a rumble down the empty, palm-lined street under the reddening Florida sky.

# CHAPTER 4

# The Other Wild Kingdom

Wonder Woman is taking a break in the lobby of Tampa's downtown Hyatt Regency. From what, isn't clear, but apparently she is invisible to everyone but me. None of the passing, casually dressed conventioneers give her a second look.

Nearby on the escalator, a gray-haired man in red latex pope vestments is trailed by a vixen in a saucy rubber nun's habit. I follow them up to a kingdom of kink.

On the convention floor, leashed sex slaves and nearly nude exhibitionists weave through the aisles of kinky clothing and sex toys. Young fetish models with breasts like basketballs and names like Bloodbunny, RubberDoll, Velvet Slave, and GhettoButt push website memberships and pose for fan photos. A legless man wearing a T-shirt that reads "Walk on Me" flattens out like roadkill on the carpet to let a fetish model do just that.

Is that a man or a hefty woman shrink-wrapped head to toe in a latex Orphan Annie outfit? And how does he/she breathe? Something that looks like the EverReady bunny is cinched in a black leather body harness and striding up the aisle like a mascot about to break out in a cheer for the fetish team.

I have fallen down the rabbit hole and landed at Fetish Con, the largest fetish trade show in the eastern United States. Every year, the kinky event takes over the Hyatt for four days, drawing more than two thousand Floridians and visitors from around the globe who dare to act out the strangest of sexual fantasies.

I'm a Vanilla, as lifestylers call those of us with more conventional sex lives. I'm seeking those whose sexual obsessions have a Florida bent and hope to later visit them in their element, wherever that may be.

In the process, I'm getting a fast introduction into deviant desires. Dressed in jeans and a black shirt, I blend in with the mere dabblers who shop for whips and sex toys to spice things up in the bedroom.

Given that you can buy leather bustiers at many swap meets, toying with the basic tie-me-up, spank-me, leather-and-whips BDSM fetish is practically mainstream (BDSM being shorthand for bondage/discipline, dominance/submission, sadism/masochism). Florida, the capital of make-believe, can do better. In the subtropical sunshine, the most obscure fetishes flourish to national prominence and the more common morph into cutting-edge strange.

Case in point, the hulking transgender redhead coming up the aisle dressed as a woman and a horse, a ponygirl.

The 6-foot 3-inch ponygirl is dressed in a black bustier, red leotard, red tights, and a bridle get-up with pointy ears. Her teeth clench a rubber bit the size of a hotdog. A red feather plume tops her head, and a long, red-haired tail hangs from her rump. Wearing over-the-knee black boots, she marches with the gait of a draft horse, although she later tells me she's an Arabian.

And if her dress isn't eye-catching enough, she's also pulling a two-wheeled cart that holds a buxom leather-clad fetish model. A pear-shaped man with a crop follows up the rear, intently watching his towering pony's every move.

I trot after them and he hands me his business card: "Ponygroom Tim." He's too busy to talk. His pony is at work.

I soon learn from a small herd that pony play is one of Florida's claims to fetish prominence. Such assertions are hard to verify given that there isn't an official census for human ponies. However, several online fetish registries back up their claim; Florida has the most

Ponygroom Tim and Ponygirl Lyndsey following a pony cart performance at a Largo fetish dungeon. Photo by Lori Ballard.

human ponies per capita of any state. Even still, serious pony players are rare. Online sites indicate Florida has more than 250 pony players. San Francisco, New York, and Los Angeles are also hotbeds.

Some semblance of equine costume play—or "cosplay," as it's called in the lifestyle—has been around since before Christ. In her book *Deviant Desires: Incredibly Strange Sex,* chronicler of obscure fetishes Katherine Gates notes an Assyrian frieze from around 2000 BCE that shows human ponies pulling chariots. Legend also has it that the Greek philosopher Aristotle liked playing pony; a famous fourteenth-century bronze statue *Aristotle Ridden by Phyllis* depicts him on all fours with his wife on his back holding his hair as if it's a mane. Around the turn of the nineteenth century, erotic ponygirl shows were a hit with British colonists.

Then came novelist Anne Rice, who under the pen name A. N. Roque-laure cracked open the stable door again in the 1980s with her erotic trilogy *The Claiming of Sleeping Beauty.* Rice told of nude princes and princesses being turned into harnessed sex slaves who wore hooves and horsetails plugged into their rears and pulled carriages.

By the late 1990s, a small subset of the BDSM community was living the fantasy, horsetail butt-plugs and all.

In pony play world, the submissive is the beast of burden, the one controlled by reins, the one who pulls the cart and rides the dominant on his or her back or even shoulders, which looks a lot like kids playing chicken.

In the hallway outside the trade show, a small Florida herd nays, can-ters, and snorts. One ponygirl prances on all fours, her hands gloved in shiny plastic horse fetlocks and hooves, and her feet covered in match-ing boots soled with horseshoes.

Prize ribbons like ones given at a state fair hang on the top rail of a purple and black pony stall. Ponygirl Lavender is taking a break. She removes her bridle headdress with purple braids, silver medallions, and a plume of black hair that spews from the top like a mane. A match-ing strap-on tail sways as she walks. The well-known children's toy My Little Pony has grown up.

Lavender is middle-aged with a matching shape clearly outlined by her leotard, dark stockings, black boots, and lacy bustier. She lives in Largo and has a professional, mainstream job and a teenager. She pre-fers to go only by Lavender, her pony play name, saying she wants to be discreet about her fetish. I don't point out the obvious: Parading around a convention hall in downtown Tampa dressed as a horse might blow her cover.

Lavender and her boyfriend, Logan, are newbies to pony play, having only gotten into the scene a couple of months earlier. They already have the fanciest of tack plus the purple corral. Logan, a professional set builder, constructed it for her as a romantic gesture and set it up in her living room.

"We didn't wade in. We dove," Lavender says and laughs. "When we started we couldn't do anything."

"Agh, we were horrible," Logan says.

Turns out pony play involves even more than modified horse tack and an abundant imagination. Learning how to canter, trot, and respond to the reins and bit takes practice. Even tougher is forgetting that you are a human who is pretending to be a horse. I am not being facetious. The pinnacle of ponydom is mental transference, a horse-autopilot, which they call "pony space."

Lavender hasn't achieved that stage and is not sure she wants to. "To me it's a little intimidating because they actually become ponies," she says. "They actually have problems with mirrors. They look into a mirror and don't know who they are. They think it's another pony."

To Lavender, pony play is more about control and performance, an extension of the BDSM lifestyle she's been into for about four years. Logan was playing master long before they met. They are both Florida natives.

"There have been many nights when we've spent hours on the phone going over what we did the night before, talking about what we liked or didn't like, where we want to go with it," Logan says. "That's the thing with this relationship—you have to spend time working at it."

Lavender suggests I talk to more experienced pony players and points out Foxy, an Ocala cowboy who trains equines and human ponies. She speaks of him and his wife, Sherifox, in a reverential tone. They are the reigning Grand Champions of International Pony Play.

This explains the ribbons hanging on the stall. Human ponies compete. But what does one do to win an international pony play title? And is competition another fetish in itself?

The answers will have to wait. Sherifox isn't around, and Foxy is leaving for home.

Being a former owner of a real horse—or bio-horse, as human ponies refer to them—I'm intrigued by the bridle headstall. The thick leather tack with its colorful doodads is fancier than anything my horse ever wore.

Lavender says it and the tail cost $650. She bought the custom-made gear from Foxy, who's also a leathersmith.

I run my fingers across the coarse black hair of the plume that mimics a mane and marvel that it feels natural.

"It's real horsehair," Lavender says. "It's from a real horse's tail."

These people take their role-playing seriously. The person who wears this Gucci of pony play tack also isn't likely to get away. The steel bit and curb chain, which fits under a bio-horse's chin, are heavy gauge and appear to be made for an actual equine. In real-horse world, the bit forces the animal to be submissive. The metal bar fits in a horse's tender mouth so that if the steed resists, it will feel a slight pain.

At the moment, the symbolism doesn't fully register. Lavender and Logan are jolly, and their pony play seems more like child's play than a fetish. When Logan offers to let me try on the headstall, the idea seems silly and innocent, like trying on someone's absurd hat. Plus, how many opportunities does a Vanilla get to try on a human pony bridle?

The headdress is as heavy as a basket of fruit. Once atop my head, the weight of the plume forces me to stand straight, shoulders back, and for a second I imagine this must be how a Las Vegas showgirl feels wearing a gargantuan display of glitz. Then before I realize what's happening, Logan pulls the bit across my laughing mouth and fastens it. Suddenly, I am not a happy pony. A submissive I am not.

Lavender doesn't look enthused, either. Her boyfriend just put her bit in another woman's mouth.

After a couple of minutes of Logan fussing with the fitting, I politely ask, as plainly as possible with a metal bar in my mouth, to be unbridled. Lavender helps Logan free me.

All is well, nice and giggly, but as I leave the pony people I wonder if maybe I wasn't being recruited to join their herd.


**Buddha of Love**

Back on the exhibit floor, Wonder Woman is at work crushing humanity. She stomps a miniature city, breaking plastic cars, high-rises, and 2-inch people. A video camera projects her rampage onto an adjacent television screen. She appears a giantess in the same way a toy lizard looked like a goliath monster in Godzilla movies, except with even less realism. Fortunately, her macrophile fans—men who fantasize about being dominated by larger-than-life women—by necessity have big imaginations.

They pay about forty dollars a month to watch similar performances by Wonder Woman and other giantesses on a private website. "It's a pretty good job," Wonder Woman says while resting her obliterating feet. "I mean, all I have to do is step on these little men and stuff."

"Do you ever want to laugh while you're doing it?" I wonder aloud.

"Yeah, at first. But then I started thinking about it psychologically. I think people like it because it takes them back to their childhood when they watched movies with giant women, King Kong. So, so what? It's not hurting anybody."

Touché.

Or not.

Wonder Woman's giantess videos are good clean fun compared to crush films, a closely related erotica. At the dark end of the fetish spectrum, these taboo films show living things being crushed to death: insects, small animals—even humans. And yes, that fetish has an infamous Florida story. In an extreme case of sexual stupidity, an Okeechobee man with a crush fetish had someone drive over him in a Honda Pathfinder. He later died, and the resulting investigation revealed that he had been operating a small crush-film business and shot videos of his wife stomping small animals to death.

Crush films are illegal in the United States and Europe. Not surprisingly, no one even whispers about them at Fetish Con. Under the bright lights of the convention hall, sex seems merely playfully twisted.

Jim "the Buddha of Love" Torvea, a fixture on the sex trade show circuit, explains that congeniality is what makes Fetish Con unique—and fun. "You have DomCon in L.A., which is a lot of BDSM; sci-fi kink at Frolicon in Atlanta; and Mr. Leather in Chicago. But here you get everything, a lot of diversity," he says. "There's a lot of acceptance of one another."

A portly man with a ceaseless smile, Jim owns Torvea Toys in Atlanta, which is one of the sponsors of the event's after-parties. He stands proudly amid a vast inventory of dildos, anal plugs, rubber vaginas, remote-control vibrating panties, and various other sex toys and seems not to notice that the couple perusing his wares are cross-species; the plain-dressed man leads a bikini-clad woman who is painted like a leopard and wears plastic whiskers.

The leopard purrs as her master examines Torvea's line of I Rub My Duckie Toys™, which look like a children's bathtub rubber duck, except it also vibrates for Mom's pleasure.

Jim carries on to me about trends in the sex-toy industry like a car manufacturer might talk of his top sellers. He says that kinksters are moving away from traditional plastic sex toys to hypoallergenic gels and latex-free pleasure tools. Even fetishists are going green.

The sex-toy business hasn't been immune from the Great Recession, he laments. The trade show circuit has been cut in half. Fetish Con continues to thrive because it is "the best party of the year," he says, transitioning from businessman to the Buddha of Love. "If we only went to one show a year, I'd want to come to Fetish Con . . . I get to see all my friends. You've got the after-parties in Ybor, and then there is the pool party after everyone comes back to the hotel." Jim says he's made good friends with the fetish models at these pool parties and describes himself as their protector and somewhat of a boy-Friday, retrieving odds and ends and assisting them in any way they ask. "I got my nickname at a pool party here one year," he says, grinning like a Buddha of Lust.

Having attended the Vamps and Vixens after-party the night before, I can envision what those after-after-parties may entail.


## "I Am a Whore"

Nighttime fetish parties are a highlight of the kinky lifestyle. Fetishists get to show off their creative costumes as well as their bodies. It's exhibitionism on crack. For the sake of those who have never attended and to better understand Jim's love of the after-hours scene, I must diverge with a snapshot of how surreal these affairs can be.

For starters, the Fetish Con after-party was held at Ybor City's Castle nightclub, which has a regular cast of patrons right out of children's fables and dark comic books. Peter Pan, Batman, a coven of fanged vampires, dozens of Goths, and a man known as "The Senator," who wears nothing but sheer teddies, all make weekly appearances. Add two thousand visiting fetishists in full regalia and the two-story club became a Mad Tea Party.

A male-female couple wore only leather body harnesses; male and female mimes in Victorian gowns; an Elvira look-alike sauntered around in a low-cut plastic evening gown; a shirtless man wore a furry horse head.

Busty women cinched in corsets and pouring out of leather bustiers were as common as witches at a Halloween party. Rubberists—latex and PVC fetishists—paraded around like royalty. Many are part of south Florida's glam fetish scene, where the epitome of fashion is four-hundred-dollar-and-up revealing latex wear that fits like a sausage casing.

In the Dungeon bar, a blindfolded sex slave with clothespins pinching his nipples was spreadeagled and tied to a cobweb of chains. Woman lined up to write graffiti messages such as "I am a Whore" on his unnaturally tan body.

Upstairs, fetish go-go dancers—saucy wood nymphs, postmodern geishas, and a host of indescribably costumed nubile women—gyrated to the frantic beat of the house mix above a sea of leather, latex, and skin. Occasionally the stage lights came up, silencing the crowd and introducing sexual sideshows; Gypsy Rose meets Jim Rose Circus.

Kinky uses of otherwise normal objects are standard in fetish performances. One breast-tasseled performer's shtick was fruit. After fingering a cantaloupe held between her legs and deep-throating a peeled banana, she pulled a stemmed cherry from her panties and dropped it in her mouth.

The hourglass-figured headliners got busy with power tools like those found in a garage—well, almost. A porn star rubbed a spinning foot-long dildo attached to a drill all over her scantily clad body. A former *Penthouse* model stripped to a metal torpedo bra, then did what comes naturally to women in steel underwear: She put a power grinder to her DDD cups. Grrrrrr!!! Sparks flew like in a welding shop, and for more than an instant, she lit up like a Fourth of July sparkler.

Although somewhat daring, these acts were exactly that—acts.

Jim's a fetish-show veteran, and I gather his enthusiasm comes from the after-after parties back at the Hyatt where the false eyelashes, latex, and steel underwear come off. During Fetish Con, the hotel houses fetish performers, latex models, superhero wrestlers, and the twenty-something anime schoolgirls who look fourteen. They have been on display all day as human sex toys, signing autographs, posing for model shoots, making fetish videos in hotel rooms, and performing kinky acts onstage. In the early-morning hours at the hotel pool, they are free to party without their temptress facades. No wonder Jim is crazy about Fetish Con.

## For the Love of Fur

At the convention, the scenery gets furrier as the hours bump by. I'm referring to fetishists like the leather-bound EverReady bunny who get turned on, or "yiffy" as they call it, by anthropomorphic characters.

Furries have their own language and porn, which in furry-speak is called "furotica." In jest, furries refer to furotica lovers as "furverts," although the moniker isn't so funny when coming from Vanillas.

Before you beat up Mickey Mouse for posing for a photo with your child, it's important to note that not everyone who enjoys dressing up like a team mascot gets sexually aroused by it. Fur fans are so for a variety of reasons; sometimes sex is a component, sometimes not. Though odd in any context, the world of furry fandom is quite complex. Most simply, "furry" is an umbrella term for people who have an extreme passion for anthropomorphic characters. For some, furridom is merely a geeky pastime that they play online.

The percentage of furs that fetishize cartoon animals is widely debated even in their community. In the universe of fetishes, furversion is so obscure that even the National Coalition of Sexual Freedom, which advocates for the kinkier set, hasn't attempted to measure it. Attempts to quantify the fetish are complicated by few furs being willing to openly admit they fantasize about Sonic the Hedgehog or Renamon the fox. Not just because it's strange, but the Vanilla world sometimes confuses the fetish with bestiality, which is altogether different. Anthropomorphic characters are completely fictional. They have qualities of humans and animals. They can even be morphs of multiple species, some of which are purely mythological. Because of that, interspecies furry mating is common if only of necessity. Finding a fellow furry zebra-dragon to yiff with is like discovering Cinderella's slipper in Lake Okeechobee.

Despite the cloudiness over the degree of fetishism in fur fandom, it is safe to say that Florida has a relatively large furry jungle. An online Orlando furry community lists more than 450 members, and another statewide group has more than 800, about a fourth of whom actually dress up in fur; they are called fursuiters.

The Orlando area has more makers of anthropomorphic costumes

As evidenced by the bunny's bondage wear, sometimes one fetish is not enough. Photo by Lori Ballard.

than anywhere else in the world, according to the Fursuit Database, a comprehensive online registry conceived by a fursuiter known as the raccoon Growl. The registry doesn't include creators of theme-park costumes. One of the largest fursuit makers listed, a nonfurry arts major living in central Florida, didn't want to be named and preferred not to know her customers' motivations.

Although no one can definitely say why the Sunshine State has a large furry community, it's no coincidence that central Florida thrives on the industries of anthropomorphic characters—theme parks and computer animation. Furs tend to be guys under thirty who are into video-game marathons and comic-book conventions. They sometimes work in the industry. Disney World is a favorite outing. And yes, some do work there.

In his book *Cast Member Confidential: A Disneyfied Memoir*, former theme-park photographer Chris Mitchell wrote that Dale of the Chip and Dale chipmunks once teased him with her bushy tail. He claimed two cast members, Mickey and Minnie no less, sneaked their costumes home for furry sex.

Many Florida furs seek companionship online. In fact, the state also has more furries per capita registered to the popular fur personal ad website, Pounded.com, than any other state in the union—nearly two thousand. Only California and, oddly, Texas have more.

Furry personal ads are not fundamentally different than Vanilla personal ads. Some Florida furs seek fellow furries to simply hang out with in fursuits and play video games. One Orlando fur wants to take furry motorcycle rides. (Finding a mate who shares a passion for baseball is tough enough. Just imagine how hard it is to connect with someone who likes riding a Harley dressed like a squirrel.) And yes, some admit they are blatantly searching for a quick yiff, which in the politest of terms is a one-night stand. Furries into BDSM advertise for a fur slave or pet. One Florida fur couple with a hip-thrusting pony avatar wants to swing.

That said, a furry's presence at a fetish convention implies he or she gets off on it. But since you can't trust appearances in Wonderland, I stalk a beagle in an attempt to learn more.

The Snoopy dog with long, floppy ears bounces from the exhibit hall like a plush toy that's come to life.

"Excuse me, can I ask you a few questions?" I ask the beagle, who, by shape and stride, is clearly male.

He nods his muzzle up and down, then points to his mouth with one paw.

"You can't talk in your suit?"

The dog shakes his oversized furry head side to side, implying "no."

"Maybe I can ask you some 'yes' and 'no' questions?"

The beagle waves his paws in a doggy version of "bring it on."

I ask if he's from Florida.

The beagle waves a paw back and forth as if to say, "no, no, no."

"You're not from Florida?"

He coyly shrugs his shoulders.

"What?" I ask, wishing I spoke fur.

He shrugs and cocks his head to one side in that cute way dogs do.

Realizing that two-way communication with a human-dog is as

futile as trying to converse with my biological golden retriever, I thank the beagle for the attempt. He lopes off to the men's room. How irritated can you get with a cuddly-looking dog that doesn't bark, bite, hump your leg, or lift his leg by a potted plant? At least, not in this setting.

It's not until after leaving Fetish Con that I discover that the most bizarre aspects of furridom and pony play—or any fetish for that matter—aren't recognizable by costume. Like most things sexual, the turn-ons are psychological. To see how strange, yet organic, the fetishes really are you have to do more than try on a horse bridle or watch a giantess superhero stomp on toy cities.

The pony play herd and their furry friends let me peek inside the fetish psyche in the following months. After a little cajoling, Ponygroom Tim and Ponygirl Lyndsey agree to an interview at their home in Deland, a quaint college town between Orlando and Daytona.

## A Well-Rounded Pony

Sitting between an auto repair shop and a dilapidated house, Tim and Lyndsey's tiny rental home with weedy landscaping and tattered window screens is about as inviting as a barn on a dark country road. I have traveled 150 miles to come into the home of two people whom I know nothing about other than they get sexually aroused by either pretending to be a horse or controlling someone who dresses like a steed at Pompano Park. As I stand on a small, makeshift stoop of landscape timbers and question my judgment, the door opens.

Tim, dressed in slacks and a dress shirt, greets me like a deacon at the church door on a Sunday morning. He could pass for a rounder and gentler Bill Maher with a similar receding gray hairline and knotted nose. His skin is pink and fair, and his voice is filled with the giggles of a child.

Lyndsey is dressed like a deacon's wife in black size-13 pumps, sheer black nylons, a flowing black skirt and matching white sleeveless polyester top. A silver pony pinned in the center of her chest adds a feminine touch while her foghorn "hello" belies her lingering manhood.

Their living room is neatly arranged and clean with modest furnishings. Shelves of faux-wood bookcases like you find at Wal-Mart are lined with novels and accented with stuffed animals. Bridle headdresses on Styrofoam heads are stored on top. Disassembled wooden pony hurdles are stacked against one wall. An upright piano holds an antique family Bible heavy enough to knock out a horse. The only seating is a cushioned garden swing hanging from a metal stand and red dining chairs arranged around a dining table covered with a fresh tablecloth. A poster of a giant black boot against a red background hangs on the wall behind the table, one of the few hints of their BDSM lifestyle.

Tim and Lyndsey turn around a couple dining chairs and sit. I take the swing that doubles as their couch and a pony play/BDSM hitching post.

Tim is loquacious and eager to educate me on the background of pony play and his evolution into it. Before that, I learn more about their lives outside kink.

They are both Christians and active in a local United Church of Christ. Lyndsey is an ordained minister, plays the organ and piano at church, and sings the lead operatic role in the church's Christmas musical.

Tim's active in politics and is conservative with a libertarian bent. He engineers implements for paratroopers, but doesn't want to share too many details, implying it's classified. Lyndsey was a school music teacher for twenty-five years and also taught at a college. She has two master's degrees in music, has completed doctoral courses, and she's a trained opera singer, hence her nickname—"the singing ponygirl."

They don't drink, smoke, or do drugs.

Tim says that a large concentration of pony people live in the Ocala area, which not coincidently claims to be the "horse capital of the world." More than two hundred farms there produce Kentucky Derby–winning thoroughbreds and some of the world's finest Arabians, warmbloods, quarter horses, and numerous other breeds. Perhaps it's only natural that the county also fosters a prominent herd of human ponies. International Champs Foxy and Sherifox live on a farm with real horses outside Ocala.

Tim explains that pony play competition ribbons go a long way toward establishing a trainer's reputation and an area as a pony play hotbed, much like winning the Kentucky Derby does for a bio-horse farm. Florida pony couples have claimed international titles three out of the past five years, with Foxy and Sherifox being the reigning champs. Foxy has a stable of four ponygirls, including Sherifox.

Florida's perpetual warm, sunny weather also makes the state attractive for human ponies. They like that they can be whipped into a gallop year-round in the outdoors. Trotting through beach sand to the sound of the ocean's roar is a particular treat. For emphasis, Tim shares a photo of Sherifox and another filly wearing bridles, tails, hooved hands, and little else as they cart Foxy along an empty Florida beach.

"Ponies like to work up a sweat," Tim says. "A lot of them like to work and like to feel something is going on. I get e-mail contacts fairly frequently from people who want to come to Florida to train because they imagine the harsh environment and heat."

Tourist ponies are sometimes in a mixed relationship, that is, their partner is a Vanilla. While vacationing in Florida, a pony spouse will hoof around a private farm with a trainer for a day while his or her Vanilla mate suns on the beach. "That's their idea of a great vacation," Tim says. "Then they go home and it doesn't happen much there."

As Tim launches into his kinky background, Lyndsey, like a good submissive, keeps an invisible ball gag in her mouth. He tells her we will get to her story later.

Tim didn't become a pony master until he moved to Florida in 2004, but he's been a kinkster since puberty. He started with self-bondage and moved on to role-playing with his then-wife. Their cosplay grew beyond the bedroom, and they started traveling to other states for small BDSM gatherings.

By the time Tim moved to Florida, he was bored with the standard tie-me-up-and-whip-me scene. "I've done a lot with kink," Tim says. "I began to think, 'What do I want to do?' Do I want to retire? Just give it up?"

Tim met his first ponygirl through his then-wife at a BDSM party. "She was getting tacked up, and I thought, 'Oh my God, this is an actual ponygirl!'" The young filly was having trouble fitting her harness. "I bent over and said 'would you let me adjust that, and adjust this,' and it was just as sexy as all get out. It was the sexiest thing I had ever seen in my life."

During the course of the party, Tim and Ponygirl Anna made a contract, which in the BDSM world involves partners agreeing to fulfill certain roles in a relationship. "Keep in mind, I'm still married while this is going on and I have her (his then-wife's) consent to do this and she introduced us. It's kind of spicy 'cause it seems a little weird," Tim says, referring to his bond with a woman other than his wife, not training a human to act like a horse.

Tim immersed in pony play. He taught "Pony101" at munches, which are informal gatherings of kinksters, often newbies. These fetish primers are held in nonsexual environments such as a restaurant or a park. People might bring cookies, homemade casseroles, potato chips, and Cokes. They share tips like how to whip safely or tie a square knot. Florida has more advertised munches than any state except California.

Tim and his former ponygirl schlepped homemade rope bridles to these kinky meet-ups all around Florida searching for other human ponies and trying to recruit new ones. "Sure enough, here and there, we found this one and that one," he says. "They were all across the state. We had people drive from Miami to Ocala so they could meet a pony. Gradually we accumulated a group of about two dozen people. That's how Florida pony play has developed."

While Tim was building his credentials in pony world, Lyndsey was beginning her public life as a woman. Lyndsey is a transsexual, a person who feels he or she was born as the wrong sex.

Lyndsey explains her gender and sexuality, which are a lot to process: Lyndsey is physically still a man. She feels she's a woman and finds comfort and arousal pretending to be a horse. She is what the BDSM world calls a "switch," someone who can play sadist or masochist, although she prefers to only perform sadistic sex acts on others at Sir Tim's command. She has been bisexual her entire life. These layers may seem interconnected, but she emphasizes they are not. Transsexualism is not a fetish, not a kinky sexual fantasy. Pony play and BDSM are. Transsexuals can be bi, straight, or gay.

Before she met Tim and got into pony play, Lyndsey planned to have sexual reassignment surgery. She continues to take hormones, hence her large breasts and softer lines, but decided not to surgically change her penis into a vagina. She says their pony play has made her more comfortable with herself, and she's resigned to the fact that surgery can't fully give her a woman's body. "You are never going to have everything a genetic female does."

Like Tim, Lyndsey got into BDSM at an early age. She saw her first photo of a human pony as a teen. "I was one of those kids who liked to find magazines that children aren't supposed to see. I found one of these early BDSM magazines. As I was paging through it, I came across this girl decked out in full pony gear. I thought, 'you mean people do this for fun?'" Lyndsey says. "She was holding herself so proud, and I thought, 'Oh my God, I'd love to do that.'"

As the son of a University of Virginia music professor and part-time Southern Baptist minister, Lyndsey tried to suppress her desires and attempted to live a conventional life. She married her college sweetheart, and they raised two children in Indiana while Lyndsey taught school.

Privately, she cross-dressed and enjoyed being bound and whipped by her wife. When her masochistic needs became too extreme, her wife turned her over to a professional dominatrix for a few years. Their marriage eventually crumbled.

Divorced, Lyndsey moved to Florida in 2003 to start a new life. She publicly came out as a transsexual woman. Four years later she met Tim and other things came out of the closet, too; namely, a pony.

Lyndsey listed an interest in pony play on her profile on a Yahoo.com fetish group site. Tim, a member of the group, pounced. He already had a ponygirl, but what's not to like about having a small herd? After some online chat, he called Lyndsey and asked, "Do you want to be a pony?"

Without hesitation, Lyndsey responded: "Yes, Sir!"

Tim drove across the state to meet Lyndsey at a munch. They arranged their first training session. Lyndsey remembers the date as if it were branded into her hide. On April 14, 2007, she became Tim's ponygirl.

"What I wanted for Lyndsey was to become comfortable in her skin," Tim says of their early days. "As I was getting to know her, I thought that a lot of what she had done with kink was about wanting to be a pony, but not knowing how to ask for it. So I thought, 'Let's see how she takes to this.' Boy! Did she ever take to it!"

With little practice, Lyndsey achieved the Zen of pony play. When in tack, she goes into pony space and loses awareness of her human self. She later doesn't remember anything she did as a pony. "I can say I did something as a four-legged pony because I have my four-legged pony gear on," Lyndsey says matter-of-factly. "I can't tell you how many rides I might have given."

Because of her trance-like state, Lyndsey is at the mercy of her master's care. As Lavender and Logan earlier mentioned, this goes to the core of every BDSM relationship: trust. The emotional bond that develops is one of the appeals of the fetish. "You have to be able to trust the person who is handling you. You have to know that they aren't going to do something that will injure you or harm you," Lyndsey says. "You become very close emotionally. For me, when I do pony work, I'm not here as a human. I have to put my trust in him."

Lyndsey finds being a pony very relaxing, even cathartic. It takes her back to her childhood. "I had a pony when I was little," Lyndsey says. "Nobody could ride her but me. Now that I'm into pony play I think that maybe she knew something that I didn't at that time."

As unusual as Lyndsey's gender and desires are, down in the rabbit hole with them it all seems almost natural. That is until the couple reveals that they believe that while in pony space Lyndsey becomes her childhood pet Buttercup, an Arabian mare. "She acts like Buttercup, sounds like Buttercup, and responds like Buttercup as she has told me Buttercup acted," Tim says.

No doubt reading the puzzlement on my face, Tim tries to explain. "It's an alternate personality, and it wants to come out, but it can't come out on its own. Twelve years ago, this wasn't talked about even in the kink circles. It was thought to be witchcraft, magic," he whispers for emphasis. "For most people, being a dominant or a master is about training somebody when they are conscious all the time. I'm talking about training somebody when they are another personality." He giggles. "There's no guidebook for that."

Not all ponies go into pony space. Many just enjoy the role-playing, the leather get-up and pageantry, even the competitiveness. Human ponies identify with specific breeds of bio-horses, all based on their skills and temperament rather than appearance, of course. "You can often figure out, 'Oh, I've got a Clyde,' or 'I've got an Arabian.' Some of 'em are hard to determine, and they call themselves paints. They say, 'Oh, I'm a paint of any of six different breeds.' There are those that just race, the Thoroughbreds," Tim explains. "Everything you can imagine from the equine world has been replicated in the human pony world."

This includes the competitions Lavender mentioned at Fetish Con. Human ponies barrel race, perform dressage, pull carts, harness race, and every other traditional equine competition along with some added challenges such as blindfolded performances. There's even a human pony steeplechase, which Tim says Lyndsey is quite good at, given her long legs and hurdling experience in high school.

I picture Lyndsey's hulking frame in leather tack, red horsetail floating behind as she gallops across a field, passing petite human ponies, her size-13 feet launching her over steeples. Yes, she could be a Grand National champion in pony play world, except she's the wrong breed. Steeplechasers are Thoroughbreds, not Arabians.

Lyndsey and Tim practice gaits and pony routines in their open backyard. They live in a semi-commercial area of town with no adjoining neighbors. Lyndsey pulls the red two-wheeled cart that Tim built, maneuvers around pylons and sometimes jumps the hurdles. In winter, when it gets dark early, they carry a flashlight.

Tim has high aspirations for his pony, but he keeps them secret. "I have a plan and she doesn't even know it," he says as she sits silently. "It would actually harm things if I told her."

He's proud of her progress. She picked up a third-place ribbon in her first pony play competition held on a Texas farm. "She feels very confident with the cart. She can do tricky things with it," Tim says. "She gets competitive when she jumps. She likes to run, likes to run fast. She is a well-rounded pony, which she knows is part of the program."

It all sounds like people playing as children. After all, many pre-video-game-era kids rode a rocking horse or played with a stick pony. What's so sexual about playing horse in your backyard or even in a large arena?

The sexual aspect seems clearer when Tim shows me a photo essay that he arranged for *Equus Eroticus*, an international pony play magazine. A pretty young woman in tack is leaning down on all fours and drinking like a horse from a murky stream. Aside from her horsehair tail and bridle, she is totally nude, her female sex fully exposed to the Florida sunshine.

My Vanilla mind assumes, given the pornography, that after the high-stepping, barrel-racing, and general horseplay is over, these scantily clad ponies end up being mounted by their masters.

Tim says, no.

Pony play for him and most others doesn't culminate with a sexual act, he explains. "It's never even been foreplay. It has roughly the same chance of becoming sex as dancing does. That's true of most of what I do in the scene. I do a lot of strange things with people, but it's not foreplay. It might excite me, but we don't go home together."

Vanillas might consider this the most mind-blowing aspect of fetishes, and it is worth repeating: Fetishists, not just pony players, rarely have genital contact with their partners, at least during cosplay.

Orgasm isn't necessarily the goal. Some may later have conventional sex, but during fetish play, particularly BDSM, the only fondled sex organ is usually the mind.

Fetishes also often overlap, Tim explains. While pony play for Tim and Lyndsey is an extension of their BDSM lifestyle, it also involves exhibitionism, hence the competitions. "We're sluts out in the open with pony stuff, but we keep the rest at home, and that's true with most of the others you will meet," Tim says. "At Fetish Con I'm a show-off. She's an exhibitionist. It's a fetish all to itself. Most of the people there are exhibitionists. That's what we all have in common."

Tim says there is also kinship between pony play and fursuiters, in that they share animal cosplay. Tim founded a pansexual group, Florida Critters, that is open to all animal/anthro cosplayers and has more than 350 members. He said a small group of BDSM furries who are ostracized by the wider furry community regularly attend their monthly meetings held at various fetish clubs and farms in central Florida. They have make-believe hunts where human ponies chase the furry canines, felines, and even a dolphin. Tim says the furs invariably give up too easily because they want to be tickled and scritched—fur language for affectionate scratching. "It usually ends in a big puppy pile."

Tim and Lyndsey offer to introduce me to the BDSM furries at an upcoming gathering. I later get an e-vite to "The Menagerie" being hosted by Master Logan and his Ponygirl Lavender. The agenda promises a presentation by three furs and pony play performances by Ponygroom Tim and Ponygirl Lyndsey and the revered world champions from Ocala, Foxy and Sherifox. I mark my calendar.

### Finding the Inner Animal

I've never been to an official fetish dungeon before, much less one in the middle of the afternoon. For all I know, it could be like the Fetish Con after-party, or people might be running around wearing nothing but horse heads. Since the invite noted a potluck, I bring cookies.

The private club is tucked at the back of a half-empty industrial building on a dead-end road in Largo, a middle-class city and retirement locale of about seventy-five thousand that abuts Clearwater. The metal building with its big garage doors owes its rise to the 2000s Florida real estate boom. Next door, pillars of an unfinished structure are overgrown with weeds, a skeletal reminder of that folly.

Inside, a bearded man wearing a black collared shirt and a shiny silver pendant sits at an old desk and acts as the gatekeeper. The entry room doubles as a fetish quick-stop retail center with a small selection of torture implements for those who may have accidentally left their cat-o'-nine-tails or crop at home.

The gatekeeper is the owner and only agrees to let me enter under the condition that I don't use his name or that of his club. He doesn't want publicity for fear that "religious extremists" will run his business out of town—trepidation not completely unwarranted given the moral outcry after the city manager came out as a transsexual woman in 2007. The City of Largo fired her.

An odd mix of about thirty people mill around the make-believe dungeon that under fluorescent lights could pass for a Disney day-care center. Walls are painted to look like the inside of a castle complete with crests. Folding chairs line the room. A bridle-less pony nibbles on Little Smokies near the buffet table.

About half the crowd is dressed in street clothes, clearly the audience, and the others are in some degree of performance-prep.

That is except for Kevin, an older, bearded man and his chunky, much younger submissive. She wears only panties and a black leather hood. Her hands are crudely mitted in pink tape, and it's impossible to tell if she is supposed to be a pony or just a run-of-the-mill sex slave. Kevin doesn't allow her to talk to anyone other than him. "She has to ask me to go to the bathroom," he says. They aren't on the agenda.

The world champion pony couple are tacking up in the far corner beside a table of their Native American Exotics handicrafts: human pony gear made with leather, feathers, and bone handles. Foxy is a man of many talents. He's also a taxidermist and a professional turkey and alligator hunter. Ponygirl Sherifox is half Native American and claims to be a direct descendent of the celebrated Chief Joseph of the Nez Perce tribe. She and Foxy met on his cowboy travels through the West.

Foxy is hard to miss. He looks like he just walked off the set of *Lonesome Dove*. He has a graying handlebar mustache and a beard parted in the middle and twirled to a point on each side. He wears a cowboy hat, a bib-front collar shirt, and his jeans are tucked into knee boots.

His DD-cup wife, a former stripper, spills from a leather bustier and matching thong. Her long auburn hair is hidden beneath a black leather headstall with a blonde plume that flows to the top of her matching tail. No doubt both are made from real horse hair.

John's dolphin, Calafin, and Dennis's Clygar Silverhooves fursuit heads. Note the stripes; Clygar is half Clydesdale and half tiger. Photo by Lori Ballard.

I discovered earlier through a simple Google search that Sherifox is far more than a pony-play kinkster and bio-horse lover. She's posted all over the Internet, every orifice exposed and turn-on explicitly stated. She performs in low-budget XXX porn videos sold on 50plusMILFs. com. On another website she sells her panties and gives away images of her feet in everything from peek-a-boo white platform boots to dirty tennis shoes. Her pay-per-view site promises to show more, whatever that may be.

As Foxy slides faux fetlocks and hooves over Sherifox's hands, she starts shuffling her feet back and forth and literally chomps at the bit.

Meanwhile, three furries in neoprene dive suits cluster around a table covered with the large, furry heads of a bottlenose dolphin, a Clydesdale, a killer whale, and three dragons. The matching bodies hang limp from a bondage rack like giant unstuffed toys.

John, the youngest of the furs, hardly looks a day over eighteen even though he's twenty-eight. He has a smooth, rosy complexion and curly brown hair, and wears wire-rimmed glasses. He speaks with the precise articulation of a precocious child loved by teachers and despised by bullies.

"Primarily, I'm a bottlenose dolphin. I'm also a dragon and sometimes a tiger. I growl," he says, deepening his voice for effect. "Dennis is a Clydesdale sometimes," he adds, pointing to a much older mustached man standing nearby. "But he is actually a killer whale most of the time."

Dolphin/dragon/tiger John and whale/Clydesdale Dennis are a couple. They are also into pony play, with Dennis being the horse, Sleipnir, again, a Clydesdale. The last of the trio, Dragon Takumori Softwing, is their roommate and pet.

In the BDSM world, human pets are fashionable. Pets typically never have sex with their masters. They just enjoy being dominated. Furry BDSMers take it further; their pets pretend to be actual animals. A furry BDSMer pet might walk on all fours, bark, and sleep in a dog crate.

Dragon Takumori doesn't look like someone who could be dominated. He's stout in a beer-drinking-brawl kind of way and is an assistant manager of an auto parts store. He says he's always loved dragons. The tattooed scales on his arms and visible beneath his buzz-cut hair testify to the depth of his obsession.

The men share a house in Mulberry, a speck of a town surrounded by towering phosphate mounds east of Tampa.

I am about to broach the furry-sex question when they share that their extended furry family also includes Dragon Takumori's teenage sister, who is a black-and-white hamster. His graying mother is a saber-toothed snow leopard. She came along for their presentation and stands quietly aside. She nods her head hello as they mention her, continually smiling like a proud mom. "We're making a suit for her," John says. "She's doing it so she can spend more time with her son."

The teenage-sister hamster and mom leopard added to their furry mix are hard to digest. This implies they aren't fur fetishists, but we are in a fetish dungeon.

The men explain that, similar to Ponygirl Lyndsey, they feel they have an animal inside them. But unlike the human ponies, they don't forget they are humans when in costume. "It's a mixture of human and animal," John says. "I still have a rational side but act in more animal ways, with stronger instincts."

"Everyone has one inside of themselves," says Dragon Takumori. "They just have to find it."

"Some people feel they have more than one," John adds as the buxom world champion Ponygirl Sherifox whinnies loudly behind him. Ignoring her, he looks toward his pet dragon and says, "He's a dragon in a human's body. He's not someone who will mind you. He has three dragon suits. Taku is his playful side. Agthorn is more like a grumpy old man and Solaris with wings is . . ." Sherifox, now closer, interrupts with another whinny as she high-steps across the floor. John merely grins, repressing a laugh or perhaps a dolphin chomp.

John's fascination with bottlenose dolphins began as a child, when his family, living in California, went on vacation to SeaWorld. "In some ways I indentified with them," John says. "A dolphin plays; it's mischievous and tends to get into trouble at times. I can also be a little bit proud of myself."

He claims he once swallowed a dead fish at SeaWorld after a dolphin refused to eat it. He jokes that on another occasion, a dolphin made a naughty advance toward him.

In the human world, John works in retail at Clear Channel and still likes playing with LEGOS. He writes anthropomorphic fiction and claims to have copyrighted two sci-fi universes. He hooked up with Dennis and Takumori in Texas. Together, they moved to central Florida.

I tip-toe back to the sensitive subject of fur fetish by mentioning the *CSI: Crime Scene Investigation* episode "Fur and Loathing," which depicted a murder victim as a kinky furry. They get defensive. "Many in the community were upset by that because it is not a fair representation of furries," John says. "It is not about sex."

Dennis acknowledges there are furries into it for the kinky sex, but that they are a "very small percentage." These three furs say they aren't part of that subset, which is still confusing because, again, they are showing off their fursuits in a fetish dungeon.

John says their fetish is BDSM. They are furries and pony players because they feel connected to an animal's nature, or in the case of the dragon, the characteristics created by a writer since dragons are completely imaginary. Dolphin John stresses that their two lifestyles couldn't mix if only because their BDSM roles are opposite their furry animal natures, which they call "fursonas." "In the BDSM lifestyle, I'm the dominant. When we're in fur, it's actually the opposite," John says. "When I'm a dolphin, he's a killer whale. He's my natural predator!"

For the moment, I somewhat comprehend. It's not until later, when I find John's online references to Dennis as his "herm orca mate" and his "mistress, at least in the furry side of things," that cognitive dissonance sets in again.

Trying to understand the attraction to an object that's fictional is a challenge in itself, but in the context of the online world, it's even harder to know where fantasy begins or ends.

The men go on to share some of the benefits of being a furry, such as anonymity. Behind the mask of fur, they can act like children and show affection in ways they would be too embarrassed to do otherwise. "In fursuit, I can lie with him and snuggle for two or three hours and watch TV," John says.

Dragon Takumori says, "If I go out and shoot archery in my backyard, my neighbors might think that's weird. But I can go out and do it in my fursuit and my neighbors just laugh."

The men claim that in costume they are physically stronger and have the instincts of the animals they dress as. Dennis recalls pulling a heavy cart as Sleipnir in a pony play competition underneath a blazing Texas sun. Out of tack he says he couldn't have pulled that much weight, that far.

No contests or hunts today. The three are here to show and tell. Their presentation is heavy on the mechanics of fursuit-making. As they go through the minutiae, I study the lifeless creatures hanging behind them. The cetaphins, as the water mammal characters are called in furry world, aren't remotely anatomically correct. For one, they are covered in fur. The finned, fursuit bodies have human legs, arms, and six-pack abs.

Fursuits cost in the tens of thousands of dollars. Even a modest one will typically set a fur back a grand. This furry family has started making their own, spending nights gluing tiny fake dragon scales by the blue light of the television.

**Bridled Enthusiasm**

Their presentation gives way to the pony shows. Ponygirl Lyndsey performs her cart-pulling routine to Paul Simon's "One Trick Pony."

"See how he dances, See how he loops from side to side," Paul Simon sings as Lyndsey does 360s with the cart. "See how he prances, The way his hooves just seem to glide."

By the time Lyndsey takes her final bow on one knee, she gleams with sweat and has a little trouble standing up.

Finally, it's time for the much-anticipated grand finale performance by the reigning World Pony Play Champions. Sherifox prances out on

Foxy tries to guide a blind-folded Ponygirl Sherifox over a hurdle that she doesn't know exists. What could go wrong? Photo by Lori Ballard.

her bare tiptoes, arms arched in front of her, hoofed hands tilted toward the floor like the feet of a carousel pony. Her shoulders are back, her head high, and her long blond plume and tail wave with each step.

Foxy tells the audience he's going to show a variety of pony moves. Then he subtly flicks the reins launching Sherifox, huffing and snorting, into what's supposed to be a high-stepping gait but is more like a majorette's pointed-toe march.

As for a breed, Sherifox seems more a spirited Mustang than a Royal Lipizzaner. She gives all the snorts and sounds of a horse being made to do something it doesn't want to do. But for all her horsey bluster, there's slack in the reins, and Foxy doesn't look the least bit worried that she will balk at a command or head for the barn. He lightly pulls and she marches in reverse, mimicking the showy move of a bio-horse backing up. Then she bounces forward again. He puts her on a lunge line, and she gallops around him in circles. She weaves through orange pylons. She ends the routine with a bow, bending one knee while keeping the other straight before her.

The small audience applauds.

Sherifox stays in pony character, huffing and restless beside Foxy as he talks to the audience in his Sam Elliott cowboy voice that makes even the most inane comment sound profound. "Those of you with a paper, we are going to take your commands in a minute," he says, grinning deviously as he glances over at his pony.

Eager to participate and see if Sherifox is indeed channeling an inner pony, I concentrate on coming up with a command.

He goes on to explain more about pony play, the psychological bond and such. "I have a high bar, but there is no right way or wrong way to play," Foxy says.

I write "JUMP" on a blank page of my notebook; human ponies do compete in steeplechases. It doesn't cross my mind that Sherifox would be blindfolded and jumping might be difficult.

"It doesn't matter whether you do it in the living room or on 100 acres in the woods," Foxy goes on. Of course, public play is better. "We've been in Central Park in New York City introducing pony play to people. Now that's as good as it gets."

He blindfolds Sherifox. He's going to show the audience just how well he's trained his little show pony. "Those of you with a paper will you please hold them up."

I lift mine high like a kid in class excited to know an answer. Then I look around the room. All the other commands are plants, predetermined by the pony pair. Clearly Foxy had passed them out earlier while I was caught up in furry world.

The snickers from the audience are not my imagination. I want to disappear inside one of the furry costumes. Foxy shakes his head. "We'll see about that one," he says.

He puts his blindfolded pony through the other commands using a subtle movement of the reins and an occasional light tap of his crop. Without error—or even much hesitation—she canters, bows and gallops to pony play perfection.

Being a sadist, Foxy can't pass up honoring my command. It would be an act of mercy to Sherifox and me. He spreads apart a couple of orange traffic cones and balances a thin pole across the tops.

The headstrong pony is restless and snorting. This deviation from routine is unexpected and unwelcome. I think she's knows it was my instruction. Could the blindfold have holes?

Positioned at the makeshift hurdle, Foxy taps behind one of Sherifox's legs with his crop. She lifts her knee and he taps her leg forward. She hops and knocks the pole off-balance. It clatters loudly on the concrete floor.

I want to vanish, but the exit is across the room, a room now so quiet in tense anticipation that everyone can hear Sherifox's heavy, horsey breaths.

After a couple more false starts, she step-hops over, a little sideways, but without knocking off the pole. Foxy, being a stickler for proper pony form, apparently thinks she can do better. He leads his pony around and lines her up for another.

She comes straight at the hurdle, but at the last moment her foot touches it. She tries to retreat as the pole falls but tangles in it. She loses her balance, and goes down hard, taking out an orange pylon.

A couple of people run out to help her up while the rest of us collectively hold our breath in fear that the ponygirl is injured. She dramatically rips off her blindfold, and her face is bright red. Foxy whispers something in her ear, and she snaps her head up and glowers at me, the interloper to this human menagerie. Caught up in their pony play drama, I cringe in humiliation and fear, yes, fear that this wild-eyed pony might just come over and belt me with her hoof.

The killer whale gives the author a big furry hug while his mate, Dolphin John, and pet, Dragon Takumori, look on. To the right, Ponygroom Tim adjusts Ponygirl Lyndsey's bridle. Photo by Lori Ballard.

Instead she turns and hobbles off with Foxy to their corner table. Afterward, I muster the courage to face them and formally apologize. Sherifox turns her back. Foxy, in his folksy way, says it's OK. He indicates he doesn't think Sherifox's accident is my fault, but doesn't say it within earshot of his angry pony—that would mean accepting some of the blame. Their relationship depends on total trust, and I worry that my ignorance combined with his pride wounded hers. I slink away like a whipped pup.

Across the dungeon, Dennis has transformed into Naketa Orcan, a black-and-white killer whale. He's wrapping his furry arms around anyone within reach, which soon includes me. It feels like being hugged by a giant plush toy, and I almost forget that there's a man inside and that we're standing in an S&M dungeon. The comforting embrace is welcome after the pony mishap and triggers childhood teddy bear memories. For an instant, Wonderland doesn't feel so kinky.

# CHAPTER 5

# Radical Rednecks

It's Saturday at 9:00 a.m., and the dusty farm road is solid muddy-bumper-to-muddy-bumper. My husband, James, and I idle in our Honda CVR, squeezed between dual-wheel pickups towing even larger vehicles. Stereos boom an odd mixture of bass-thumping rap and country twang. The toxic smell of diesel exhaust hangs in the air.

Somewhere in the distance is the entrance to the Redneck Yacht Club, an 800-acre mud park. A friendly guy in the next pickup says it's at least an hour's wait to reach the gate. "They have to search everybody's vehicle," he says.

Signs along the road lay out the park laws: No firearms, no glass, no pets, no underage drinking, no illegal drugs, no burning of tires, and no chain saws.

Given that everyone around us is chugging beer for breakfast, the reason for the prohibitions is fairly obvious, although you have to wonder how many people have brought in a gas-powered saw for it to make the list. Nothing like a drunk, pissed-off redneck wielding a chain saw to kill a good beer buzz.

The Redneck Yacht Club, twenty miles inland from Punta Gorda, allows mud lovers to camp overnight and haul in RVs, tents, grills, food, furniture, and all the canned beer and plastic bottles of liquor they can carry. Trucks and swamp buggies are loaded with oversized coolers, some multiple, and one buggy has a full-sized refrigerator in back.

No beer for us, yet. But an earlier pot of coffee forces me to join the pilgrimage of beer drinkers walking along the road en route to distant Port-o-Lets. The portable toilets are so rank that a girl comes out gagging. Some things can't wait. I hold my nose.

As mud parks go, the Redneck Yacht Club is luxurious. Matt Steele, whose production company videotapes and hosts event parks all over the world, sold me on a visit to the park. "It's the most elaborate place in the country. If that's the only one you ever go to, it will spoil you."

Matt's Orlando-based company is hosting the event today, and his crew's footage will undoubtedly make it into another DVD in his series called *Trucks Gone Wild*, porn for mudders.

Matt also hosts *Truck U* on the Speed cable channel. The fact that he can make a living chronicling mudding is a testament to the popularity of the backwoods culture. His home base in central Florida speaks to its prominence in the state. Florida has ten mud parks, and counting.

"A lot of it has to do with weather and the fact you can do it year-round," Matt says of why mudding is so big here. "A lot of states might have one or two parks. But here in Florida there are probably two events a month within an hour's drive."

Local newspapers report that the Redneck Yacht Club draws as many as twenty-two thousand in one day. The park's owner, Danny Kelly, says rednecks tend to exaggerate. The max has actually been around five thousand. This particular November weekend is expected to draw the largest crowd to date.

Dozens of mud lovers were so eager to get inside that they camped outside the park's gate Thursday night for the Friday-morning opening.

A truckload of young revelers from Okeechobee, about 80 miles east, lament that they couldn't make it until the weekend. They are towing a mud-caked swamp buggy—a flat-bed, open-air vehicle with giant tires that sits high enough above the ground to keep passengers' feet from getting muddy. Swamp buggies are Florida's unique contribution to the world of modern transportation.

This one is being trailered by a pickup so tall that I can barely see them through its open windows. The twenty-two-year-old driver sporting a rumpled straw cowboy hat shouts over the truck's rumbling engine, "We like to hunt deer and hogs, ma'am," he says, explaining the primary use of his buggy. "We use curs and pit bulls."

No dogs today. Instead they have a couple of giggly young women along for a ride who don't seem the least offended by the guys' blunt honesty about why they are here.

"I like the titties," says a guy in the backseat, referring to women who flash their boobs at passing revelers.

Another chimes in, "I jus' like getting drunk."

For as little as forty dollars per person, mud lovers can spend three days and two nights in the woods, drink as much as they want, swim in muddy ponds, and run around nearly butt-naked. Some equip their buggies with stripper poles and hold amateur contests.

Partying aside, off-roaders have few other options if they want to play in the mud. Most south Florida prairies are fenced and farmed. Wetlands are protected. Neither the Park Service nor farmers take kindly to vehicles cutting through boggy fields, leaving a trail like a backhoe.

Danny Kelly, the owner of this mud lover's dream, knows far too well the plight that young boggers face in finding a place to churn up mud. A self-professed redneck and third-generation Floridian, Danny and his four-wheel drives were chased out of many a field when he was growing up.

His grandfather was a farmer who built his own swamp buggy. Danny is so proud of this that he e-mails me an old photo showing him and a horde of other grandkids gathered around the contraption that looks like a combination of an old pickup, tractor, and small barge.

Danny always dreamed of opening a park where man, mud, and machine could mix with abandon. After making a small fortune through his marine construction business in Fort Myers, he turned the family potato farm into just that.

He says he spent $1 million and more than two years developing the park. He built miles of fences and roads, drilled wells, flooded fields, and put in bridges and dams. He created mud pits, a man-made silt-bottom stream, a muddy racetrack, and trails that snake through thickets of longleaf pines. For overnighters, he added a huge stage and campsites. Recognizing that someone might get seriously hurt, he put in two emergency helicopter pads.

## Redneck Royalty

My husband, a central Florida city boy, doesn't quite get the appeal of mudding but is adventurous enough to try. Being a north Alabama farm girl, I have a little red clay mud in my veins. I've four-wheeled over hills and through muddy creeks just enough to get a taste of the adrenaline rush. Unlike a roller coaster, where the experience is always the same (and you know you'll survive), no two off-roading challenges are alike. There's always a chance that something will go wrong, that you will get stuck or, worse, topple over. When the tires sink into the mud, the vehicle becomes an extension of your body. You're on edge, pressing your feet on the floor as if that will help give you traction. The engine roars, and you let out a primal yell. Smoke comes off the tires, you pray, you cuss. Once you escape the clutches of muck, there's a brief *yeehaw!* moment that's immediately followed by an impulse to ford something bigger, deeper.

James and I have no illusions about taking our wimpy SUV through the mud. We're hooking up with a mudder to ride on a bona fide swamp buggy.

The odd-looking amphibious vehicles rolled through the state's mosaic of wetlands and prairies long before monster trucks and ATVs were conceived. It was rugged and soggy south of Orlando, Florida, when the buggies were invented early in the twentieth century. The Everglades, not yet channeled by the U.S. Army Corps of Engineers, was twice as large. Half of south Florida was a grass-filled river part of the year. Not many people dared living in the region. The 1910 U.S. Census registered only 32,300 residents south of Sarasota and Lake Okeechobee. Those hardy few were an independent lot: either they or their parents had sought refuge in the Glades for various, sometimes nefarious, reasons. They hunted badgers, skinned gators, gigged bullfrogs. They cleared virgin forests of towering pines and killed tropical birds for the colorful feathers that ended up on women's hats in New York City.

By necessity, these south Florida pioneers were an inventive sort. So, after mass-produced Model Ts took to the road, they figured out ways to adapt them to wheel through the bogs.

Various Florida crackers claim their ancestors invented the first buggy, but Naples's historians like to credit the late Ed Frank, a Naples mechanic who built *Skeeter* around 1918 out of Model-T parts and used an orange crate for a seat. "I had no money. I built it out of junk," Ed later recalled to the *Marco News*. He lived inland of Naples on a 220-acre farm that adjoined untamed wilderness. He drove *Skeeter* through a break in his thicket and disappeared into the Everglades on weeklong hunts. Perfecting it after each trip, he added an extra transmission, more gears, dual rear wheels, and tire chains. He turned the axles upside down to give more clearance over stumps and cypress knees, and he swapped the orange crate for an aluminum World War I airplane seat. His most noticeable modification was the wheels. He replaced the spindly auto ones with bulbous tractor tires. His monster wagon looked more like the modern swamp buggies around us in line than the buggies that race in Naples.

Legend has it that Ed and fellow hunters gathered to compare notes on their vehicles the week before hunting season began. Somewhere along the line, they started racing them for fun. Word got around, and locals started gathering to watch.

When the races moved to a soggy sweet-potato farm closer to town, city leaders jumped on board and encouraged buggy owners to stage a parade. An official Swamp Buggy Days festival began in earnest in 1949, complete with a swamp buggy queen. Racers competed for guns, turkeys, and camping gear. The *Collier County News*, the local newspaper of the day, declared the swamp buggy was "as important to Florida as the cow pony is to the West . . . [T]hey are the only practical means of transportation once off road." ABC's *Wide World of Sports* started airing the races in the mid-1950s. Cary Grant showed up. Prizes became money, encouraging backyard mechanics to build buggies more for racing than hunting. Racers installed larger engines, propellers, and sometimes even water skis, whatever they thought might give them an advantage. Like NASCAR rides, the modern Naples racing buggy little resembles its humble origins. Bodies are long and narrow, wheels are thin, and racers wear helmets.

"They haven't been buggies in ten years," complains Mike Fox, a third-generation Florida buggy builder. "They're more like boats."

Mike, owner of M.C. Ventures in LaBelle, isn't exactly a swamp buggy purist. Sure, he builds more than fifty buggies a year, which he claims is more than all other Florida buggy builders combined. He constructs hunting buggies, eco-expedition buggies, and utilitarian models for the Park Service. But Mike also builds flashier show buggies that are used for nothing but parading and partying at mud parks. They look like luxury pontoon boats on tractor tires, complete with names airbrushed across the back.

Mike's crowning achievement, *Redneck Royalty*, is to be our ride for the day. I spotted the outrageously redneck buggy for sale online. List price: $99,000. The price, though, wasn't the eye-catcher. The buggy's back panel is airbrushed with voluptuous women in itsy bikinis, stockings, and high heels—something along the lines of a trucker's strip-club fantasy. As if the motif weren't parody enough of redneck culture, the photo includes three pretty, teenage girls in cut-offs and tied-up shirts posed around the buggy in Daisy Duke fashion. Mike later tells me they are his daughters.

At 13½ feet, the buggy is as tall as a house. The tires alone are 5 feet high. Every square inch is detailed. Gauges change colors with the push of a button. The exhaust pipes running through its open belly are chrome. The gold-painted wheels are laser cut with an intricate design of crowns and the letters "RR." *Redneck Royalty*, indeed.

Appearance isn't the only thing that sets *Redneck Royalty* apart from hunting buggies. The mudding vessel is equipped with more luxuries than a stretch Hummer. It has a built-in flat-screen DVD player, an overhead stereo system, an icemaker, a wet bar, tilt steering, and an electric retractable royal-blue canopy. The four, cushioned passenger seats mounted along the outside have rising armrests with cup holders. The center captain's chair swivels so the driver doesn't have to get up to reach the bar.

Mike admits he got the idea for *Redneck Royalty* during a late-night get-together. He was downing Crown Royal with friends and started pontificating about his dream buggy. His drinking buddies made suggestions. As best as he can recall, the brainstorming session went something like this:

"I'm going to build a buggy so big that when I pull up to a mud hole everyone's going to be looking at me," Mike declared, then added it would include a bar.

One friend joked, "As much as you drink, you're going to run out of ice."

"So, I'm going to build one and put an ice maker on it," Mike responded.

"Hey, if you're going to put running water on it, you might as well put a wet bar on it, too," one added.

*Redneck Royalty*, our ride for the day. Photo by James Harvey.

Another chimed in, "Let's put a TV on it so we can watch games!"

In the light of day, the plan sounded, well, like a crazy drunken idea. "You mean you're going to build a buggy with 700 horsepower and a rolling bar, and drive it through the woods?" another friend asked Mike.

Yes, Mike confidently replied. His friend shook his head and said, "Well, I'm just going to tell law enforcement to go the other way if they see you coming because the paperwork would take way too long."

No one laughed at Mike when his redneck masterpiece took first place in the show buggy competition in West Palm Beach. Turns out, there's an east-west Florida rivalry in swamp buggy culture. The West Palm swamp buggy community had long taken the trophies and considered theirs the biggest, badass buggies of Florida. But then along came Mike, a small-town boy who raised the Florida creation to a new level of decadence.

Mike laments that he can't make it to the *Trucks Gone Wild* event. He's too busy filling buggy orders and dealing with cable-channel producers who want to shoot a reality show based on his business. He's generous enough to hook me up with Tony Barnes, the buggy trader who now owns *Redneck Royalty*, and offers a few words of advice: "Be careful who you ride with. They have to medevac people out of there every weekend . . . And I'd get out before dark."

His warning explains the full-page liability waivers we have to sign after finally arriving at the entry gate. Guys in Redneck Yacht Club shirts check our driver's licenses and do a cursory search of the SUV for guns, knives, and chain saws.

A woman in a wooden booth takes our thirty-dollar-entry fees, the one-day rate. At last we are inside the mecca of mud.

Our ride, the tallest vehicle in sight, is waiting in a grassy parking lot just inside the gate.

Given the buggy's *Redneck Royalty* name and saucy design, I expect Tony to be loud and crude with a beer belly the size of a small country. Instead, he and his wife, Lacee, are soft-spoken, trim, and look like young suburbanites. Our meeting is not without some awkwardness. They are wearing University of Florida shirts and caps. James and I are wearing Crimson Tide caps.

Southeastern Conference rivalries run deathly deep, and in recent years no contests have been fiercer than Florida and Alabama's. The two schools have in essence battled for the national championship. I can take comfort in Alabama's whipping Florida in the last match-up to the point of making their quarterback Tim Tebow cry. But when I see Tony and Lacee dripping in Gator garb, and they see our Bama flash, it's a little like the Hatfields finding themselves sharing a cab with the McCoys.

We're all too polite to talk smack about one another's team. James and I climb up the pull-down ladder and settle into the cushiony captain's chairs along the rail. Tony mounts a large Florida Gator flag to the buggy's roof. I tuck a beer into my Roll Tide cuzie.

Clay, another rider, hooks his iPod up to the buggy's stereo system. Clay is a Florida cracker whose family has been in the state for five generations farming large swathes of land near Lake Okeechobee. He's a chemical salesman for a Florida phosphate giant. Given his dress—a casual designer shirt and shorts, silver ghetto chain, and flimsy Gator-emblem flip-flops (yes, another Florida fan)—he hasn't spent much time in mud.

The two men met when Tony sold Clay a house in Fort Myers. Tony is a man of many trades.

During the week he runs computer networks for U.S. Sugar in Clewiston. On weekends he sells real estate, and somewhere in between, he deals in swamp buggies and staghorn ferns.

Lacee is a legal assistant for a criminal defense attorney. They work hard and earn more than a decent living. The rock on her finger could cut steel wheels.

With the cooler stocked, Tony cranks up the buggy. The engine rumbles like a tractor on nitro, drowning out conversation. Clay cranks up the stereo. Tony hits the gas. We're off to the tune of Creedence Clearwater Revival's "Fortunate One." Yeehaw!

## Mudderdome

ATVs, four-wheel-drive trucks, and lesser buggies scatter like insects to make way for *Redneck Royalty*. Forget driving on the right side of the road or yielding to the vehicle on the right. The only rule of the road here is that the biggest vehicle has the right-of-way.

On the dusty thoroughfare that splinters the park, Tony opens it up. I hold onto my hat with one hand and grip the rail with the other. The buggy is only going about 20 miles per hour, but with no windshield it

*Redneck Royalty* owners Tony and Lacee Barnes. Note the Florida Gator garb.
Photo by James Harvey.

feels more like 50 mph. Tony shouts that the buggy will go up to 60 and jokingly asks if I want to experience it.

I laugh, half-hoping that he will take it to the max.

It's a short ride to the heart of the action. Tony points out a family campground along the way. Yes, some bring their children along for the weekend. Since the partying goes on all night, there's a small wooded area for those who want to spare their kids the mayhem, which is a little strange considering there's no shortage of it in the light of day.

Tony whips into a watered-down field named Pine Island Sound, a mudder's replica of the estuary and islands off the coast of Fort Myers. The open, 40-acre field is pocked with deep mud holes and mounds of mud named after real islands. Most are identified with metal signs, but a few markers are missing. Danny told me earlier that revelers constantly uproot them for souvenirs.

Considering all the vehicles barreling this way and that across the field, there's a good chance that many just disappear in the mud.

Tony slowly circles the field to give us a panoramic view of the mud mayhem; *Mad Max* meets redneck spring break.

ATVs whiz in all directions like panicked ants. Huge fancy buggies with names like *Southern Swagger* and hunting buggies with built-in cages for dogs up top and kill below tour the perimeter. Others congregate by mud holes that are like small ponds. Lurking in the midst are amalgamations of metal, rubber, and flesh that defy a sober city slicker's imagination.

One buggy topped with a loveseat moves on rolling track like an army tank. A decommissioned U.S. Army truck has "Show me your tits," painted on the door and a plywood bar and bench car seats in the back. Stuffed pig toys decorate one Jeep's hood. An old yellow bus with monster tires and the name "School Trip" in multicolor looks like the result of a mudder's acid trip.

Two white guys cruise the field in a rusty, baby-blue Cadillac with tractor tires and a tag that says "White City Boys." Their windshield is emblazoned with "H.N.I.C.," which stands for "Head Nigger in Charge," a racial slur that dates back to the days of cotton plantations. A George W. Bush bumper sticker is plastered on the rear: "Miss me yet?"

Orange-and-blue Florida Gator flags hang from buggy rails, truck antennas, ATV safety arms. The team pride is so overwhelming that I momentarily think a pickup spray-painted with the message "NO-BAMA" is a knock against my alma mater, rather than the current president.

Most of the crowd is under thirty-five and drunk, or on their way to it. Men wear T-shirts with messages like "Titties & Beer" and "I Love Boobs." Women wear string bikinis and tall rubber boots. No inhibitions. No shame. They party standing-room-only on swamp buggies. They sit on buggy steps and hang their legs off the side. They ride on toolboxes in the back of pickups. They take in the scene from living room couches squeezed into truck beds.

A group of teens ride in a makeshift tall, narrow cart with small wheels and bench seats from an old car. A chubby boy standing on the back repeatedly shifts his weight, causing the buggy to pop wheelies like a Shriners' parade car. Riders nearly slide out the back, but they beg for more.

Parents zoom around on ATVs with kids loosely clutched in their laps. One family in a show buggy rests their infant in a car seat on the steel floor.

Two rectangular parachutes eyebrow the sky. Ultra-light fliers are taking in the scene. No one on wheels seems to notice them. Perhaps it's sensory overload, drunkenness, or just part of survival.

Mud boggers are exhibitionists, and bragging rights aren't worth anything if no one can see you conquer. So, mudders tend to congregate around the field's deepest holes and watch one another slog through, or at least attempt to.

Beside the largest hole, a toddler pats muck around a parked truck tire four times her height. Her siblings wade along the edge of the murky water.

The mud isn't black from decayed foliage like in the Glades. It's not even tawny like the farm's natural wetlands. Those are off-limits, environmentally protected. Danny created these bogs, and they are the color of a pig's sty.

Danny bedded the mud holes with silt he'd dredged from the Caloosahatchee River. Getting mud the consistency of cake batter isn't easy, he says. He mixes clay, river silt, sand, and well water. "Some people come out there and complain it's too thick; others fuss it's too thin. They're like a bunch of old women trying to please," Danny said. "People get very anal about mud and if there's too much water there's not enough challenge, but if it's too thick it slows them down too much. It's not fun if you don't have a risk of getting stuck."

There's no shortage of people willing to take that chance.

Saying the *Royalty*'s engine needs a rest, Tony parks alongside one of his friends at the deepest hole. We get to watch the action up close. That goes as much for the people as the vehicles taking on the mud hole. Each buggy has its own little redneck drama.

Tony's friend in the smaller hunting buggy brought along his female roommate. Despite having a girlfriend on a buggy elsewhere in the park, the female roommate is getting cozy with a young woman in cowboy boots and tiny cut-offs that show off her belly-ring and tattoos.

Tony's friend laughs that they don't know who the cowgirl is. She just climbed aboard after they arrived at the park.

Someone cranks up rap music and the two women start dancing suggestively. They grind front to back, wave their arms in the air while holding onto their beers. Guys in buggies and trucks across the mud hole cheer them on. Mystery Girl gets so amped that she climbs up on the steering console and thrusts her pelvis a little too enthusiastically. Losing her balance, she takes a tumble back into the front seat. Pickled to the pain, she merely laughs, gets up, and dances more, though avoiding the buggy's edge.

Meanwhile, the testosterone show carries on in the mud pit. By necessity, the chaos is more organized. Drivers wait their turn to pass through the murky water. Most are in trucks and Jeeps. Tony tells me he wouldn't dare try to go through the deep hole in a swamp buggy. They are too top-heavy, he says.

I'm a little disappointed. Maybe it's my roots, or perhaps the beer, but I'm itching to ride through a mud hole.

A few swamp buggies dare to try the hole anyway and teeter dangerously close to flipping over. Inevitably it happens. A packed buggy takes the water at an angle, tilting to one side along the slope. As if in slow motion, the tall vehicle topples over, and riders fly through the air. The buggy slams on its side in the mud. The occupants plop into the cloudy muck. Rather than wading to rescue the female passengers, one man rushes to salvage the cooler.

Having seen enough for the moment, Tony backs *Redneck Royalty* away from the hole. Clay watches out for any ATVs or smaller vehicles behind. There are no rearview mirrors.

As we move through the horde of vehicles, people stop, point, and snap pictures of us, or rather the buggy. It's like being on a parade float, and we are the royalty of the redneck kingdom. Of course, the Florida Gators flag on the roof heightens the adoration. As we pass, other buggy riders salute us with arm-scissoring Gator chomps. The only Roll Tide! shout-out would come from a guy wearing a red Teletubbie™ costume.

Tony bypasses the drive-thru truck wash on the way out of Pine Island Sound. A well feeds the continuous vehicle shower and the overflow keeps the field flooded. Tony notes that everyone on a buggy gets wet, and that sometimes it's a welcomed bath.

*Redneck Royalty* doesn't need a wash at this point. Tony has been light on the pedal since we entered the mud field. Lacee says he hates getting the vehicle dirty, even though it is, after all, a swamp buggy. "I

Mystery Girl, pre-fall.
Photo by James Harvey.

thought he was going to kill his brother for bringing it back dirty last time," she says.

Tony didn't own a swamp buggy until 2009. Now he has six, all for sale.

Unlike most of the guys he grew up with in LaBelle, Tony's not a hunter. He never needed a buggy for sport or even joyriding since his friends owned them. But when mud parks began opening around 2004, demand for buggies grew. Tony, like a lot of other Floridians, recognized there was money to be made in mud.

"I bought one and turned around and sold it in three days and made $13,000," he says.

Tony credits the parks for growing the market of the party buggies. Since the mud attractions started opening, builders have gotten orders for swanky $75,000 to $150,000 buggies that rarely roll through anything deeper than a mud puddle.

Commerce, obviously, played a role in the rise of parks, too. Most park owners' families have owned the land for generations, but for one reason or another have found the mud attractions more profitable than farming.

Plant Bamboo in Okeechobee started the trend in 2004 when owner Ed Underhill opened up his struggling dairy and bamboo farm to more than eight thousand mud boggers. The farm has been in Underhill's family for six generations, but encroaching development was making it harder to operate. His first mudding weekend was considered to be the largest on the East Coast, but Ed admits the crowds had a lot to do with unwanted publicity stemming from a lawsuit his mother filed against him to try to prevent it.

Many of the mud boggers' families also go back generations in Florida. But the younger set hunts for sport, not out of necessity, and they like a little P. Diddy mixed with their Lester Flats. Some live in urban subdivisions and big-city condos. Others live in farm towns where hoes and shovels were long ago replaced by air-conditioned tractors and harvesters that dwarf any swamp buggy.

Parkgoers get in touch with their roots even if they are fabled. That goes for the Confederacy as well. Florida is part of the South despite how many northerners make it their retirement home. Many Florida boggers take pride in Confederate heritage, however racially divisive it may be. It doesn't matter if their ancestors fought for the Union, the southern rebel rules.

I see more Confederate flags in these muddy fields than I've seen in my entire life, and I grew up in a town that was briefly the national headquarters for the Ku Klux Klan. The Stars and Bars is on ATV flags, car tags, rear windows, shirts, and hats. A woman in a rebel-flag bikini and cowboy boots parades throughout the park on the hood of a truck with a Busch beer in her hand. When she goes on break, a blow-up doll in a rebel-flag bikini takes her place.

One buggy flies a pair of rebel flags imprinted with Hank Williams Jr.'s face. "If the South Woulda Won." Yes, imagine.

Not surprisingly, the crowd is more than 99.9 percent white.

### Redneck Rock Stars

As Tony steers us to the next play area, he shouts that we'll come back after the races. "It really gets busy in the pits then." Busier is hard to fathom, but the main parking lot and campground give a sense of the potential. A mass of steel and horsepower covers more than 40 acres. Everything from million-dollar RVs to towering pickups with flatbed trailers.

The amount of money invested in the sea of recreational vehicles is unfathomable. Tony says his buggy tires alone cost six hundred dollars each. It costs a hundred dollars just to fill up the buggy for one day in the park. Even small ATVs sell for around $5,000. Then there's the cost of constant maintenance and upkeep. Breakdowns are a given.

A fancy buggy nearly as large as *Redneck Royalty* is stalled by a broken fuel pump. The owner says it was the only replacement part he didn't bring. He had to send someone all the way back to Punta Gorda to pick up a new one.

Tony nods his head in commiseration; he's been in that spot before.

A row of vendors in travel trailers borders the huge campground. The smell of fried food overpowers our buggy exhaust. This is one of the few areas where people dare set out on foot, and not just for a burger and fries. A mudder can pick up a copy of *Mud Life*, an Orlando-based magazine distributed around the nation and a big seller at U.S. military bases in the Middle East. A few entrepreneurial, self-professed "bubbas" of central Florida hawk Bubba Rope®, a towing strap adapted from ones used by military helicopters. And what event would be without a T-shirt vendor? A family-based business from Myakka started small, but soon incorporated as Sloppy Holes Mud'n Club. They sell

For those times when waving a rebel flag just isn't enough. Photo by James Harvey.

mud fan wear at parks all over the state and online. One of their big sellers is a camo T-shirt with a silhouette of a topless cowgirl and the slogan "Sloppy hole hunter . . . always lookin' for a wet spot."

Nearby, the races are at full throttle. They are billed as the primary attraction, but most mudders are too busy entertaining themselves to watch. Those who do, simply pull up to the rail—no need to disembark. Seats on the elevated trucks and buggies offer unobstructed views and convenient access to party supplies. The sweet, musky smell of marijuana floats through the air.

One by one, giant trucks spin around the soupy track, shooting up tails of muddy water as they round each curve. A far cry from the ad-covered trucks of Monster Jam, these vehicles look like something constructed in a backyard garage. Some are missing hoods, one doesn't have a bed, and several lack side windows. All have massive engines and tires.

A stage large enough to accommodate an orchestra borders the track. The giant fire pit beside it smolders from the night before. After dark, motorized traffic is forbidden, and the park attempts to keep the rowdy crowd entertained with country bands.

A steady string of revelers ride past, seeing and being seen like high school kids cruising a downtown strip on a Saturday night.

Tony's friends pull up in another massive swamp buggy. Anticipating getting smashed, they hired a designated driver. Tony had told me the day before that they were grilling out with friends. I had envisioned a cozy campfire in the woods. His buddies are firing up the charcoal grill on their rolling front porch.

Plastic Mardi Gras beads hang from their buggy's rails and dangle around their necks. Like at the hedonistic New Orleans festival, men toss baubles to women who bare their breasts.

Mike had warned that there would be a lot of mammary flashing, and that the *Redneck Royalty* attracts it. "It's a chick magnet," he told me. "I feel like a redneck rock star when I'm on it." He said a teenager once asked why he didn't put a gun rack on *Redneck Royalty*, and he responded: "I've seen more racks in one day on that buggy than you will ever see in your life."

Maybe it's because there are two women on board, but *Redneck Royalty* isn't drawing any boob salutes today, at least not at this point.

A Jeep parades past with two young women with breasts as firm as grapefruits spilling from skimpy bikini tops. Like beauty queens, they stand in the back, holding onto the roll bar with one hand and waving to men with the other. Tony's friends go wild. They holler, dangle their strands of beads, and practically jump up and down to get the women's attention.

"I think we're fixing to see some beans come out," Tony tells Clay.

The girls only flash smiles.

"Aw, wimps," Tony says.

The races nearing their end, we head back to Pine Island Sound where the only prize is bragging rights. Tony was right in his prediction. The field is getting packed.

Buggies, trucks, Jeeps, and ATVs are parked two and three deep around the deepest pond.

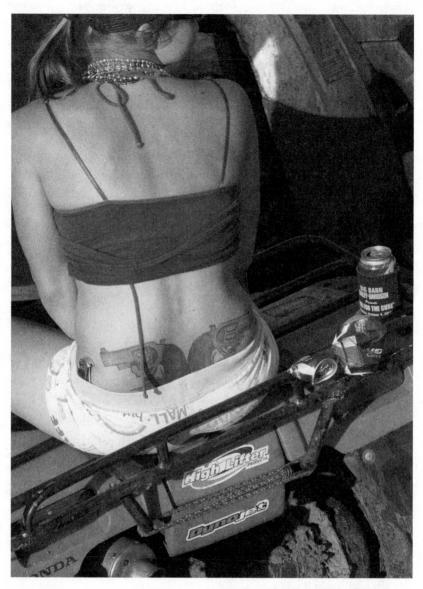

Some guns are allowed.
Photo by James Harvey.

The hole has deepened throughout the day with each drag of tires. As the sun lowers over the Australian pines, it is now at least 5 feet deep. Only trucks equipped with snorkels attempt it, and by snorkels, I mean literally. Each vehicle has a long pipe sticking up through its hood that allows the engine to breathe. Otherwise, the engine would choke.

I fight the urge to climb off the buggy and chase down a truck owner who will give me a ride through the muck. Before I work up the nerve, we leave Pine Island Sound to drop off Clay at his truck. On our way back, a sobering sight on the side of the road kills my enthusiasm. Paramedics are loading a man in a neck brace into an ambulance.

Back at the deep hole, the crowd is captivated by a Jeep that flipped upside down. Only the wheels and under carriage are visible above the muck. Amazingly, the occupants weren't the ones hauled off to the hospital. They are up to their necks in the stew of muddy water, petroleum, and who knows what else. The Jeep is so mired that it takes two trucks straining in tandem to upright it. As the mud-coated vehicle flips over, the crowd hollers, whistles. "Hell, yeah!"

The trucks stop, and the Jeep, right-side-up, sinks back into the muck, listing to one side like a boat run aground. Onlookers groan.

Like a dark knight, the biggest truck on the field—at least two feet taller than *Redneck Royalty*—rumbles to the rescue. The crowd lets out more hillbilly cheers. The young Jeep riders go through another round of hooking up tow straps, which clearly goes slower when you have to work in muck up to your ears.

Connected, the black truck backs up as if to get a running go and allows slack in the tow strap.

"Uh oh," Tony comments. His friend in the next buggy laughs. The consensus is the driver is all truck and little experience.

He guns his engine hard. The line snaps.

Undaunted, the Jeep guys, still up to their necks in muck, retie it. The truck keeps the line taut this time and digs in, black smoke spewing from its towering exhaust pipe like a coal plant in China. The Jeep frees, but by now the crowd is too engrossed in their beers and talk of "titties" to give more than a half-hearted cheer.

The scene grows more postapocalyptic as the sinking sun casts a golden light, illuminating diesel exhaust and swirls of oil film atop the muddy water. A young buggy crew disembarks by a mud hole, and they drag one another into the muck. One guy belly-flops in and then floats around on his back as if he were in a resort swimming pool. The girls stumble out of the water looking as if they had been dipped in chocolate.

"You see that?" Tony asks. "They'll still be like that in the morning. There aren't any showers out here. But they don't care. They probably won't sleep all night."

Naively, I ask, "But don't they pass out from drinking all day?"

"Well, I think there could be some drugs involved."

Duh.

James and I decide to escape while there's still light. We have an Alabama game to catch. Plus, it's pretty obvious that things get even crazier after dark. We've just had our first bare-boob sighting. Tony's friends in the next buggy finally coaxed a couple of women to flash them.

Tony and Lacee drop us off back at our SUV. They are going to return to the depths of the chaos and join their friends for a grilled dinner. (He, of course, is taping the Florida game.)

They invite us to join them again, but Tony adds: "Just do me a favor. Don't wear the hats next time."

CHAPTER 6

# Spirits, Fairies, and
# a Blow-Up Mary

Floridians are on average about as religious as the residents of any other state, and they worship dominant faiths to roughly the same degree. But in a land of individualists prone to the fantastical, ordinary often isn't an option.

Florida has entire small towns and significant portions of larger ones devoted to religions that are mere blips on America's spiritual radar.

The nation's largest commune of Hare Krishna sits just outside Gainesville, for example. Bald practitioners swathed in ponchos come into Gainesville to serve free vegetarian lunches daily to hungry University of Florida college students.

The church of Scientology, a religion started in the 1950s by a science-fiction writer, owns about half of downtown Clearwater and considers the city its spiritual headquarters. Some two thousand followers a week come to the coastal town to be cleared of psychological implants, which they believe are the root of all their problems.

Some of Florida's religious imports are obscure even in the countries where they originated. In Hialeah, a leader of Ifa Orisha, a South African religion, preached the virtues of drinking giant African snail mucus to cure medical ills and allegedly smuggled the highly invasive species into Miami inside his suitcase. Federal and state authorities raided his yard, seizing the snails after several of his followers claimed the snail fluids made them sick. State wildlife officials since have had to deal with a neighborhood giant snail epidemic.

Florida has homegrown faiths as well. A Jewish Brooklyn woman says Jesus Christ told her to start the interfaith Kashi Ashram in Sebastian. *Newsweek* profiled a former heroin addict turned south Florida reverend who runs his ministry on a biblical Etch A Sketch®. First, he claimed he was the reincarnation of the Apostle Paul. Then he declared himself Jesus Christ and changed his name to Jose Lois De Jesus, "The Man Christ Jesus." Not long afterward, he said he was the Antichrist and got a "666" tattoo. Many of his followers, who he claims number 2 million across thirty-five countries, also wear his brand.

Florida has such a history with unusual religions that it even memorializes one. The defunct Koreshan community—a late 1800s commune that proselytized that man lived inside a hollow Earth—is now the Koreshan State Historic Site in Estero.

The majority of Floridians are Christian—Catholic or Protestant. Florida, particularly the northern portion, is definitely in the Bible Belt and filled with fire-and-brimstone fundamentalists. The practices of those mainstream faiths sometimes also take on a relatively extreme bent.

A creationist theme park with fake dinosaurs operated in Pensacola until the founder was hauled off to jail in 2009 for not paying taxes, something he claimed wasn't commanded by God's law.

The controversial Christian minister Terry Jones, whose anti-Islamic rants caused international incidents, bases his ministry in Gainesville. His plan to burn Qurans in 2010 prompted a call from the White House asking him to stand down.

As for Catholics, a pizza magnate turned remote scrubby pastures in southwest Florida into a town exclusively for the faith. Ave Maria is complete with an elaborate cathedral, schools, a university, $300,000 homes, and a chain grocery store.

In the documentary *Florida: Heaven on Earth*, Stetson University religion professor Phillip Lucus attributes Florida's diversity of faiths and practices to the state's image as a land of dreams. But it also doesn't hurt to know that whatever you believe isn't any weirder than something you read about in the local morning paper. It's a shared delusion. Nothing is impossible.

My journey into the fringe of Florida's spirituality leads me to two religious hotspots—the Cassadaga Spiritualist Camp and the Holy Land Experience. They represent the extremes of the state's unconventional faiths, a juxtaposition of old and modern, New Age and Bible-thumping Christianity, earthy and plastic.

While the Cassadaga Spiritualist Camp embraces tourism, at its core it is a residential community of about fifty practicing mediums, psychics, and healers. They practice a religion outside the mainstream in a bucolic setting that is more Old Florida than the majority of Florida churches. Founded in 1894, Cassadaga is the oldest active Spiritualist community in the South.

Meanwhile, the biblical-themed Holy Land Experience in Orlando could hardly be more iconic of modern Florida tourism as it's based on a Christian faith that, while not entirely mainstream, has thousands more followers than Spiritualism.

Conveniently, the two religious destinations are only about forty-five minutes apart along I-4. My husband, James, and I start in Cassadaga and work our way home.

### Age-Old to New Age

Spiritualists believe in God as a higher power. Like Protestants, they don't see a need for an intermediary for divine connection, and like many New Agers, they don't believe in hell in a literal sense. Rather they think hell can be a place on Earth, a sentiment with which anyone who's ever been stuck on I-4 for three hours between Tampa and Orlando might agree. Where Spiritualists diverge from most conventional religions is in their belief that a person's soul hangs around after they die and that trained mediums can communicate with them.

Over the decades, Cassadaga residents have apparently communed with the dead more easily than they have with one another. The founder was booted from a trustee meeting for swearing not long after the camp was officially established. In modern times, a debate over finances led to a scuffle and police being called to a camp meeting. Over the decades, scribes from local papers have chronicled Cassadaga residents' squabbles over medium protocols, appropriate behavior, finances, and real estate. The purpose of this trip, however, isn't to examine their differences, but to learn what they share—an unconventional faith based on the paranormal—and why so many seek their services. To that end, an overnight stay in Cassadaga's allegedly haunted hotel (the only lodging within miles) and a Sunday service are on the agenda. Of course, a Spiritualist reading is a must.

Cassadaga is about a forty-five-minute drive northeast of downtown Orlando. Modern Florida quickly gives way to cracker culture once you leave Interstate 4. Handwritten signs advertise horses and goats for sale. A rebel flag hangs from the front porch of a weathered farmhouse. The land even becomes hilly.

Downtown Cassadaga is little more than a four-way stop with a bathroom-sized post office and a couple metaphysical shops on one side of the road and the hotel and camp-owned bookstore on the other. To an outsider it isn't clear where the official historic camp begins and ends, but residents won't hesitate to tell you. "Those are the leeches," one says of the shops on the post-office side of the road. By leeches, she means non-camp-sanctioned psychics, many of whom set up shop outside the camp proper after the rise of the New Age movement in the 1980s made Spiritualism more popular.

An aura as thick as the summer humidity hangs in the air. The unsettling quiet and stillness are punctured only by the occasional chirping of a blue jay or sparrow perched in the branches of oaks that drip lacy Spanish moss.

A drive on the camp's unmarked roads takes less than ten minutes, a walk less than a half hour. There aren't any camping facilities; the name "camp" comes from the old-time tradition of religious "camp meetings." Many of the early camp residents were Spiritualist snowbirds, staying the winter and returning north in summer.

The architecture and style closely resemble early-twentieth-century Christian assembly retreats across America. At least half of the homes are that old, many Victorian. Landscaping is a collage of rural bizarre, and décor is whimsical—a St. Francis statue overlooks gaudy golden sphinxes, and a Buddha wears sunglasses and Mardi Gras beads. One yard is planted in plastic flowers; another is edged in tiny American flags. A quilt covers a window of one home; an Obama poster blocks

It's hard to get lost at the
Cassadaga Spiritualist Camp.
Photo by James Harvey.

another's. Neon lights hang on screened porches. Hand-painted signs identify mediums' residences by saying "walk-ins welcome" or "by appointment."

Since it's a holiday weekend, the place crawls with tourists as well as regulars. The hotel is booked. Small, dusty parking lots overflow. Curious sightseers check out the bookstore and grab a bite in the hotel's Lost in Time Café, the only restaurant in town. Others move with purpose. They seek closure with a deceased loved one, help finding a lost pet, or guidance from their dead mother, God, Native American spirits, Mother Earth, or whatever higher power holds their faith. They crave assurance that there's existence on the other side of life, something a medium can address for a donation of around $120 an hour.

The camp bookstore has all the metaphysical tools and knickknacks. Prayer beads, fairy figurines, Native American dream catchers, crystals, healing rocks, and an array of books on the paranormal. As if there were any doubt the community is a tourist attraction, the store also sells T-shirts with the slogan "Cassadaga, Where Mayberry Meets the Twilight Zone."

James and I feed the tourism machine by buying tickets to a history tour, one of several the camp offers. Christina, the clerk, says we are the only ones signed up.

Christina is getting off work and is able to share a little about her life at the camp. She has an earthy fashion sense, elements of a bohemian look that's been around since the 1970s. Her dark hair is long and straight with a hint of gray. A handkerchief skirt brushes her mid-calf. She wears oval wire-frame glasses, a twinkling rhinestone in her nose, strands of prayer beads, and loads of sterling-silver jewelry on her ears, wrists, and fingers.

Although she's only lived and worked in the camp about a year, she was drawn to Cassadaga even as a child. "[My sister and I] used to beg my mom to bring us here for our birthday," she says.

A year ago an inexplicable gut feeling led her to a Sunday service. She met and started dating the leader of the camp's Native American group, which practices tribal rituals for healing and general harmony. These include rain dances known as Turtle Dances, healing drum circles, and wood flute music. Christina moved into a garage apartment of a camp home built for Abraham Lincoln's carriage chauffeur, one of the more illustrious former camp residents.

Christina and the leader of the tribal healing rituals broke up, but

Christina, the friendly bookstore clerk. Photo by James Harvey.

she believes her attraction to him was the universe's way of getting her to the camp. She likes living here so much that she says she would work in the bookstore for free if she could afford it. She's studying veterinary care at a state college and aspires to work with exotic animals, particularly reptiles.

Christina plans to take medium classes at the camp. She has always been intuitive, and with training believes she could further develop her clairvoyance. She adds that she can pick up people's thoughts from their body language. I suddenly become paranoid that she's reading mine.

Tours begin in a small room off the bookstore. It also serves as a place to shop for mediums and is not unlike a real estate office with home listings posted on the walls. Rows of business cards embossed with fireflies, fairies, daisies, licenses, and degrees line the Spiritualist sales wall. Spiritualists suggest that one should select a medium by waving a hand over the cards and choosing the one it feels drawn to.

Mediums also advertise their daily availability on a whiteboard. A medium at the bottom of the list only gives her first name, Nellie. Maybe it's the simplicity or that Nellie is a common name for a horse, but I'm drawn to this medium. Using the phone in the room that's specifically for making appointments, I reach Nellie and discuss the terms—time and cost. She has a youthful voice that's at once calming and authoritative. A half-hour reading requires a $60 donation, she says; an hour will cost $120. She only accepts cash, but you can pay with a credit card at the bookstore, which charges another $5 for processing. I hold on to my cash and book a half-hour reading for the next day.

### In Search of Fairies

A burly man in jeans and a loose-fitting camp-logoed golf shirt marches in and announces he's our tour guide. With a gruff voice, shaggy salt-and-pepper hair past his shoulders, and a thick handlebar mustache, Dan could easily pass for a rough-and-tumble biker.

He quickly lets his two customers know that he is a medium, but because he hasn't been formally trained and licensed by the camp, he can't give readings there. He's a "natural" medium, he says, noting that he's had the gift since the age of three, when his family moved more than 1,000 miles so his mother could study under noted Cassadaga Spiritualists. He says he still lives with his mom, along with a yellow-naped parrot and a macaw that calls him "Psycho."

"Have you looked at the orb book yet?" he asks. He grabs a photo album from the coffee table and flips to an image that's almost pitch black except for a wispy white vapor, which he calls ectoplasm. Without any explanation of what that is, he turns to a picture of trees at night. This photo has three translucent dots—"orbs," he calls them—floating in the sea of darkness.

"You see the woman's face?" he asks, pointing at the larger orb.

There's a slight pattern within the cloudy ball that in a stretch could be considered a distorted face.

"Kinda," I say hesitantly.

"That's my mother," Dan says. "She passed on years ago."

He studies us for a reaction.

James and I withhold comment. How does one respond to a stranger's revelation that his departed mother's face floats around in a ball of light?

Dan moves on to another nighttime photo with pastel-colored orbs. "Orbs come in different colors, not to be confused with a horse of a different color," he says in a way indicating he's said it hundreds of times before.

"Do you believe in fairies?" he asks.

"No, not really," I answer.

"What if I showed you a picture of one, then would you believe in fairies?"

"Well, I don't know. Maybe."

He grins and splays photos across the table. They are a series of enlargements of the same image: a wooded area at night illuminated by a camera flash. A cluster of tiny lights rests on a tree limb. They are the size and color of fireflies, but this is no insect. No fairy, either, that I can tell.

"You see, there are his wings." His fingers trace the outlines of light.

At this point it's not even like finding Jesus's face on a piece of burnt toast after someone points it out to you. If there are wings, they seem to be in an entirely different place from where he's pointing.

"One of his legs is hanging down there. I see him like this on the limb." He demonstrates by going into a crouched position that no grown man should ever take in public.

I struggle for something quick to say: "So are fairies male, female, or are they asexual?"

Poor choice of a question for Dan's comeback is not only puzzling but makes me want to hide under the sofa: "She's talking sex over here," he yells across the room to a Middle Eastern camp resident who's explaining Spiritualism to a German tourist couple.

They pause, bewildered, and look over.

Dan simply moves on.

"Why does it matter?" he asks me gruffly.

"It really doesn't, but I thought since you were referring to it as a he, maybe there is a significance to that. What is fairies' purpose? I mean, what do they do?"

"Why do they have to have a purpose?"

The Middle Eastern man comes over and borrows the fairy photos to show the German tourists.

"Hey, what are you doing?" Dan asks him. "You can't take those. You're not even American."

The Middle Eastern resident, apparently used to Dan's unfiltered comments, ignores him. The German tourists look horrified.

Thus begins our two-hour tour with Dan.

## A Trek in Time

We spend about half the tour inside the stuffy meeting hall at the back of the bookstore. The narrow room with worn heart-of-pine floors and faux wood paneling reflects the camp's evolution, which seems to have stopped somewhere in the mid-1970s. Eight-by-ten photos, many of which are cloudy enlargements of old lithograph postcards, hang on the walls. Dan stops at each image, reciting a narration loaded with dates—birthdays, groundbreakings, ownership changes, fires, expansions, deaths—and names of residents and Spiritual bigwigs long since passed. Questions fluster him. "You're getting me off my narrative," he says.

The crux of the history is that a guy named George Colby, a seer and lecturer, was led there in 1874 by Seneca, his Native American Spirit guide. Seneca instructed Colby to form the Spiritualist camp there in the then-unclaimed wilderness. At the time, Spiritualism was in vogue and Colby was riding the trend. He had made the Spiritualist circuit throughout northern states in the late 1860s and early 1870s, giving readings and lecturing about communicating with the dead.

The American Spiritualism movement began in 1948 when two Hydesville, New York, teens showed neighbors that they could communicate with a ghost by asking questions and getting mysterious knocks in return. Within a couple of years, Kate and Leah Fox were demonstrating their medium skills before large audiences around the United States and Europe. They gave Spiritual advice to First Lady Mary Todd Lincoln, famed newspaper editor Horace Greeley, and New York Supreme Court Judge John W. Edmonds.

Then, in 1888, one sister admitted it had all been a hoax; they had created the noises by snapping their knuckles and cracking their toes. Although she later recanted, her admission dealt a hefty blow to the Spiritualism craze. But it didn't dissuade hard-core believers like Colby or modern camp residents such as Dan.

"She did that because they needed the money," Dan says when asked about the Fox sisters' admission. "When someone comes to you in the late 1800s and says, 'We'll give you a thousand dollars to say this,' they say it, especially when they are making five dollars for each reading or two dollars per reading to support themselves and to travel."

By the time the sisters confessed their fraud, the Cassadaga Spiritualist Camp was already established with graceful homes, a general store, a forty-room hotel, water lines, and a railroad station. Wealthy Spiritualists could board a train in New York, Iowa, or even Maine and ride it all the way to the front door of the Cassadaga Hotel without ever having to change seats.

In those days, more than a half century before interstates and passenger planes, the railroad was the king of transit and played a crucial role in the development of Florida, including Cassadaga. Across rural America if your town had a railroad station, it prospered, and if a Florida town had one, it had tourism potential. Colby wasn't blind to that. When it came time to certify the camp as a Spiritualist church, he had little problem getting approval from the National Spiritualist Association. A renowned Spiritualist came down from the North and identified Cassadaga and two other locations—ones near Bradenton and DeLeon Springs—as Spiritual vortexes. She certified Cassadaga because it was easiest to reach.

National certification had greater advantages than just giving credibility to highfalutin Spiritualists. It's one thing to claim you're a religion and quite another to prove it to Uncle Sam, as Scientologists found out decades later. To that end, Dan says certification and calling their auditorium a "temple" helped the Spiritualist camp get tax-exemption as a recognized religion.

Still in the meeting hall, Dan explains the faith as we sit in what's come to feel like a sauna. "Spiritualism is the science, philosophy, and religion of continuous life," he says. The science involves those such as professional ghost hunters who measure energy and shoot photos of orbs, wood nymphs, and fairies. "It's the proof of continuous life on the other side," he says. "They actually see these things, and they know that science is getting close to proving this stuff."

The philosophy follows the traditional do-unto-others-as-you-would-have-them-do-unto-you directive. "It's natural law," Dan explains. "We have to live by it."

"The religion is that we do have ceremonies and rituals to go along with it," Dan says. "We go through the rituals and prove this by communication with the so-called dead."

The Spiritualist camp also has a paranormal school, offering classes and certification for mediums, psychics, and healers. "When you get your papers here, they are accepted anywhere in the world without question," Dan says. "The National Spiritualist Association and a few others all question some medium schools because they don't all work with Spirit, but work with tools, runes, throwing of bones, the reading of knobs on your head."

The tour finally continues outside where a ticket booth once stood and visitors paid from one dollar to three dollars to come in and look around. "They could wander the camp from sunrise to sunset," Dan says. "You'd be able to go to the library or bookstore, but come sunset they ushered you out, sorta like a zoo."

Dan motions to the historic Mission-style hotel and tosses out tales of hauntings. Sometimes guests smell the cigar smoke of a long-dead Irish tenor who used to vacation there. The spirit of a little old lady walks the halls at night and turns on bathroom lights. The ghost of a little boy who died at five sits on guests' beds. "If you talk to him or read to him he will actually stay for a while."

Ambling down the quiet unmarked lane, Dan points out some of the unique architectural details of homes. One incorporates numerology. Several have second-story outer doors with no stoop or stairs. He explains that the doors are only for "spirit guides." I'd like to ask why spirits would need a door and not stairs, but don't want to get him off his narrative again. Plus, the tour is headed toward overtime.

The Eloise Page Meditation Garden is a small, shady lot filled with statuary, benches, and memorials to noted Spiritualists who have passed over to the other side. Dan shares that Mrs. Page was the reason his family moved to Cassadaga from Detroit. Sentimentality isn't tourist fodder, so Dan quickly shifts to another medium memorialized in the garden, June Mahoney. She gave readings to professional race-car drivers. "Richard Petty was one of her favorites," Dan says. "Maybe that's why Richard won so many races and stuff."

Sightseers on Harleys rumble past. For the most part, Dan says, the camp stays quiet. It closes to the public at 10:00 p.m., although there are no gates or barricades to prevent entry. Crime is rare, and to make sure it stays that way, Dan acts as an unofficial neighborhood watchman. He often gets up at 3:00 a.m. and cruises the neighborhood in his pickup, watching for out-of-town teen pranksters.

Daytime visitors are more than welcome since most are customers, and well-heeled ones at that. A Jaguar sports coupe convertible rolls past with a young female driver. Dan says she's typical. Two other women regularly drive their Austin Martins over from Orlando to see mediums.

The camp has always had ties to affluence. A Civil War hero and accountant for wealthy industrialist J. D. Rockefeller built a grand 4,000-square-foot mansion in the camp. The expense seems particularly unusual given that the camp association owns the land beneath all homes within its boundaries. Not just anyone can buy or build a home there. You have to be an association member.

Down the lane outside a more modest residence, three generations of a family—grandmother, daughter, toddler and teen boy—are coming and going. Dan says the teen once died in a motorcycle accident. "He was waiting for his body at the hospital. He had a total out-of-body experience," Dan says. "He couldn't talk or walk and now he's without a cane or anything."

They smile and wave hello, no doubt used to the curious eyes of outsiders.

Dan points to the small, wooded Black Hawk Park, where the Native American group communes for healing ceremonies. He says, "That's where the fairy picture was taken, believe it or not."

No comment.

Orbs, like the one he pointed out with his mother's face, often appear at Spirit Pond, where the ashes of many camp mediums have been scattered. Dan mentions that he also leads a nightly orb tour for twenty-five dollars a head.

You cannot see orbs with the naked eye, he says. They can only be seen in flash photographs. He looks at our professional camera gear and warns that orbs probably won't show up well even in our photos; higher-end flashes are just too intense.

At last we reach the Colby Temple, home to Sunday services and séances. Like much of the camp, the interior is rather basic and looks as if it hasn't been updated in decades. Fans hang from high ceilings, and rows of slatted wooden benches slope to a stage topped with a simple podium.

In the back there's an old metal water fountain and a sign-in book for anyone who wants to be healed of some physical or spiritual ailment. First name only, Dan says, though it is important to list your zip code so that the healers will know where to direct their energy.

Dan sternly warns us not to touch floral arrangements and peacock feathers on the stage as we head to the heart of camp mysticism, the séance room. The narrow, windowless room has only wooden chairs, a black curtain, and a heavy wooden round table, known in the Spiritualist world as a "tipping table." A tipping table is supposed to lift to one side by strictly a spirit force in response to questions posed by a medium. We aren't allowed to test it.

"You can't go in because you're not certified to do so. Put your arm in because there's usually a temperature difference," Dan says.

A duck inside is met with the warmth of a closed, windowless room with little, if any, ventilation.

Walking back to the bookstore, Dan points up a street toward some trees. "That's where someone saw a wood nymph."

### Message from Afar

The next morning, parking is at a premium. SUVs with TVs, luxury sportsters, old pickups, and granny sedans park along the lanes' grassy shoulders. Dollops of people wearing everything from designer heels to flip-flops, Sunday best to faded hip-huggers, migrate down the hill to Colby Temple. Sunday service is about to begin, and the church has a special speaker, a young Maharishi from India.

Colby Temple fills with more than two hundred people, from crying babies to the ancient. About two-thirds are women, many dressed and coiffed as if plucked from a Presbyterian congregation.

Since it's Memorial Day weekend, the service starts with a group singalong of "My Country 'Tis of Thee" led by a young soprano who has trouble holding a note. As standard, a fifteen-minute healing ritual precedes the Sunday message. Those who want to be healed move to metal chairs along the outside walls and wait to be summoned to the back of the temple. There are only a half-dozen healers and about four times that many are seeking a cure.

Having no idea what a healing entails or what I want to be cured of other than procrastination, I get in line. The tan reverend who looks like a New Age Ben Franklin, spectacles and all, instructs all to close their eyes and relax in meditative prayer. I struggle to come up with an ailment and settle on something heartfelt, sadness over the recent death of an uncle. Granted it's not hard to fixate on someone you've lost in a place that lives on connecting with the dead. In mourning, tears roll down my cheeks.

When it's my turn, the red-haired healer offers me a tissue, probably thinking I'm dying of something like a brain tumor. She turns my palms up in my lap and lightly lays her hands on my back, the sides of my head, my face, my legs, my hands. This goes on for about three minutes. I feel no energy flowing to me or from me, but it feels pleasant just the same, as a kind touch is apt to do. She clinches my hands and leans close. "You know what to do," she says softly. "You just need to tell it."

Does she intuitively know that I am a neurotic writer? Or is it something she tells everyone? Such vague directives, open to interpretation, are common in the world of Spiritualism.

I return to my seat not feeling much different than when I had left. I'm told that the effects of a healing aren't always immediate. Improvement may take more than one session.

Time for the guest of honor—Shri Vibhu Ji Maharaj. The slender young man is the grandson of the late Shri Hans Ji Maharaj, who was considered by his followers to be the "perfect master." Shri Vibhu looks every bit the part, wearing white pants and a long powder-pink shirt. He sits in a tapestry-draped chair that looks like a throne. He is twenty-eight, with hair and eyes as black and shiny as obsidian, and skin as smooth as chocolate pudding. The reverend invites attendants onstage to welcome their guest. A half dozen go up and lay white roses at his feet and bow. One woman from Nepal even kisses his socked feet.

He smiles and nods to each. When he stands, the parishioners rise, too, and give him a hearty applause. Their enthusiasm is contagious. After all, what could be more enlightening than the words of a young guru who comes from the land of Gandhi, no less? He has spoken to crowds of 100,000, spreading the ancient wisdom of how to get right with the universe.

He tells the audience that they must look deeper within themselves for meaning. Learn to remove the labels of a profession and family roles and see the world as it is. "What is the mind? What is the spirit?" he asks rhetorically.

Yes! He's going to tell us.

He speaks of how all religions follow the same noble codes and the golden rule: "Do unto others as you would have done unto you." But it's the concepts beyond that rule that cause dissension among faiths.

"Concepts can be their own trap, you know," he says. The key to understanding life, he says, is "Man, know thy self. Looking deeper within yourself because everything you need to know you are born with."

"The spiritual journey is very individualized, you know," he says. "That's why it is important to accept the actual truth. For the essence of knowledge is not words. It is not concepts. It is your being. All the answers you seek you are born with, you know."

Eureka! I feel a divine message has been revealed and join in the crowd's applause and another standing ovation.

The guru bows his head and demurely walks back to his throne. It is not until reflecting on his message outside the sheep-following energy that I realize how general it actually was. That he had put into words, so plainly and simply, something all want to believe is true.

His oration is followed by a shrill soprano solo of Cat Stevens's "Like the First Morning." Senior men in blazers like Baptist deacons pass offering plates brimming with cash, donations for the Maharishi.

The normal service is cut short, but the reverend still manages to throw in a couple of psychic readings of audience members. He calls out to a woman in the crowd. "I feel a very strong connection to you," he says. "You have been through a loss and have her with you."

He moves on to another younger woman several rows farther back. "You feel everything is going faster and quicker and at times you feel life is moving past you, but it is all working for good," he tells her. "I feel something concerning learning with you. Maybe it's books and school. Embrace it."

Afterward, regulars catch up on small talk as they exit. Visitors make their way up the hill to the bookstore and shop for spiritual trinkets and texts. Some head to their cars for a 30-to-40-mile drive back to their suburban homes in Orlando, Deland, Mt. Dora, and Daytona Beach.

One Deltona woman in a conservative suit says she doesn't attend service regularly, but she didn't want to miss the Maharishi. She's been a Spiritualist for about five years and is taking medium classes at the camp. "I'm just a baby," she says. The gift of clairvoyance runs in her family. "My mother has dreams that come true, and my sister is a healer but doesn't know it," she says. "I think like he said, the truth is within ourselves."

For regulars like Kristi, a vivacious single mom, the service was a weekly dose of positivism. "It always makes me feel really good when I come here," she says with a sincere enthusiasm that overshadows her awkward appearance: curved spine, long dishwater-blond hair, and gangly bowed legs filling faded bell-bottom jeans.

"Usually when I thought about going to church it was a dread. But I want to come here. It's rejuvenation. There's no signs telling me I'm a sinner and no one telling me I'm going to hell. It's always positive."

Kristi came to the temple seeking guidance a year before. "I was going through some unhappy times in my life and I went online looking at different religions." Nothing she found appealed to her, but she had heard about Cassadaga. One morning she mustered the courage and drove over for a service. She's been back most every weekend since with her young daughter.

"You are all in control of your brain. If you think life sucks and is horrible, then your life is going to suck and be horrible. It's all about control of how you look at things. That makes a lot more sense to me than believing you are going to hell for all eternity."

Kristi is studying to be a nurse. Since she discovered Spiritualism she's is also contemplating pursuing a psychology degree. "I think this will give me a step up," she says. "It will be interesting to see how the two combine."

Her family isn't thrilled about her participation in the church, especially her father. "They think I'm joining some kind of cult, and I tell them it's nothing like that. My Dad and I get into arguments all the time. I wish I could just get them to sit down and listen to a service and they will see it's not some crazy cult."

Kristi may believe in communicating with the dead, but she isn't sold on the whole fairy business. "I think the people who are into it are more on the fringe. I saw the same photo and I didn't want to upset him or anything, but I didn't want to say I had seen fairies when I didn't."

### I Am a Rainbow, I Am Doomed

Nellie's home is only a five-minute walk from the hotel. Perched at the top of a hill, it is a mishmash of painted and bare clapboard siding with a tiny front yard of wildflowers. Despite its eclectic form, or maybe because of it, it has a cozy vibe.

A knock on the heavy wooden door triggers the yip-yips of a small dog. The door opens, and Nellie, with her long, wavy gray locks and youthful, steel-blue eyes, welcomes me inside. She looks sufficiently old and has a warm, confident aura. Her front parlor looks like a fortune-teller's set in a movie—dark and filled with antiques. A small table draped by a scarf sits between two high-back chairs. All of this seems to promise an authentic reading.

Nellie has lived at the camp for more than a dozen years. She trained and received her license here. She does not use tools—tarot cards, runes, Ouija boards, tea leaves—but does not condemn them.

Everyone does a reading differently. Nellie likes to read a person's energy first then consult about their particular concerns and follow up with a communication with a spirit if there is someone they wish to connect with. I pass on the latter. I prefer not to drag the dead into my little dramas.

She instructs me to put my hands on the table, close my eyes, and take three deep breaths. Her bony hands grip mine and she asks my full name. Then she softly says a simple prayer: "Divine Spirit, we ask for your presence with us. Walk with us, guide us, and comfort us. Protect us from all evil. Send to us some information that this our beloved child seeks. For how it is and best."

She sits back in her chair and crosses her legs underneath a long, flowing black skirt. "I see energy as a form of color," Nellie says. "I'm not talking about aura. It is an electromagnetic field that changes. What I see is the way God created you, who you are inside. We always are created to attract people, places, and events that are going to give the lessons that we are here to learn."

She first sees an iridescent shade of royal blue, which she associates with "committed people," those who are bound to their word and for whom keeping their word can be more important than to what they are committed.

My next colors are red and orange, the first of which she says signifies that I'm goal-oriented with lots of physical energy. My dusty elliptical machine comes to mind, and I have my doubts.

"Orange is intelligence that you want to use your mind and energy to power the part of life that relates to loved ones, family friends, coworkers. The first is your world involvement. This part is more about how you drive your life. Some people kinda let life happen. That's not the way you are. You want to drive your life. You want to create your life.

You want to be able to have a plan for life. It can be difficult to achieve but you still have it."

Mmm. Could this relate to the healer's message from the morning church service?

My last color is a pale, clear yellow. "What that tells me is you have the capacity to make judgments based on fact. That you can look at everybody's input on a situation including your own and say this is the best thing to do here."

Yes, I am principled, fair, and caring! I'm starting to appreciate Nellie's powers.

Then comes the downer.

"The whole problem here is that you don't always do the best thing," she relates. "You have these other parts of you that are drawing you to do things that you don't want to do. The way we always should make a decision is to make it for ourselves. When you are making these decisions, the universe puts in your opposites. You are going to attract people who are users and people who are needy." Past boyfriends come to mind. "You are also going to attract procrastinators, big time."

She goes on to tell me ways to overcome my issues, suggestions I know instinctively and have read in way too many self-help books. Recognize what you are doing, stop and say to yourself, I'm not going to let *xyz* interfere. Not exactly the magic pill I was hoping for.

The reading evolves into a question-and-answer session about Spiritualism. Nellie provides logical explanations for phenomena that many consider completely illogical. "It has to do with energy," she says. "Some people have an extrasensory perception (ESP) that allows them to pick up on others' energy. It's not so out there when you consider that animals have senses that people don't have, such as dogs being able to hear frequencies of sound undetectable by humans," she says.

Mediums have this naturally, but also must learn how to develop it. Contrary to depictions in fairs and Halloween tales, mediums aren't fortune-tellers, she says. "We don't predict the future. What we do is tell you about the path you are on. Because you create your future with every decision you make every single day."

Like several other Spiritualists in the camp, Nellie also applies her abilities to animals. She helps people find lost pets and says she used to communicate psychically with her previous dog. "She taught herself. Not only certain words but how to use them. She was very good at it."

"Dogs do think. It is something beyond intelligence. The one capacity that they all seem to develop first is ESP. And they learn when you are hearing them. Now this dog that we had learned right away that I heard her."

It begged the question, "Did she actually talk?"

"It's not a voice. Everything we do is a vibration. In order for me to hear it, she is mentally sending me the vibration. You can see the films about how thoughts progress in the brain, and they light up and run across. That is an energy impulse, electromagnetic, and it does not stop at the skull. It emanates out. But animals learn to direct it, and people who learn to exchange information by ESP learn to do the same thing."

I kick myself later for not asking what the dog had to say. Bacon? Sausage? Walk me?

### Orb Etiquette

After the session, it's time to check into the hotel. Aside from a couple of stylish men on the verandah smoking organic cigarettes and downing Coronas, the hotel feels quite dead. The Lost in Time Café is closed. The only sign of life is in the gift shop. A young woman behind the counter doubles as a front-desk clerk. The spirits have been quiet lately, she says, handing us a room key. She doesn't rule out the possibility we will see ghosts.

The long, narrow hallway is eerily silent. The small guest room, though not luxurious, is clean and has character with high ceiling and a simple antique bed and a wardrobe. But there is no TV, telephone, or radio. We're not even able to get a cell phone signal. The *Twilight Zone* reference on the bookstore T-shirts begins to make more sense.

The room opens outside to the long veranda. A child's gnome-like rubber toy lies at the threshold. Is it a plant by the hotel or a welcoming gift from a young ghost? I'm positioning the toy cross-legged on a porch bench when Dan passes.

He's not doing the orb tour tonight, commenting that we were the only ones interested and didn't sign up. It's unlikely we would see many orbs anyway, he adds. Nothing, anyway, like the large group last night that included a boy. Orbs respond to human energy and children are naturally brimming with it, he says. "He was snapping orbs all over the place," Dan says.

We tell him we might try it anyway. This launches a whole discussion and lesson in the art of orb interaction. "You have to take deep breaths and call them to you," he says. You also have to be careful, he adds, because the spirits can drain you of energy if you allow them. "You have to conserve."

"Maybe I'll down some energy drinks to speed me up," I joke.

He evidently misunderstands me. "Speed. That's a term I haven't heard since the '70s. Remember Black Beauties?"

Since there's nowhere to buy a soda in Cassadaga, much less speed, we're forced to travel to Deland for dinner and libations. We hurry back to try our luck at finding orbs before 10:00 p.m., when the camp officially closes and Dan starts his patrol.

The two men are still drinking on the veranda. There's no one else in sight in all the camp. Only four cars are parked in the hotel lot. The handful of hotel workers have locked up and gone home. Residents have retreated inside their Victorian homes and apartments. It could be a backwoods Kentucky community in the 1920s. No drone of car engines or throbs of rap bass rattling windows. The chirp of crickets gives the camp a pulse.

We follow the croaks of bullfrogs toward Spirit Pond. Our muffled giggles pierce the darkness. Energy we have, but not the optimistic sort of the faithful orb hunters. More like the daring excitement of schoolkids who sneak out to toilet paper a yard.

James photographs shadows of trees. Even after lowering the camera flash, no fairies or wood nymphs show up on the digital screen. No orbs either, save for a distant yard globe that radiates through the trees. Maybe we are too old and drained of energy to be of much interest to such apparitions.

## The Seekers

Back at the hotel, a couple of plump women devouring Italian takeout have joined the men on the veranda. The table is cluttered with packs of cigarettes, overflowing ashtrays, plastic cups, and bottles of booze.

"Isn't country life grand!" pronounces the older man wearing a white, flowing button-down and broken-in Bermuda shorts.

"Oh, right," the younger one huffs. "When we got here yesterday he was 'there's no TV! No bar!'" They quickly alleviated his agitation with a visit to a liquor store in Deland.

Carlos and Randall (not their real names) drove up from south Florida but could have stepped right out of the film *The Bird Cage*. Carlos, in a fitted knit shirt and designer jeans, is a dark-haired, svelte twenty-seven-year-old Latino who, Randall trumpets, "could be a model." Carlos got his green card only a few days before. He quickly relays that he's a trust-fund child who doesn't have to work. He's flirting with college and in love with an older man who is in a committed relationship with someone else.

Randall is nearly twenty years older and also flamboyantly gay. They are not a couple and have separate hotel rooms. Randall came along to humor Carlos, who needed to get away.

The men met the women at the hotel the night before. Given their bawdy jokes, you might assume they had been best buddies for years. Of course, a six-pack of beer, three bottles of wine, and a liter of vodka go a long way toward establishing friendships.

Diane, a nurse, from the east coast of Florida, had been to Cassadaga before and talked her lovelorn friend Betsy into coming along for girls' weekend getaway. (Again, these names are pseudonyms.)

As spontaneous as the vacationers' trips are, their adventures are obviously not without motive. None are hard-core Spiritualists, but all have varying degrees of belief in the paranormal, although calling Randall a Doubting Thomas is an understatement. Carlos says Randall mocked the psychic during his reading to the extent that he was asked to leave. Randall later had a blow-up with fairy-and-wood-nymph aficionado Dan on the orb tour.

Betsy has the most paranormal experience of the lot. She took photos of orbs on a previous Cassadaga visit and is convinced that a ghost visited her and Diane's hotel room. "I was dreaming that Diane was at the foot of the bed. I woke up and felt something down there and thought, what is she doing?" She rolled over and saw Diane across from her, then looked down and saw the form of an old woman rise up. By the time Betsy woke up Diane, the apparition was gone. "I hope she leaves us alone tonight. I want a good sleep," Diane flatly adds as she lights a cigarette.

Everyone is past the point of eloquence, and the conversation jumps and skips from subject to subject. One minute they laugh about Randall's temper tantrums, the next they hint of the darkness that led them to Cassadaga.

Diane says a medium told her what she already knew. "I have to leave my husband of thirty-five years," she says. "My youngest son (of four) just graduated from college. I couldn't leave before because I have always been the buffer," she says, leaving the details between the lines.

Carlos says an off-camp psychic told him that his current affair is ill-fated and predicted he will meet a new man, who Carlos hopes will be his Mr. Right. He laments that he hasn't had a committed relationship in years.

Slowly the group peels off to bed. It takes Carlos a few trips back and forth from his room to the table to find his key, which is in his pants pocket. Betsy clears the table on her way to bed, leaving a swaying, drunk Diane and a phenomenally awake Randall to carry on into the wee hours.

"Diane and I are going to stay here and have lesbian sex," Randall shouts to all. Diane sticks out her boobs, then laughs so hard she almost falls out of her chair.

Not surprisingly, there is no sign of any of them the next morning and no time to wait around. The gates to the Holy Land beckon. Being Memorial Day, it should be packed.

### Jesus Christ, Tourist Attraction

The Holy Land Experience theme park is a twist on the opposite end of the state's religious bell-curve. An urban theme park, it reflects modern Florida, where most visitors expect a condensed, action-packed experience—even if that involves standing in hour-long lines.

Knowing a little about the Bible from an upbringing in a Baptist church, I ponder how one makes a theme park from biblical history? Does it have a Jesus roller coaster and Noah's Ark log ride?

The questions seem less absurd when you consider the park's locale. Just off I-4, it is only a dash from Walt Disney World and Universal Studios. International Drive, the Vegas Strip of Orlando, with Wet n' Wild, designer outlet malls, and spaceship-shaped T-shirt shops, is only a ten-minute drive. The nativity scene at Holy Land's entrance, featuring a club-footed blow-up Mary doll and a mechanical baby Jesus, fits right in.

At 10:00 a.m., the parking lot fills quickly as the gates to faux Jerusalem have just opened. Caribbean tourists pour from buses. A Trinity Broadcasting Network van pulls up with the park celebrities—Jesus, Mary, and the gang.

They don't look historically accurate and aren't modestly dressed like the holy crew pictured in most Bibles. More like if Jesus and friends had won the lottery and gone on a Winter Park shopping and salon spree. The Christ actor has blond highlights in his light-brown hair. His beard is meticulously groomed, and his eyes are strikingly blue.

Pretty Mary and the posse of other young female performers are made up and wear fine, jewel-tone silks and chiffon veils, all dotted with sequins and seed beads. They chatter to each other but shun my questions, much like other Holy Land actors and park workers I've tried to interview. Perhaps their reticence has to do with comedian Bill Maher's gonzo mockery of the park in the film *Religulous*, or a pending high-profile lawsuit against the park owners, or maybe today it has to do with my wearing a "Big Spender" T-shirt and a cowboy hat. Probably not the best choice of attire, but it's hard to grasp the decorum of a place that depicts the Garden of Eden as a land where lions pal with sheep, and deer curl up on butterfly-shaped benches.

From the looks of those lined up at the ticket window, others have the same problem. An unnaturally tanned mom in a sundress flashes massive cleavage. Her noisy pigtailed daughters wear matching red, white, and blue bell-bottom outfits straight from 1976. A man behind them is covered from neck to ankle in tattoos of Jesus and topless women with cherry-red nipples. The cashier seems not to notice and takes his thirty-five-dollar entry fee.

Outside the gate, dark-skinned families converse in French. One church group of mixed age and race pose for a photo with a park employee in a furry lamb suit that has seen better days.

Just past the turnstiles, the gateway to Jerusalem is clogged as patrons stop to pose for a picture with a life-size cardboard replica of another Jesus actor, who has an uncanny likeness to Fabio from the cover of romance novels.

Small by Orlando theme-park standards, the park is about one-eighth the size of Disney's original Magic Kingdom. The condensed ancient Jerusalem has everything from carts bearing fake fruit and replicas of the mount to a children's play area with a walk-in whale filled with a suspended Jonah.

Holy Land attempts opulence, as much as a theme park can. Metallic gold covers columns and Romanesque statues. The man-made lake is filled with fountains that shoot a rainbow of water toward the heavens, choreographed to Christian music. Along the lake's bank, a large

The nativity scene outside the Holy Land Experience. Photo by James Harvey.

topiary spells out "He is Risen." The $6 million Church of All Nations auditorium was built to look like an ancient coliseum on the outside. The white-and-gold Grand Temple, Herod's Temple, houses a state-of-the-art theater where visitors watch a slick film dramatization of the Last Supper. At other times, they take the stage for Christian karaoke.

It's hot as hell, but that doesn't prevent the crowd from passing, one by one, through a tight, narrow passageway into a replica of the Calvary Garden Tomb to see the fake rock bed where Jesus's body was put to rest. "I've seen the real one and you can definitely see the outline of his body," a man in shorts tells a friend as they squeeze out to let others get a view.

We join about two hundred park-goers gathered around an outdoor stage to watch hunky Jesus Christ in action. The play is called *Woman at the Well*, but the park takes creative license. Jesus recites the

Beatitudes from the Sermon on the Mount to a Samaritan woman and friends, played by the glittery actresses from the parking lot.

The deviation from scripture doesn't appear to bother the crowd. Many hold their arms high in the air and sway to the recorded music as if in a trance. Their demonstration of faith is so earnest and strong I can almost touch it. Regardless of your spirituality, there is something powerful about being surrounded by people with such unified belief that there is something better beyond this life.

But as this is Orlando, theme-park capital of the world, something unusually surreal is unfolding on stage.

Jesus is saying good-bye, and the three actresses make over him like he's Elvis Presley in a 1950s beach flick. They giggle and one gives the line, "Everyone is going to be so jealous."

The crowd applauds. They seem so oblivious of the sexual undertones that I later have to watch a video replay to be sure I wasn't imagining it.

Such elaborately costumed biblical plays and musicals are the park's primary entertainment. Turns out there aren't any thrill rides, only about a dozen shows throughout the day all around the faux holy city. Although the music is canned, the songs are original. The actors are pros. They sing! They dance! They are also a very Caucasian bunch. African American performers are rare, and mostly play bongo drums in the marketplace.

## Cosmic Vending Machine

Such glitz wasn't a part of the park when it opened in 2001, though it was quite controversial given that the founder was a Messianic Jew whose ministries tried to convert Jews to Christianity. As might be expected, the act was rather unpopular with Orlando's twenty-five thousand Jewish residents. The Jewish Anti-Defamation League protested outside the park on opening day. One rabbi quoted by *Messianic Times* went so far as to call the park founder a "soul-snatcher."

The original park's more authentic costumes and somber plays also didn't attract large enough crowds. Tourists who come to Florida and particularly to Orlando have come to expect hypersurrealism. If not terrifying rides or wood nymphs and ghosts, at least give them uplifting, glitzy shows. In that regard, the Trinity Broadcasting Network (TBN), the world's largest Christian television network, may have been the perfect buyer for the struggling park. The ministry bought it for $37 million in 2007 and quickly turned the park into a reflection of its razzle-dazzle theatrics. That goes for the founders as well as the network.

Paul and Jan Crouch started their network ministry in partnership with Jim and Tammy Faye Bakker, whom Jan Crouch closely resembles, big hair, raccoon eyes, and all.

The Crouches run the $225 million TBN empire on the generosity of followers. Requests for donations run across the bottom of the TBN programs and the Holy Land Experience's park map. The thirty-five-dollar entry fees don't cover the park's expenses, the literature says. The Crouches preach the "prosperity gospel," meaning you give God, or rather TBN, all your money, and God will reward you with riches, health, and success in return. Prosperity gospel has been compared to treating God as a cosmic vending machine—you put your coins in, and pray to get more back (literally). But like in casinos, the only thing for certain is that the house always wins.

The *New York Times* reported in 2012 that the Crouches have his-and-her multimillion-dollar mansions in Newport News, California. They have use of TBN's corporate jets, two multimillion-dollar homes in Orange County, Florida's exclusive Windermere community, homes in Texas, and Conway Twitty's former estate in Tennessee.

Jan Crouch spends much time in Orlando. Her *Praise the Lord* show is frequently taped there, and she was highly involved in renovating the park. She insisted on remodeling one of the restaurants six times in three months, according to the *New York Times*. During the process, she rented two suites for more than a year at Orlando's Loews Portofino Bay Hotel—one for her and one for her clothes and her Maltese dogs.

But biblical faith is much bigger than its leaders, and many park-goers find inspiration in the story of Christ told through the attraction, however synthetic or glittery it may be.

## Gifts of Faith

In a rose garden by the lake, several park-goers quietly pray beneath a towering cross that is covered in handwritten prayers. For a moment, I'm reminded of the healing list at Cassadaga's temple.

A Latina woman who has difficulty with English asks me to pen a message for her. She prays for Jesus Christ to help her son. "He has problems with drugs," she says. She is Catholic and says she doesn't watch TBN, but is enjoying the park's shows and decorated grounds. She points to a statue of an angel playing a harp. "I feel his love here."

The line for the park's $12 million Scriptorium museum moves more slowly than one for a Universal Studios roller coaster on the Fourth of July. Tours are fifty-five minutes, and several in line say they have been waiting that long.

Even park critics herald the museum due to its authentic biblical antiquities such as pages from a Gutenberg Bible and ancient scrolls. This being a theme park, it also has flashes of animatronics, including biblical characters that appear to talk. It is a small world, indeed.

Those who don't want to wait in line can snatch up a DVD of the tour for $24.95 in Scriptorium's gift shop. Like at any theme park, gift shops are everywhere.

One shop also houses what's touted to be the largest indoor model of ancient Jerusalem complete with hundreds of two-inch toy figures posed in various daily activities: a miniature woman scrubs a patio; toy Roman soldiers are lined at attention; tiny robed men work on flat roofs, albeit under cobwebs.

Visitors can't seem to get enough. They circle mini-Jerusalem in droves, taking snapshots. A prim, red-hatted lady rubs shoulders with a Sammy Haggar lookalike in Day-Glo green shorts and Hawaiian shirt.

Mixed messages abound. Nearby, a young man poses for a photo with his dukes up beside a painting of Jesus as a boxer. Jesus's gloves are inscribed with the word "mercy."

Prize-fighting Jesus isn't the only odd artwork. A prominent photo from a TBN show hangs on the wall over the checkout counter. Jan Crouch is pictured wearing her big, pink-tinged wig, and standing beside her is Fabio Jesus and someone dressed in a furry camel costume.

No one gives it a second look. Those who aren't focused on the model city are mostly spellbound by the play in the adjoining Shofar Auditorium—*The Four Women Who Loved Jesus*.

The female actresses are dressed like they came straight from Bollywood. The lead, dancing in a brilliant red midriff costume, sings about being a harlot and how much she likes it.

Hunky Jesus convinces her that her soul is valuable. They have a touching moment where she gazes into his eyes.

"I love you, Jesus, and I will always love you," she cries as she tightly embraces him. He removes his scarf and places it tenderly around her neck. The women in the crowd "awww" as if they are watching a Lifetime Network movie.

The harlot goes on to tell the other bejeweled actresses, "There's no mistaking him. His voice is so gentle and that touch, I've waited twelve years for that touch."

The crowd laps it all up; when the play ends with Jesus being dragged away by Roman soldiers, they applaud loudly.

Afterward, as they pour into the gift shop, one woman in the audience wipes away tears. "That was just beautiful!" she tells me before disappearing into the aisles of tourist trinkets.

The park souvenirs aren't much different than the tchotchkes sold at massive nonsecular parks just up the road. Instead of Cinderella snow globes, Holy Land Experience sells Arc of the Covenants that fit in one hand. For the flashier set, an ornate denim jacket with more bling than a hip-hop video hangs from the ceiling, the back covered in the word "Israel" outlined in rhinestones. There are serious religious books, copies of religious text in scrolls, men's ties with apostles' names, and naturally, DVDs of TBN and the Crouches' TV shows.

In the children's section, Jesus and the disciples are action figures, biblical substitutes for Barbie and G.I. Joe. A little boy swings a plastic sword and begs his parents for it and the matching Roman-soldier breast shield and plumed helmet.

A family of five from Ohio gathers at the clearance shelf, where an assortment of biblical dust-catchers—miniature scrolls with the Ten Commandments, alabaster perfume jars, plastic figurines of Jesus on horseback, and miniature temples of Solomon—are on sale, two for three dollars. The father explains biblical history as they make their selections.

Barbara, the mother, says her husband is in seminary and they are visiting their oldest daughter whose military husband is stationed near Orlando. "We love the shows," she says as she places a couple of the Jesus-on-horseback figurines on the checkout counter. "We come here every chance we get."

As performances are the hallmark of the park, Jesus's crucifixion is the highlight. The park is near, if not at its capacity of 1,500, and everyone wants to watch. But like the five virgins late for the wedding, James and I, along with dozens of other park visitors, find we have been shut out. A passageway for the actors—Jesus to carry the cross, Roman soldiers to remove his lifeless body—is cleared. Those who didn't get on the front side of the stage, like James and I, who were too busy downing four-dollar hotdogs from Simeon's Corner, are trapped behind guarded ropes.

We have a good view of the massive crowd, several of whom are taking snapshots of a bloody Jesus as he carries the cross to the mount.

The show lasts for a half hour.

Jesus, wearing only a loincloth, is nailed to the cross to the sounds of stereophonic pounding, cast members' operatic voices and an orchestra sound track. After his last breath, the Christ actor is removed from the cross, completely shrouded in a fake-bloodstained cloth, and carried off overhead by Roman soldiers wearing plastic breastplates. They parade him around back to the other side of the staged area, place him in the tomb, and roll out a faux rock to seal it. Dialogue and song intertwine. At last, Jesus appears again. He lives!

Meanwhile, most of the crowd is dying from the heat. People are practically panting. One woman has to be helped to the shade as a family member scrambles to a concession for water. Holy Land Experience employees usher everyone away from the stage and begin cleaning up for the next horde. No rest for the weary.

# CHAPTER 7

# Swing State

The liquor and beer have been flowing all morning around the rooftop pool of the Miami Hilton Hotel. More than seven hundred swingers are loosening up beneath the glass eyes of the downtown office buildings and condos. A beach ball bounces over the crowd. Bare breasts and scrotums jiggle and sway to the island beat of house music.

Some are simulating sex acts, and, yes, some are actually doing it. In fact, a young couple is having porno sex in the lounge chair right next to my husband, James.

He and I are paralyzed in disbelief and anxious despite the copious amounts of alcohol we are downing. We're not swingers, nor do we have the desire to be. Yet here we are—James in jeans and a button-down and me in a knee-length dress lugging a purse that could hold a litter of puppies—at not just a swingers' convention, but one that claims to be the largest in the United States.

I wasn't sure what to expect from a businesslike event complete with a trade show, seminars, and speakers that centers around something so intimate and, for the majority of America, deviant. Swingers having sex? Sure, in hotel rooms and themed playrooms. Promotional swinger blogs and YouTube.com clips pretty much confirmed that. But sex around a crowded pool under the bright October sun and eyes of surrounding condo dwellers wasn't something we were prepared for, as if Vanillas could ever be prepared for such a thing.

I had attempted to educate myself about the "lifestyle," which is how they refer to their practice of swinging. I discovered that swinging is a robust, largely underground cottage industry in Florida. Swingfest isn't even the state's only lifestyle convention.

If you rated each state in the nation on a scale of 1 to 10 for swinging, Florida would be a 15. According to NASCA, an international association of swinger clubs, businesses, and travel agents, Florida has more lifestyle businesses than anywhere else in the United States, including California. SwingersClubList.com, which claims to be the "world's largest adult lifestyle directory," lists thirty-seven Florida nightclubs and party houses that allow couples to have sex on-site. There's also another layer of discreet clubs that only advertise by word of mouth.

My friend Larry Siegel, a Boynton Beach clinical sexologist, says the magnitude is a little freakish but quite understandable when you consider that Florida is already the largest tourism state in the nation. "People come to Florida to play. Swingers come here to play and to play around," Larry says. "Many like the fact that they can go to a sex club, explore their fantasies, hook up with another couple, then fly home and not have to worry about running into them at the grocery store."

Swinging Floridians are more than happy to entertain the tourists. Some have turned their homes into mom-and-pop weekend pleasure palaces, which for legal reasons they call "on-premise parties," as opposed to clubs. They can't serve alcohol, but some do serve dinner buffets. They have regular hours, websites, and names like Orlando Love Loft, Ranch4Play, or Playful Couples.

One swinging entrepreneurial couple near Orlando planted a string of portable sheds in their backyard and floored them with mattresses. Another in a middle-class Cape Coral subdivision converted their living room into a black-light dance hall, complete with a stripper pole. A Largo party house advertises twelve bedrooms, a sex dungeon, dance floor, pool room, lockers, showers, massage tables, swimming pool, hot tub, a sound and light show, love swing, and glow-in-the-dark volleyball. Peeking at the two-acre spread through its rickety wood fence, you would never suspect the one-story house on the edge of a subdivision is the site of megaromps.

"Donations" open the door to most swinger house parties. Party hosts technically can't charge an admission fee without a business license. One party host goes so far as to label his home-based club a religious non-profit, saying that donations are tax-deductible and help keep the sexual fellowship parties going. He takes credit cards, though single ladies need not donate. Presumably the fellowship finds their mere presence a gift from God.

## Where's the Party?

I got a glimpse of a controversial swingers party house during my early days of alt-newspaper reporting, and it wasn't "the lavish playground" the owner claimed it to be. I gained entry with a forty-dollar donation, which went on my expense account, and my signature, which promised among other things that I wasn't a cop. Other than a gaggle of young guys with their eyes glued to porn on TV, there were only two couples in sight. Refreshments were limited to Oreos and lemonade served in Dixie cups.

The host assured me that "Things usually don't heat up until after midnight." It was still early at 10:00 p.m. on a Friday night. She gave me the tour—the "voyeur room," where several full-size framed mattresses formed a massive bed and an assortment of whips hung on the vanilla-colored walls; the 1920s bathroom with a worn tub where swingers could shower; and game room with a pool table and a chessboard set up on a small table for two. Who comes to a swinger party to play chess?

The only hint of action was a couple of grunts coming from a dark room at the end of the upstairs hallway. "You can look in," the host said. "But don't join unless you're invited." The lyrics to the Eagles' "Hotel California" came to mind: "You can check out any time you like, but you can never leave." I headed for the door.

Florida's swinger sex-on-site nightclubs play by different rules. They run on private memberships and often serve alcohol. Some have chandelier-lit dining rooms, DJs, and backroom leatherette beds, showers, and lockers, amenities sustained by a large and well-heeled membership. Miami's high-energy Club Velvet boasts an international reputation and more than twenty thousand members. Fort Lauderdale's Club Trapeze lists more than ten thousand. Tampa, being Trampa, has the kinky Eyz Wide Shut I & II that offers saddles with vibrators, gynecological tables, and suspension racks.

Florida even holds claim to the longest continuously operating swinger club in the country. Deenie's Hideway in Coconut Creek has been open for swing since 1973, welcoming randy couples to its weekly "Fuck My Wife" and "Full Moon Pool" parties.

Rounding out Florida's swinger landscape are events and clubs that meet at hotels. An especially kinky one, Club Relate, based in Orlando, claims to be the nation's only swinger masturbation club. It's been featured in *Penthouse* magazine, on Playboy Channel's *Sexcextra*, and on HBO's *Real Sex* series.

## Love Thy Self

Club Relate cofounder Lynda Gayle, a buxom, blond sexagenarian with the libido of an eighteen-year-old male, enthusiastically explains over the phone how she turned her intimate pastime into a group experience. It started when she met her second husband and confessed that she liked to masturbate fifteen times a day. For a first date, they visited a swinger club with the goal of finding a place where Lynda felt comfortable pleasuring herself. This proved to be a challenge. At most parties, oral sex or full penetration in front of an audience is encouraged, but going solo is considered poor form. One swinger party host even asked Lynda to leave when she started masturbating. She was incensed. "I enjoy watching people have sex while I masturbate, but they call that aberrant behavior. I consider it safe sex!"

Lynda and her partner started their own swinger club in 1991. Twice a month, Lynda and forty to fifty other voyeurs and exhibitionists take the show on the road. With a cache of industrial-strength vibrators, double-ended dildos, and a club favorite they call the "Relate Wand," a device that stimulates a woman's G-spot and a man's prostate at the same time, they set up in hotel suites in Orlando, Daytona Beach, and Tampa and get to business. Although masturbation is the club's theme, just about anything goes. As Lynda explains, "Everybody is doing what they want." This might include men masturbating while watching nude women dance ("Women love to see men masturbate") or a pack of wives pleasuring one another on a king-size bed ("Men love to see women together"). "New people always say they are just going to watch," Lynda says. "Everybody else laughs because they know it's not going to stay that way."

Lynda claims Club Relate's membership numbers in the thousands and hails from around the globe. Parties are limited in size and slots fill fast. One member books his reservations two months in advance and takes the train all the way to Florida from Washington, D.C. Another travels from Germany. Some have even moved to the state to be party regulars. "We're good for Florida because people fly in to come to our parties. We increase tourism," Lynda says with a laugh.

Unlike most swinger clubs, single men are warmly welcomed at Club Relate, and the membership ratio of men to women is two-to-one, something for which Lynda is thankful. "Men don't last as long as women," she confides. "When it's even, it's 'oh dear, there just aren't enough!'" That's when the electronic accoutrements come in handy.

What makes Florida a magnet for this erotic fringe? People in the lifestyle give a familiar litany of explanations: the sunshine, the sandy beaches, the theme parks. Plus, Florida has the infrastructure. The same goliath convention hotels that host defense contractors and Tupperware distributors offer ample room for risqué gatherings.

Susan Right, of the National Coalition of Sexual Freedom, explains that unlike New York, Florida doesn't have strict health codes that prohibit on-premise private sex clubs. That's not to say Florida swinger clubs haven't had their run-ins with the law. Intent on stamping out such places, Broward County sheriff deputies went undercover at Club Trapeze, the private Fort Lauderdale nightclub, in 1999. They returned armed and masked when the place was filled with about two hundred customers—lawyers, doctors, teachers, and law enforcement officers among them—and arrested twenty-four people for lewd and lascivious behavior. Most were having sex with their married partner.

The charges didn't stick. A judge ruled that the activity wasn't illegal as long as no one, other than police investigators, was offended. The judge added that "the Legislature did not make it a crime to operate a place for sexual activities." The ruling sent a message to club owners that anything goes as long as everything is consensual. Following the ruling, Club Trapeze became so popular that the owner had to turn people away at the door.

Aside from the fairly permissive legal environment, there's also a more elusive quotient, an implicit social acceptance that works to make

Florida the largest swinger playground in America. Call it a libertine aura, an uninhibited mojo that emboldens people to try anything from driving around with a pet tiger in the front seat to having sex on a crowded hotel pool deck.

## Inside the Arena

Swingfest organizers laid out my ground rules weeks in advance of the convention. No press pass, no interviews. However, I could pay my way and attend like everyone else. James insisted on accompanying me, arguing that a single woman at a swinger convention would be like raw meat in a den of lions.

To ensure privacy, the 585-room Hilton is closed to all but 2009 Swingfesters. For four days, one of Miami's premier business hotels crawls with more than 3,500 conventioneers, far fewer than the 12,000 who attended the prior year. Organizers chalk up the drop in registrations to the poor economy. "For sale" signs are posted in condo windows and lawns all over south Florida. The housing bust here was one of the keenest in the nation.

The entry fee isn't cheap. Sure, for a mere twenty-five dollars anyone can peruse the Swingfest exhibit floor. But everyone knows the real action at a convention doesn't occur in the aisles of vendors exhibiting their wares, which are not unlike what I'd seen at Fetish Con. When you're talking about a swinger convention, one can only assume the nitty-gritty takes place in the designated "play rooms" or in actual hotel rooms. We pony up two hundred dollars for a couple's day pass.

At the registration table, a convention employee hands us bags of swag, which turn out to include gels, lotions, razors, raspberry-scented shaving cream, condoms, and ads for pornos, sex-toy stores, swinger clubs, and nudist resorts.

In a twist of sexual discrimination, unescorted men pay three hundred dollars for a day pass, while single women pay only one hundred. "We don't really cater to single men," says the convention rep as she fastens fluorescent-pink day-pass bands on our wrists. "It's safer that way. The ones we do allow are interviewed and tested." She's not talking IQ tests. Single men must supply proof that they are free of sexually transmitted diseases.

"We weed them out, but we don't really want them here," she confides in a hushed tone, as if speaking of an unmentionable found in a swimming pool. "Who wants a bunch of creepy guys hanging around?"

This helps explain why there are fewer than a handful of unescorted men roaming the brightly lit corridors of the convention hall. There also are fewer than a handful of single woman, the convention rep says. "We call them unicorns."

Well-dressed and bejeweled couples with wrists ringed in multiple bands of color to signify their level of participation—a four-day full access, a day pass, and others of unknown significance—move purposely between the classrooms, the exhibit floor, the hotel restaurant. None give us a second glance.

They seem far more interested in learning how to run their own swinging enterprises and swinger parties than hooking up. Except for a handful of women in skirts that barely cover anything, the crowd is not much different from one at an Amway convention.

The list of seminars is fairly business related—creating successful adult websites, how to run a swinger party, and record-keeping for taxes, a reminder that even the most titillating subjects can be dulled by the IRS. The snoozers make our selection fairly easy. We are just in time to catch "Female Ejaculation," presented by a duo from Montana called the Squirtinators.

We join about forty couples filtering into the seminar room where rows of folding chairs hold Hilton-inscribed notepads. You never know when you might need to take notes. A pale man who looks like a small-town southern politician (comb-over, perma-press slacks and all) and his equally conservative-looking wife take seats in front of us.

Up front, a middle-aged man with linebacker biceps faces the audience, waiting expectantly. This must be Tim. His eyes light up as an attractive blonde of equal age in a low-cut, tie-dyed bathing suit cover-up sashays up the aisle. Her hefty natural breasts threaten to escape with every step, and her carefree smile suggests she doesn't care if they do. Despite the audience's attempts at small talk, every eye in the room follows her as she heads to the front and stands beside Tim. This must be Tammy, the other half of the Squirtinators.

Tim and Tammy teach women how to ejaculate like men. They work the swinger circuit from Las Vegas to Spain. They offer their up-close-and-personal lessons on adult cruises, at nudist resorts in Jamaica and Mexico, and anywhere else people will book them and pay their travel fees.

They stand beside a padded table, and Tim breaks the ice with a joke about masturbation. He then relates how he became fascinated when he was only a teenager by a woman's ability to shoot fluids from her vagina.

While Tim is still in the introduction, James accidently knocks over my full drink. As I pick ice cubes off the soggy carpet, James cracks the tension by whispering, "Watch your fluids."

The seminar is clinical in many ways. Tim explains the physiology of women and what happens in the process of arousal, offering that he gained much of his knowledge from a porn director. He describes how a woman's ejaculatory fluid comes from an area in the female anatomy akin to the male prostate. Despite the scientific biology lesson, he's a funny guy and keeps the audience entertained.

I'm assuming the seminar is about to end when Tammy stretches out on the table. Then it hits me. They are actually going to demonstrate.

Tim lifts Tammy's skirt and his hand disappears between her bent legs. She immediately starts to moan. He narrates what he's doing with his unseen hand as if giving instructions for fixing a faucet.

And then, there it is. No sooner than he had started, a stream of fluid shoots up about six inches above Tammy's crotch. It happens so fast that I barely catch it and turn to James for confirmation. His red face tells me all I need to know.

Mission accomplished, Tim puts his hand to his mouth. "Tastes like chicken," he jokes. The audience laughs.

He asks for volunteers, adding he once squirtinated a stranger in front of two hundred people. An up-close view was projected onto a large screen. James elbows me. I give him a death look. With no volunteers, Tim offers to give one-on-one lessons in their hotel room.

Instead, we head straight for the bar.

It's one thing to see extreme sexual lifestyles on a cable channel or even pantomimed in a Fetish Con stage show. It's quite another to watch someone have an orgasm in front of a crowd of people in folding chairs in a bland hotel seminar room. As the lunchtime crowd of swingers begins to surround us, I lose myself to a screwdriver and the college football game on the TV above the bar.

So far, we have yet to see any couples showing the slightest interest in other twosomes. But it's only noon and we still have other areas to explore.

The "play rooms" are set up behind closed doors right across from the seminar rooms. This is where Swingfesters get the chance to practice what they've learned and show off any old tricks. The Chocolate Room is billed as a perennial favorite. A conventioneer explains that couples pour chocolate sauce and cream on one another's privates and then lick it off, satisfying two cravings at once. We screw up our courage and open the first door. The room is empty. A few homemade, glittery, poster board stars and cloud cutouts—like you might see at a high school prom—are taped to the walls.

The exhibit floor is a one-stop-shopping center for swingers. The cavernous hall is filled with more than seventy booths, in essence small storefronts pushing everything from vibrating gloves to a variety of the sex-toy standards—lubricants, dildos, vibrators. Women are getting flowers and butterflies painted on bare breasts. The Shoe Guy pimps red platforms with a 7-inch heel. A man in a white ship captain's uniform tries to sell us a chartered couples cruise out of the Port of Tampa. Florida, a capital of cruises, is quite naturally a jumping-off point for those who want to swing at sea.

Twenty-somethings in string bikinis dance around a stripper pole to promote rental stages for swingers who want to take their house parties up a notch. I recognize several of the vendors from Fetish Con, and they seem to remember me.

Swinging clearly isn't just a pastime for many conventioneers: It's a business. Dixie Does Florida, an attractive middle-aged blonde from Pompano Beach, specializes in swinger travel. Today she's promoting her "Splash Parties," which are in essence weekend swinger takeovers of various hotels around Florida. The profit potential is nothing to sneeze at. Dixie charges $125 and up for day passes, and two-night hotel packages can run north of $700. Swinging clearly isn't a poor man's lifestyle. No wonder hotels allow the clandestine events, especially when they are knee-deep in a recession.

But even on the convention floor, the crowd is surprisingly light. Where is everyone?

We take the elevator up to a floor of private hotel rooms. The long, carpeted hallway is as quiet as a school on Sunday. No naked people running from room to room. No blaring music. No trail of undies. But a handwritten sign on one door hints that the stillness is deceptive— "Come On In."

Instead, we head down to the pool for fresh air and another drink. An attractive couple in their forties, dressed in swimsuits and sporting wristbands of every color, ride with us. They're contemplating a jaunt to Miami's Haulover Beach, the only official nude beach in Florida. I initiate small talk and immediately declare my research purposes to establish that I'm not hitting on them. They're happy to talk once I agree not to use their names.

"We've only hooked up with one couple," the husband says. "But the scene really turns us on, and the party last night was totally crazy, in a good way."

"We have to get to know people and both like them before anything is going to happen with them," the petite wife says. "But we're only into soft-swapping anyway." She gathers I'm lost. "No penetration," she explains. "It's much safer that way."

Later, another swinger gives me a lesson in the lexicon. Hard-swinging means full penetration with a nonspouse. Although the definition of soft-swapping can vary, generally it means sex with a spouse in the presence of others who are also having sex or heavy petting with someone other than your spouse. Each couple sets their own boundaries for what's permissible; for example, some forbid their spouse from kissing another sex partner.

Our elevator companions got into swinging six years into their marriage, which is typical. Studies show that most swingers get into the lifestyle around their seventh year of marriage or commitment, when mystery has left the bedroom.

"Do you swing?" the husband asks, studying us a little too closely for comfort as the elevator doors slide open.

"No," James barks, a bit hastily.

They look at one another and grin back at us before sashaying into the crowd.

James doesn't think they bought my story about being there for research. "They were probably thinking, 'Yeah, you're writing a book. Sure. Wink. Wink. Whatever your fantasy.'"

I pretend he's being paranoid.

Elevated above the pool crowd, a topless girl hula-hoops to reggae and is silhouetted by the sun. The potted palms, pulsing island house mix, and Latino waiters in crisp white Habaneras ground us in Miami. Even though November is just hours away, the sun is piercing and the air, sticky. So much for catching our breath.

The pool deck is packed with oiled bodies. We squeeze through to the bar on the far side on the pool, hopelessly out of place in our conventional wear.

Couples line up at the low poolside stage when the spiky-haired emcee announces the contest for Mr. & Miss Swingfest. Their challenge is to demonstrate as many sexual positions as they can within one minute. Accompanied by a throbbing musical beat, couple after couple whizzes through every position in the *Kama Sutra* and more. Handstands, back to front, feet to earlobes, 69, and a few contortions beyond description. The women are topless and the men more modestly dressed in swim trunks, with the exception of a gray-haired hippie couple who chose to do their entire routine painfully nude.

The crowd cheers for each couple with a vigor that suggests they're already half-lit. Beside us near the bar, a young couple who look not far beyond college years grind to the music as they watch the salacious show. The young man wears wraparound sunglasses and plaid Quiksilver shorts. He keeps looking over at me, which I assume is because I am dressed like a schoolteacher amidst the crowd of skin.

We move away to isolated lounge chairs at the far end of the pool, the closest ones to the exit in case we need to make a quick getaway. Only a sip or two into our screwdrivers, the scene devolves into bacchanalia.

I blame the blonde in braces. She, with the rigid melon breasts. She started the sex wave.

"Is that girl actually giving that guy a blow-job?" James asks incredulously as Blondie's head bobs over the lap of a naked man sitting on the pool's edge. Her long hair spreads flaccidly on the water with each dip.

All at once, head-bobbing, breast-fondling, and bare-buttock massages spread around the pool like a sexual flu. Most appear to be playing with their mates, leaving the rare singles, like an older fellow dressed like a Nantucket yachtsman, to circle the pool and watch. It doesn't occur to me that people might assume we are also sexual voyeurs. Lust keeps all eyes on the action. So despite our self-consciousness, we feel invisible.

Mr. Wraparound sunglasses and his girl change that delusion.

They saunter over from the bar and take ownership of the chairs adjacent to James. She removes her thin top and stretches out her tiny nude body on the lounge chair. Wraparound lies down on top of her. She squeals with pleasure. Loudly. I attempt not to notice.

I'm sure it's some unconscious defense mechanism, but I start to worry about missing the University of Alabama football game. I turn to ask James the time and—bam! Mr. Wraparound's fully erect penis in penetration mode is in my line of vision. I look up. He's grinning at me! I cannot look away fast enough. My cheeks burn with embarrassment.

"What is it?" James asks, somehow oblivious to the carnal pleasures going on just inches from him.

Without turning to face James, for that would mean another penis view and possibly invite some interaction, I whisper, "They are actually doing it."

James glances over his shoulder and snaps his head back around. "Yes, they are."

Mr. Nantucket strolls by, ogling.

A passing waiter carrying a tray of empties notices the couple, too. His eyes bulge in shock. He moves quickly. He has seen enough.

I have, too. For me, this sexually charged environment is about as arousing as changing a baby's diaper.

James and I sit in silence, facing straight ahead to avoid eye contact with Mr. Wraparound, whose gaze I still feel on my blushing cheeks.

"I kind of have a headache," James offers.

I welcome the cue.

There's no dabbling in swinging. You can't playfully try it on like a human horse bridle or feel the excitement of it by climbing atop a rolling pontoon boat. You are either into it, or you're not. We are clearly not. So, I grab my half-ton purse and we tiptoe away from the pool with our plastic bags of swinger swag, hoping that no one approaches us before we reach the car.

# CHAPTER 8

# Alien Riviera

Something bizarre is happening again outside a ranch-style home in Gulf Breeze. Blow-up aliens have touched down in the yard. A red trolley pulls up filled with a cast of characters straight out of a B sci-fi movie. Out pours a green Martian woman wearing bug-eyed sunglasses. A dorky man scurries by and appears to be incubating a football-sized egg. Other trolley passengers wear strange foil hats: one is strung with lights, another has eggbeater antennas. They wave light sabers. A gray-colored alien in a tuxedo and black fedora enters the mix carrying a sign: "I Saw Elvis in a UFO."

The merry band of local actors and UFO-loving tourists have landed at the house where Gulf Breeze's legendary UFO sightings all began. This is the former home of Ed Walters, the man who in the early 1990s put the coastal town on the paranormal map.

Local UFOlogists warned me that so-called real aliens don't visit Gulf Breeze much anymore, but I've come to town anyway, determined to soak up some of the afterglow. I find enough to keep even the most skeptical entertained.

A UFO presentation this weekend at the Gulf Breeze Recreation Center promises a chance to meet witnesses and maybe some alleged alien abductees. Not long after checking into my Pensacola Beach motel, I discover you can throw a shell and hit a local who's seen a UFO or knows someone who has. I'm halfway through my first drink at the adjoining bar when the man next to me confesses he's had a close encounter. "I don't really ever tell anybody about it because I know they'll think I'm crazy. But I know what I saw. And my mom, my uncle, and my brother saw it, too."

Back in the early 1990s, his family was heading home to Gulf Breeze from Pensacola. They were in a long line of traffic on the Pensacola Bay Bridge when they spotted a green light glowing in the bay. "There was a stream of brake lights. Everybody on the bridge just stopped," he recalls.

A glowing eerie green craft passed underneath the bridge. Once on the other side, it zoomed out of the water. "It hung there in the sky for a few seconds, then zipped one way, then another, then just shot off and disappeared." When his family got over to the Gulf Breeze side of the bridge, his mom insisted on stopping at a pay phone to report what they had seen. She couldn't get through to the police, he says. The lines were busy.

Now you might suspect his tale is induced by the Budweiser he's drinking, but it's his first, and he doesn't strike me as someone prone to conjuring fairy tales. A fisherman by profession, he adds that he's seen other strange lights out on the water at night.

The crowd begins to clear out to watch a different sky show. Coincidently, the Blue Angels, the Navy's hotdog aviators, are performing over the beach this weekend. Based at Naval Air Station Pensacola, the Blue Angels take their daredevil show on the road as an unadulterated recruiting tool for the military. Every July they give locals a buzz and attract more tourists to the area than at any other time of the year.

Thousands are gathered, some knee-deep in the surf. Blue and yellow jets whiz past at seemingly impossible speeds, leaving thin trails of smoke, deafening roars, and the smell of burnt fuel. They do loop-de-loops, face off in faux chicken fights, and sometimes climb straight up to disappear vertically into the heavens.

Their speed is a marvel of man's ingenuity; the pilots' stunts, a testament to how far man will go for the sake of giving and getting a thrill.

Living just across the bay from Pensacola, "The Cradle of Naval

Aviation," and less than 40 miles from Eglin, the Southeast's largest Air Force base, Gulf Breeze residents have a natural fascination with what goes on in the sky. But given that the sliver of a town sits in the Bible Belt, it's not exactly the kind of place you'd expect to find fervent believers in little green men.

Most tourists probably don't even recognize Gulf Breeze as a town as they pass through on their way to Pensacola Beach. The stretch is more a bottleneck of red lights and the last place to pick up groceries. Nestled on the narrow end of a peninsula and surrounded by water on three sides, it's the only stop between historic downtown Pensacola and Pensacola Beach and separated from each by miles-long bridges.

To understand how Gulf Breeze came to warrant a UFO parody takes a glimpse back at how it all started, at that bland ranch-style house on a typically quiet residential street.

### The Walters Files

On a temperate November night in 1987, Ed Walters took Polaroids of what he claimed was a spaceship hovering over his yard. Frozen in a beam of blue light, he claimed a voice telepathically told him to calm down. And then his brain was implanted with images of dogs. That's right. German shepherds, Labradors, beagles. Man's best friend. Ed's grainy photos were published in the local weekly, the *Gulf Breeze Sentinel*, which had a circulation of nearly three thousand. That was also about the population of Gulf Breeze in 1987.

Ed maintained he was being downright stalked by aliens. An array of UFOs appeared at his home in various colors and shapes. He even saw them at Gulf Breeze's Shoreline Park. He pointed to dead circles of grass in his yard and at the park as evidence they were there.

His stories became more bizarre. He claimed these gray creatures communicated with him telepathically in Spanish, which would make sense in multicultural south Florida but seems an odd choice in Florida's "Redneck Riviera." They even tried to abduct him. Once, a four-foot gray alien carrying a wand of light showed up inside his house. All the while, his photos and stories continued to be published in the small weekly, and an increasing number of other UFO witnesses came forward to add their experiences.

Mainstream media picked up the sensational story. Major television networks, reporters from as far away as Japan, and countless

UFO researchers descended on the town like flies on raw meat. Walters even got a book deal, which allegedly paid him a $200,000 advance. The book, *The Gulf Breeze Sightings: The Most Astounding Multiple Sightings of UFOs in History*, sold like tickets to an Elvis Presley concert.

By 1990, Gulf Breeze had become an intergalactic hotspot. The Mutual UFO Network, MUFON, which claims to be the world's largest UFO investigatory association, held its International Symposium at nearby Navarre Beach. But *Pensacola News Journal* reporter Craig Myers came up with what many consider the coup de grâce for Walters's credibility—a small UFO model made out of Styrofoam plates and paper that the new owner of the ranch-style house had accidently discovered in the attic. It looked almost identical to the UFOs in Walters's early photos. The newspaper's following story was picked up around the world. The model, along with a host of other unearthed details, strongly suggested Walters had committed one of the biggest hoaxes in UFO history.

You might think that would have put an end to the Gulf Breeze UFO hysteria. But it didn't. More people came out of the shadows to defend Walters, claiming that they'd seen things, too. A local UFO group formed and began hosting sky watches and regular UFO powwows. As many as 150 people would show up at the end of the Pensacola Bay Bridge and at Shoreline Park in Gulf Breeze to search the skies for erratically moving lights. A small group of diehards came out nightly, 365 days a year. They watched when it was muggy and hot and when chaffing cold winds blew in over the water. They brought lawn chairs, brownbag dinners, coolers, and increasingly sophisticated camera equipment. It became as much a social event as a scientific undertaking.

The local tourism board passed out fliers identifying places to watch for aliens. Local entrepreneurs sold glow-in-the-dark alien T-shirts, rhinestone UFO watches, bumper stickers, and anything else they could peddle to fascinated tourists.

More than five hundred people officially reported seeing a UFO during that era, including a city councilwoman, a county commissioner, judges, lawyers, and teachers—respected members of the community. Dozens reported they'd been taken aboard spaceships. So many, in fact, that a newly formed UFO group brought in a psychologist to counsel them. When he died, a member of the group went back to school and learned how to do hypnosis herself.

It was close encounters of UFO mania.

But the sightings abruptly stopped in July 1992. Local UFO stalwarts could no longer guarantee tourists a sighting within a week's time. The media moved on. The excitement was gone. The aliens had left town.

Yet they left behind quite a legacy. A robust metaphysical group, Unlimited Horizons of the Emerald Coast, evolved from the local MUFON chapter. Its monthly programs still focus heavily on UFOs, extraterrestrials, and government conspiracies to cover them up. But members are open to anything from past-life regression to telepathic communication with dolphins. A few even took a series of dolphin attunement "pods" and opened their own dolphin healing center in nearby Fort Walton. They don't attempt to cure their finned friends; instead, they try to channel the sea critters' energies to heal humans.

I spoke with Alan Abel, Unlimited Horizon's president, who says the group has about 2,500 members. Between 100 and 150 typically show up for the monthly presentations. Alan runs a small publishing business selling books on Florida and aviation. He wasn't around during the heady days of Gulf Breeze's UFO sightings, but after moving to Florida he discovered that he may have been abducted by aliens.

Shortly after arriving in Destin, he took a seminar in remote viewing, a paranormal experience in itself. During it he realized that he and his twin brother had been taken aboard an alien spaceship when they were children back in Indiana. "I always just thought I was dreaming. They were very realistic and I was dreaming the same thing over and over," Alan says. "I dreamed I'm sitting on a stool in this small, round, white room, wondering where I am. Then all the sudden these electric doors open. The alien was standing in the doorway. During the seminar they said that if you dreamt something over and over, it likely had happened. That hit me like a ton a bricks."

Though still not 100 percent sure, Alan is thoroughly convinced that if he was abducted, it's because he and his twin brother are identical. "You can't have better subjects for DNA work than identical twins." Alan's twin doesn't remember any of it, but Alan says that's not uncommon. "Aliens have the power to erase your memory."

## The Investigators

Alan connects me with a couple of members, former MUFON officers, who investigated the UFO sightings. Heading to the meeting, I half-expect to find people in black stargazer T-shirts and carrying L. Ron Hubbard sci-fi novels.

But Art Hufford and Don Ware defy my stereotyping. Art looks like the Presbyterian Church secretary and retired chemical engineer that he is. His gray hair is close-cropped. He wears pressed khakis, a button-down shirt, and a heavy Georgia Tech class ring emblazoned with the Kappa Alpha fraternity symbol.

Don's a retired lieutenant colonel and former Air Force fighter pilot with college degrees in mechanical and nuclear engineering. Based on his resume, I look for a man with extra starch and a deadpan demeanor. Instead I'm greeted by a small man in a Hawaiian shirt. He has lively eyes and a frivolity that fits his fascination with birds and other things that fly. He hands me his business card with the title, "Truthseeker and Bird Watcher."

During the sightings era, Art was president of the local MUFON chapter and Don was the organization's state president.

Don tells me he saw his first UFO at sixteen, the well-documented sighting over Washington, D.C., in 1952. He's spent most of his retirement researching UFOs along with collecting data on birds for the Audubon Society.

Art, a Pensacola native, was the local MUFON president for eleven years. He comes across as reserved, speaking in a matter-of-fact tone with a slight hint of a southern accent. He tells me his belief in UFOs didn't begin until he spotted one over Gulf Breeze in 1987, and even then he didn't think it was from outer space. He and his wife were riding back from church when they spotted something in the breaks in the trees along Pensacola Bay. "We thought, 'Wow!' But at this point I'm still convinced there has got to be some easier explanation. Due to the limitations of the speed of light, I couldn't fathom any exterritorial life ever getting here from a faraway star system. So case closed. We weren't going to get involved."

That changed after he saw Walters's photos in the *Pensacola News Journal* along with an article in which a photographic expert declared them a hoax. (The model space ship wouldn't be discovered for another couple of years.) Art says Walters's spaceship looked exactly like the one he and his wife spotted, and the photographs were supposedly shot on the same day. "I said, 'I've got to come forward.' Because I don't know what's going on, but it's not some guy in a dark room hoaxing photographs. There were no double exposures on the windshield of my car."

When *Unsolved Mysteries* came to town in 1988, Art says he began to believe these glowing crafts were actually from another planet. Most of the witnesses had never met until they were assembled for the television show and yet they reported seeing similar phenomena.

Art bought his first book on UFOs and soon became a local MUFON investigator. Though there is no academic institute for UFO analysis, MUFON prides itself on being the next-best thing. They analyze reports of UFOs as tenaciously as a medical diagnostician searches for causes of a fever of unknown origin, a FUO. MUFON investigators interview witnesses and carry a kit with everything from UFO flashcards to protractors. They sometimes take samples of grass, soil, water or even pavement if spaceships have allegedly appeared above. They attempt to rule out sightings of man-made things like airplanes, helicopters, weather balloons or, say, a wayward *Star Wars* kite.

Art says he determined that most of the Gulf Breeze reports were true UFOs or what UFOlogists refer to as TRUfos.

He also increasingly came across people who felt they'd been abducted by aliens. "One woman I talked to was so frightened that she was unwilling to go into her bedroom at night. She would get in her car and ride around all night long and come back in the morning, at daylight, and go to sleep. Her husband thought she was going wacko."

Art went to the sky watches three or four nights a week. He says it paid off with about eight to ten sightings a month, and he pulls out a binder of 8" × 10" photos to show the fruits of his diligence.

The first photos are extremely blurry, and he explains that he initially used a rickety tripod and didn't know much about photography. They look amazingly similar to shots I'd taken of flying embers from a campfire, colored streams of light zigzagged against a dark background. But in all fairness, how can you expect to capture a moving light against a night sky using still photography? Art also points out that at night, you can only see what's illuminated, which rules out the likelihood of seeing much definition or gray aliens peeking out the windows.

As Art leafs through his later photos, the patterns of squiggly lines become more defined. "Some of us would leave open our shutter to track the UFOs' paths, because you can see some real interesting patterns." He pulls out one showing three red lights in a triangular

Art Hufford in Gulf Breeze's Shoreline Park, where he spent many evenings watching for UFOs. Photo by James Harvey.

formation and notes a star in the background that was used to estimate the UFO size. "I shot this with my 35mm camera shutter at ⅛ a second to capture the light changing in intensity. You can't see that with the naked eye."

"I'm convinced that's a 2-foot diameter red light on the bottom of an 8-foot diameter unmanned vehicle," Don adds, pointing to one of the red dots. "We weren't familiar with it then, but we learned more later."

Given Art's earnestness and their seemingly scientific calculations, I begin to dance around the black hole of UFO mysticism. At this point, Art's not saying the lights are alien spacecraft. He's building the case that they don't look or move like any aircraft known to man. It all sounds perfectly plausible, especially considering that more than five hundred other people officially reported seeing the same things.

Perhaps sensing I'm beginning to follow them, they delve into the more fantastic—that these unidentifiable crafts were piloted not by humans, but by aliens. "They are smarter than we are," Art says. Once, the lights appeared exactly halfway between two different groups of sky watchers. "They knew where we were. It's like their way of saying, 'You guys think you can sneak up on us but this is the way it is.'" On another occasion for strategically placed sky watchers, he says, "They put on a show right in the middle of all of us."

The UFO sizes and colors were different, so they gave them nicknames. They called ones with quickly pulsating lights "shooter-outers"; others they called Bubba and Tinker Bell. Don says, "We did that because we didn't want to freak people out if they overheard us talking about them in a restaurant."

The red lights were most common. But the ones with rings of light in a perfect circle were the hardest to explain away as possibly man-made, Art says. "They were doing 360-barrel rolls and all this stuff silently. It's like they were saying, 'Here, watch what I can do.'"

After watching the Blue Angels stretch the boundaries of physics the day before, I wonder aloud if what they were seeing was some experimental military craft. After all, Gulf Breeze sits in the crosshairs of five Navy airfields, and that's not counting both an international and a smaller private airport. Plus, Eglin's Hulbert Field is less than 40 miles away. But Art and Don have logical answers to the most obvious questions. These aren't simple men. It's clear they've turned these questions over in their heads like rocks in a tumbler until their explanations come out polished.

"Make no mistake about it, if we've developed a new propulsion system they [the military] wouldn't have been able to keep it quiet as long as they have," Art says. (He has a point when you consider the leakage of thousands of U.S. confidential documents to WikiLeaks; Uncle Sam has a hard time keeping secrets.) He argues that the military wouldn't be able to resist employing any supersonic craft given that the nation has been in two Gulf wars since the sightings. "And even still, you don't pick a residential area to test drive your highly secretive experimental craft. It doesn't make sense."

Although they make some logical arguments that something strange was occurring quite regularly over Gulf Breeze, the questionable impetus for it all—Ed Walters's photos—can't be overlooked.

Art and Don still believe Walters's photos are authentic.

Art reinvestigated Walters's photos for MUFON after the model was found. He and Don go into great detail about the paper used inside the model, saying it was a house plan that Walters had drawn up more than a year after he took the UFO photos. "Someone apparently had been going through his trash on a regular basis and thought, 'Aha! Now I can discredit him!'" Don says. Their primary suspect is the Committee for the Scientific Investigation of Claims of the Paranormal (CSICOP), which was later renamed the Committee for Skeptical Inquiry (CSI).

Now, this may sound like the paranoid delusions of men who've spent ten years in a closet watching *The X-Files*. But it's actually the consequence of a UFO soap opera that's been going on for decades. CSI has spent as much time and energy trying to disprove MUFON and other UFO believers as the believers have exerted to prove extraterrestrial life exists.

Reporter Craig Myers details the extent to which some of Walters's debunkers have gone in his book *War of Words: The True but Strange Story of the Gulf Breeze UFO*. CSICOP (CSI) put out streams of scientific reports, press releases, and mocking journal articles debunking the Gulf Breeze sightings. And then there were the local naysayers. The Gulf Breeze mayor and police chief even flew to Chicago to interview someone who tried to confirm the photos were fake.

With no means to judge the truth of either side's claims, I figure it's time for the question people have been asking since Ed Walters's photos starting appearing in newspapers: Why Gulf Breeze? Why would aliens pick a small bedroom community on the fringe of Florida to reveal themselves to the world?

Don theorizes that maybe the aliens sensed the community is more educated and therefore more open to accepting them. He says a Gallup poll showed a correlation between level of education and belief in extraterrestrials.

Art is more philosophical: "I think part of the answer is we weren't in charge of their agenda. We were not controlling where these guys chose to appear and where not to appear. I think they just took their light show somewhere else. There are UFO sightings all over the world."

By Art's and Don's accounts, Bubba, Tinker Bell, and the shooter-outers stopped performing over Gulf Breeze in mid-1992. They didn't reappear until the end of that year, and then with no more frequency than in any other small town in America. They still hear of occasional UFO sightings over the bay, but Art saw his last UFO in 1998. Why the flying saucers left is as much a mystery as why they appeared.

Don and Art have a theory about that, too.

They gently lay out the foundation of their hypothesis. Don, it turns out, communicates with an alien friend through a New Age medium, a channeler. Through her, Don asked his alien friend why his kind weren't showing up anymore. "He said to me, 'As a military officer you should know that if you keep doing the same things over and over again, and there are people who want to interfere with what you're doing, that makes it too easy for them.'" Don looks me in the eye. "Not all those who want to interfere are human."

I later learn that MUFON ousted Don from its board in 1993 because he proselytized his channeling-derived theories to members. The board characterized the psychic technique as "fringe" and unscientific.

This was all before Don and Art came up with their second theory on why the Gulf Breeze sightings stopped. They believe Gulf Breeze was caught in the cross fire of feuding extraterrestrials.

Art and Don got their confirmation from Oscar, a man they learned about from a visiting UFO researcher. Oscar had his own alien friends— ones he claimed he could see, making him a "contactee" in UFOlogy parlance, or someone who has communicated directly with ETs. Think Richard Dreyfuss in *Close Encounters of the Third Kind*. As an aside: Oscar, a former soldier, also told a UFO investigator that the military had captured and abused extraterrestrials back in the 1960s. After he spoke out in protest, he claimed the military declared him mentally ill and discharged him in an effort to discredit his allegations.

Of more interest to Art and Don, Oscar had allegedly talked with Tau Cetians, telepathically, of course. Tau Ceti is an actual star, part of the whale-shaped constellation Cetus. Burning hot and 11.9 light-years from Earth, the faraway star has been greatly fictionalized as having strange intelligent life forms in *Star Trek* episodes and countless sci-fi novels.

Art and Don's theory takes an even more surprising intergalactic twist. "Oscar said the Tau Cetians, who were peace-loving and nonwarring, were getting fed up with the bug people," Art explains. He goes on as casually as if he were talking about the Florida Gators playing the Florida State Seminoles in football. Seems the Tau Cetians were irked that the "bug people" were manipulating and defrauding the U.S. government, so they decided to crash the party. The resulting alien war left the Tau Cetians no time to wink at the sky watchers in Gulf Breeze before they left.

The clincher, Art says, is that Oscar's alien friend told him the intergalactic war started in mid-1992 and ended toward the end of that year, the same time as the break in the Gulf Breeze UFO sightings.

Stuck on the bug people reference, I forget what relevance any of this has to their theory on why the UFO sightings stopped. My brain's been taken over by images of the giant arachnids from the campy sci-fi classic *Starship Troopers*. I get Art to elaborate on these creepy aliens. They actually aren't all that imaginative. He says they're just called bug people because they have big bug-like eyes. They look more like the gray-skinned, slant-eyed humanoid aliens typically portrayed in 1950s sci-fi films and innumerable alien novels.

I fumble for a response.

## The Faithful

Inside the meeting room at the Gulf Breeze Recreation Center, people are taking their seats for the presentation. Many are retirees dressed in slacks and dresses as if they'd come from church. About fifty people show up.

The speaker is Randy Koppang, a California UFOlogist and coauthor of the ominously titled *Camouflage through Limited Disclosure: Deconstructing a Cover-Up of the Extraterrestrial Presence*. Koppang has been studying UFOs for more than twenty-five years and looks like he's been doing it inside a cave. He's a lanky bearded man with sleepy eyes and wire-frame glasses. He speaks in a monotone, citing a litany of UFO books, reports, dates, and planetary names that I have no idea even exist. Cover-up theories are mired in the data. A couple of men in the audience momentarily doze.

During the break people snack on store-bought cookies and sip lemonade. I need a double dose of Red Bull, but settle on fresh air. Outside, Michael, a husky bearded man says he drove three hours from Hattiesburg, Mississippi, just for the presentation. He hands me a handwritten flier advertising his paranormal netcast, *Conundrums*.

Michael's been interested in otherworldly phenomenon since he saw a brightly lit alien craft about twice the size of his parents' Ford Galaxy hovering over their house back in 1973. "Seeing something like it got me to thinking," Michael says. "There's nothing we have here that could do that. So where is it coming from?"

Art comes out. He's not hanging around for the rest of Koppang's opus, but isn't opposed to talking more about his alien experience and how it changed him. He's still a man of science with a strong Christian faith, but says he's now more open to new possibilities for man's existence, potential new answers for the mysteries of life. "I was amazed when I started slowly getting into the possibility of intelligent alien life. They have been here for thousands of years. God may have upgraded our species. Who knows?"

Turns out, Art has also been to the Cassadaga Spiritualist Camp. He had a reading with a psychic whose business card I had picked up in the camp's bookstore months prior. Worlds collide.

Trying to find Ed Walters proves as difficult as spotting a TRUfo. He claimed to have UFO sightings through the late 1990s and even wrote a couple more books. One, *UFOs Are Real*, was coauthored by Bruce Maccabee, a former Navy physicist turned UFOlogist. Maccabee writes me that he hasn't had any contact with Ed in years and doesn't even have his e-mail address.

Art tells me Walters now lives in Pensacola, going by a different last name and running a telephone business. His latest address on Pensacola Beach is a $200,000 step up from his former home. But no one's around. Ed doesn't return my calls.

## Sky Watch

Despite assurances that UFO sightings are a rarity, after dark I head to Shoreline Park anyway. From the road it looks like undeveloped woodlands. Farther inside it opens up to a blanket of asphalt so brightly lit you could read a magazine in your car. Beyond, covered picnic tables line the grassy banks of the dark Santa Rosa Sound. The circle of scorched grass that Ed Walters had once photographed has grown in or been paved over. A few trucks with boat trailers are scattered throughout the lot. Water ripples up a boat ramp just beyond the picnic area.

There's hardly anyone around. A dad walks the bank with his little boy. Beneath a pavilion, a couple of Goth teenagers look eternally bored. The water is bedded with rocks and sharp-edged oyster shells mired in mucky sand. The lapping of high tide against the seawall makes it relaxing just the same. A long wooden pier reaches out into darkness. Far beyond, across the sound, hotel lights cast a halo over Pensacola Beach.

I take Alan's advice for a successful UFO viewing: "Ask them to come. Intend it with your mind." I telepathically send a welcoming message into the universe as I try to escape the shoreline lights and stroll to the end of the pier. The humid summer night sky is aglow with stars, a half moon, but nothing is moving except the tide and the Goth kids heading toward their beat-up Corolla.

I search for Cetus, the whale constellation. I can't find it. Bubba and Tinker Bell aren't flashing me, either. I stretch back on the pier and gaze above at the splatter of diamonds and feel the allure of sky watching. A rest on the water contemplating what may live on a distant star is not a bad way to spend an evening, especially if you've brought along friends and a cooler. Too bad I left mine at home.

## Aliens on Board

Unfortunately for me, the UFO Red Trolley Tour is sold out. But after spending a couple of days in Gulf Breeze, I have the sense that aliens have implanted more than mere beliefs in stargazing and dolphin healing. A corny local music video called *Gulf Breeze UFO* made in the goofy tradition of Weird Al Yankovic plays on the TV of a local bar. A midcentury Futuro house on Pensacola Beach has been fashioned to look like a UFO equipped with a ramp leading to its front door and a resident green bug-eyed alien peeking from one of its portholes.

I catch up with Denise Daughtry, the creator of the UFO tour performance. She's also the president of Winterfest of Pensacola, the nonprofit that owns the red trolleys. She tells me there's recently been a resurgence of interest in the legendary sightings. Enough time has passed that the bug people and their zippy spacecraft have reached cult status. She calls my attention to the upcoming Greyhound Pets of America annual Hound Dog Howliday, which this year is themed around UFOs and includes an alien costume contest for dogs. The promotional photo shows a slender canine in a silver lame coat with goggles and springy antennae.

A true testament of cult appeal is the popularity of the trolley tour and its onboard play, *Planet X: An Alien Love Story*. Every performance has sold out since the tour began in 2010, Denise says. People have traveled from as far as Indiana just to join the wacky spectacle. "It has absolutely no redeeming value. We're just doing it for fun."

She says she stresses that point to out-of-state callers lest they expect a serious presentation of Gulf Breeze's UFO history and get pissed-off after discovering it's a spoof. "I tell them I don't believe in UFOs. Some will say that they do, but it's OK with them. They want to come anyway."

The midcentury Futuro house, constructed in Pensacola Beach decades before the Gulf Breeze sightings, is a stop on UFO Red Trolley Tour. Photo by James Harvey.

The moving play's plot charts the adventures of Ned Walters, who is trying to escape the affections of a creepy green alien who has borne his love child. Extraterrestrials have stripped Ned's memory of his alien affair. (Ed Walters claimed to have no memory of his alien abductions until he underwent regressive hypnotherapy.) Ned tries to fight off the alien woman through the entire tour, which also stops at Shoreline Park for an encounter with a couple of Sleestaks—yes, the hissing reptiles from *Land of the Lost*. The trolley moves on to the iconic UFO beach house where alien eggs are hatched. Along the way, guests eat alien food (green Jell-O molded in the shape of baby ETs), make hats out of tin foil to prevent alien mind control, and listen to the song from the *Gulf Breeze UFO* video.

The tour host always asks if anyone in the audience has seen a UFO, and invariably someone has. "Many begin with 'I have a college education' as a disclaimer," Denise says.

Denise, in her sixties, finds the belief in aliens absurdly funny and jokes that there's a local theory that military aircraft pilots put on fake alien aircraft shows just to scare the locals. She's lived in Pensacola long enough to remember seeing the hordes hanging out by the Pensacola Bay Bridge. She originally hails from New Orleans, where she was quite the bon vivant, putting on highfalutin parties that made local society columns. She moved to Pensacola by marriage to a former local news anchor and is trying her best to bring a little Big Easy to the rather sedate local culture.

Her Gulf Breeze UFO parody has met some sour faces, including one at home. Her husband, David, a member of the theatrical group's cast, takes UFOs rather seriously. He had his own freaky craft encounter during the sighting years and even attended the big MUFON convention in 1990. When she first shared her idea for the UFO tour, he refused to have any part of it. "He didn't like me making fun of UFOs. What can you say about that? We're talking UFOs! How can you be serious about that?"

The tour also hasn't set well with city leaders, who would prefer the town to be known as a quiet upscale enclave close to the white sands of Pensacola Beach. "They hate it and are trying really hard to ignore us."

She's not exaggerating. Gulf Breeze City Manager Edwin "Buzz" Eddy denied knowing about any UFO tour when I spoke to him earlier on the phone. "From what I've heard it was a hoax," he says of the UFO sightings. "If tourists think that might be interesting, that's great. But we don't try to promote it. It's not a significant part of our local culture."

Denise is not a woman easily deterred. She's making the UFO tour a full-blown enterprise. She and her trolley crew are designing T-shirts and alien memorabilia based on the UFO theme. For giggles, her crew of aliens made a facsimile of the infamous paper-plate UFO model, which they plan to ceremoniously present to the city's historical society on the fiftieth anniversary of the release of the sci-fi classic *The Day the Earth Stood Still*. A stand-in for the film's star alien, Klaatu, will officially award the Styrofoam craft outside Walters's former home. They'll leave behind a historical marker in the front yard that says: "We came in peace for all mankind. . . ."

An advertisement for the UFO trolley tours, provided by Winterfest of Pensacola. Photo montage by Denise Daughtry. By permission of Denise Daughtry.

I later learn that although the local news crews couldn't resist capturing the mockery, representatives from the historical society were a no-show.

I hit the road with images of amorous bug people doing loop-de-loops in their green amphibious craft. By the time I'm home, it all feels like some crazy dream—perhaps implanted by aliens. I've returned to reality Florida-style in St. Petersburg, a city where about the only alien-looking things are sunburned Canadian tourists.

But as I bring my space gear back into the house, I spot something that makes me wonder if I'm still in the *Twilight Zone*. Underneath my dining table, all by itself and there for no good reason I can think of, is the business card of Art Hufford's Cassadaga psychic.

# CHAPTER 9

# Showtown's Last Showman

Along the fair midway beyond the Zipper ride, beside the flying swings, and across from a cotton-candy cart, towering walls of sideshow banners depict freaks of nature. On a small stage in the midst, a lively old man in a red-sequined coat eloquently sells the fantasy of what's inside the red-and-yellow circus tent behind him. Ride-weary adults lugging stuffed animal prizes and their antsy children crowd around to listen. Showman Ward Hall is in his element. "This is a program of the events you will see on our stage. Twelve acts alive," he says pointing to the colorful banners of Tarantula Girl, Cobra Girl, the Human Blockhead, Zamora the Gorilla Girl, and a dozen others.

In any other dress or environment, Ward would cut a grandfatherly figure. He's short with a broad face, receding gray hair, big-framed shades propped on a broad nose, and hearing aids the size of quarters in ears that are a cartoonist's dream. Here on the sideshow platform, he's giving such a spirited bally, as showfolks call the pitch, that you would never guess he's eighty.

"You're going to see the Queen of Kerosene drinking gasoline like you and I would enjoy an ice tea," Ward says, peering into the eyes of his audience. "A sight to behold is Unique Monique from Hamburg, Germany, pictured on that first painting. And ladies and gentlemen, she looks just like that picture. A woman alive who visibly does not have any head at all. And when you see her today it is a sight to behold.

"The strangest of them all is a seventeen-year-old girl from Leslie, Minnesota. Her name is Angela Perez. Angela has a normal head and an absolutely beautiful face but that is all that is beautiful and normal about her. Because from the neck down she has a body that looks like a tarantula spider. It's not pretty. It's not nice. When you look at her it may shock you. But you will never forget the spider girl."

Ward's hyperbole is so lyrical and rhythmically punctuated that you want to believe everything he's saying is real and you don't really care if it's not. As a final enticement, he introduces a taste of the show.

A toothless elderly dwarf in a silver-sequined jacket, stage name Poobah, lights the balls on the ends of two skinny sticks. They flame up like a torch.

"Watch the little man eat the fire," Ward says as the dwarf puts a flame into the back of his mouth. "There it goes down the hatch! And the vanilla is good. What a way to make lunch."

Ward then turns to a handsome young man in a fringed Western shirt and white cowboy hat holding two 27-inch steel swords. "Now watch Mr. Tommy Breen. He's all the way from Fort Worth, Texas. Mr. Breen will swallow the sword," Ward narrates as Tommy, who's actually from New Jersey, leans his head back and the blades disappear into his mouth. "Open the lips, past the gums and look out stomach, here it comes." The cowboy bends forward, removes the swords, and then holds them up for the clapping crowd.

"What a way to make a living," Ward says.

Ward should know. By his accounts he's been in the business since he was fifteen and has managed a sideshow since he was seventeen. The Gibsonton showman has pretty much done it all. He's been a magician, clown, fire eater, and ventriloquist. He's worked with marionettes, played cross saw and whiskey bottles, and posed for knife throwers. His most famous role is selling the traditional American sideshow on and off the bally stage.

Through the decades, Ward and his partner, Chris Christ, have at times had more than a dozen sideshows performing simultaneously with circuses and carnivals all over North America. They've played

Ward Hall, king of the American sideshow. Photo by Lori Ballard.

Carnegie Hall, the Las Vegas Strip, and the Smithsonian Museum in Washington, D.C. Their shows and freak performers have appeared in more Hollywood movies and documentaries than you can count on two hands.

No historical account of the American sideshow is complete without Ward Hall. He is a living legend, "living" being a key word. He is the oldest showman still working in America and one of few old-time performers still breathing in Gibsonton, a place once labeled Showtown U.S.A. for its concentration of sideshow performer residents. The Human Blockhead, Lizard Man, Lobster Boy, Monkey Girl, and the other seventy-five to eighty human oddities who wintered in the backwater community are either dead or in nursing homes. You'll find many buried in the Showman's Rest cemetery in Tampa.

Showtown's reputation lives on, in large part due to Ward Hall. I later catch Ward and Chris's full show in all its nostalgic glory at the Florida State Fair in Tampa. Tommy Breen, no longer the Texas cowpoke, has his dark hair slicked back and is wearing a black tuxedo jacket. He's working the bally and drawing adults and children away from the dizzying Zipper and Dream Catcher rides.

"Now the strangest of them all, ladies and gentlemen, is Zamora,"

Tommy says, pointing his sword toward the painted banner of Zamora the Gorilla Girl. "When she is on stage, you will see her placed in a hypnotic trance. Please watch her close because her eyes will start to sink slowly back into her head. Watch her teeth. They will grow big fangs. She will grow thick black fur all over her body. She will change from a beautiful woman to a giant screaming, hairy gorilla."

A man in the crowd holding a stuffed bunny carnival prize shakes his head. "I know it sounds crazy. It is crazy," Tommy responds. "But I've seen grown men pass out when they watch it. Sir, please don't be afraid, because she will be locked in a steel cage. That gorilla will jump at you. It might make you scream and it may make you laugh. But you will remember her for the rest of your life."

Poobah sits on the side of the stage in a miniature cushiony chair looking rather catatonic. His Facebook profile says: "All you need in life is fire, sleep, and a comfy chair," and right now the latter seems more appropriate. Of course, Poobah, who's eighty, has been eating fire dozens of times a day his entire adult life, so you have to give him some slack on his lack of enthusiasm. His real name is Pete Terhurne, and he was a Munchkin in the original *Wizard of Oz*.

My friend Lori introduces me to Little Pete. A hearing aid consumes his ear, and he doesn't comprehend when I ask him where he's from. I repeat, and his short response is so garbled I can't understand him. Eating fire for a living has its drawbacks.

The five-dollar entry fee painted on the ticket booth has been marked down to three dollars to create the illusion of a bargain. Parents unfold the cash and scurry to catch up with their kids who are bouncing into the striped tent. Inside, the walls are lined with some of the promised freaks, or rather replicas of them. The giant is just a dusty statue. Glass cabinets off to the side hold stuffed two-headed animals, a questionable mummy, and replicas of long-dead sideshow freaks.

The show is in process, as always, looping continuously from opening until close.

On the low stage a red-haired man with a ponytail is dressed as a Scottish Highlander, albeit a little rough around the edges. He's wearing a tartan kilt and scarf, once-white socks, and black loafers. John "Red" Stuart of Gibsonton is sixty, missing most of his teeth, and has ruddy skin as thick as leather.

I later learn that Red is legendary as the world's oldest performing sword swallower, according to Sword Swallowers Association

International. He holds the Guinness World Record for swallowing twenty-five 18-inch swords at once as part of a mass group-swallow. Yes, there are such things in the seams of entertainment.

Red tilts his head back and swallows long-handled, solid-steel swords one at a time. The audience claps but doesn't seem to fully appreciate that this man is actually sticking sharp blades down his throat, through his pharynx, into his esophagus, straightening its curves and coming within millimeters of his heart and lungs, and possibly into the top of his stomach. Seriously, even professionals have died doing this. And here Red is, swallowing the blades of death every twenty-five minutes, ten to twelve hours a day for eight to ten months a year in a three-dollar sideshow. He's been doing this routine—sometimes substituting blades with fire pokers and car axles—for the past forty-five years. He later e-mails me that sword swallowing "is just an exercise to keep me centered in thought." He adds that he's also an electrician.

Out comes a young woman in black with frizzy blond hair. Natalie, an art student from Brockton, Massachusetts, threads a steel hook through her tongue and uses it to lift a fire extinguisher. The kids and adults, including yours truly, squirm with empathetic pain. No matter how wigged we are, we can't stop watching. Such is the timeless allure of sideshows.

The show moves quickly with a string of acts about as old as the sideshow itself—the woman in a cabinet-of-blades magic trick and man who lies on a bed of pointed nails.

Short on true human oddities with physical deformities, Ward and Chris's show creates its own—well, sort of. Showmen call these acts "illusions," but that's actually just a euphemism for fake. Illusions don't quite live up to the images painted in the bally, which sometimes results in cries for refunds, but technically they fulfill the promise. Tarantula Girl, billed as a woman with a beautiful face and the body of a tarantula spider, turns out to be one of the pretty cast members whose body is hidden behind a black wall and her head is poked through to the front. The audience merely sees her face as the center of a faux giant spider with 3-foot fuzzy legs that look like oversized pipe cleaners. Cobra Girl? Same deal except with a fake snake body. They're so absurd they work.

At last comes the top-billed Zamora the Gorilla Girl, the freak who's made grown men faint.

Red returns to the stage to play the role of emcee and stand-in Brazilian mad scientist. Mind you, he's still dressed as a Scottish Highlander.

He pulls back a curtain. Sunshine from Long Beach, California, stands inside a cage wearing a can-can-style dress and rainbow-striped stockings. Red, who's a much better swallower than pitch man, tells how a mad scientist experimented on Zamora with shape-shifting trances. Then the man in a kilt goes into wacky scientist mode, reciting hypnotic incantations. Sunshine and the cage disappear behind manufactured fog. All at once, "Grrrrr! Grrr!" someone in a gorilla suit with fake fangs, a King Kong furry if you will, bursts out of the cage acting all crazy, beast-of-the-jungle-like for no longer than it takes the curtain to fall. A couple of grade-schoolers flinch, then giggle. No doubt they've seen scarier things at Wal-Mart, though they aren't leaving. Like Tommy promised out front, the images stick with you.

**Freaky Rebirth**

Sideshows were once the most common outdoor entertainment in America. They traveled with circuses, carnivals, fairs, and even sometimes set up shop inside abandoned empty storefronts. For a dime you could see a man born with no legs or watch a magician make a coin disappear. In the mid-twentieth century, an estimated one hundred sideshows still blew in and out of most every town in the nation. A vast number of those were based in Gibsonton, or Gibtown, as the locals call it.

Then came television and thrilling carnival rides. Circuses shrunk and stopped carrying sideshows. Disability rights groups, which sideshow people derisively call "do-gooders," started complaining that deformed performers were exploited. Advanced medical technology decreased birth defects and gave people with deformities a chance to correct them. The fat man gets a gastric bypass, the bearded lady uses electrolysis, Siamese twins are separated.

By the mid-1990s, only a Coney Island show could lay claim as a true, traditional 10-in-1 sideshow, meaning ten live acts for one price. Ward and Chris's World of Wonders show had dwindled down to basically a museum with foam replicas of its one-time freaks and stuffed and jarred deformed animals. Their only live acts were a fat man and Poobah. Ward has announced his final show many times, and each farewell generated mass publicity. The British Broadcasting Corporation even did a documentary on what was to be his last show in 1994. Nearly every season following his publicized retirements, Ward did what he's done most of his life. He dusted off his sequined jacket, loaded up the semi in Gibsonton, hooked up the travel trailer behind the pickup, and hit the road for another county fair.

Maybe it was the publicity from his repeated retirements, his media title as "King of the American Sideshow," his and Chris's online posts seeking new performers, or all combined, but around 2006 the World of Wonders began to rise from the dust. Young college graduates, actors, and performance artists from around the country, like the ones I just saw at the Florida State Fair, started contacting Ward and Chris for a job. They wanted to be in a traditional traveling carnival sideshow, the family-freak-out-the-kids kind, not the nightclub-rock-concert-shock acts like the Jim Rose Circus. Most of all they wanted to learn from the legendary Ward Hall.

"When he placed a help-wanted ad on the Internet, I jumped at the chance to work with him because he's the real deal, an actual circus sideshow man," Tommy Breen tells me. "I mean, he's the king." Tommy graduated from Rutgers in New Jersey as a theater major. You might think that joining a traditional sideshow in the twenty-first century would be a college graduate's last hurrah of whimsy before buckling into a nine-to-five grind, kind of like a year backpacking Europe. Not for Tommy. After a few years with World of Wonders, he wants to be in the sideshow business for as long as he's physically able.

He credits Ward and Chris for that. "Everything I have today as far as my dreams of being in the sideshow business I owe to him and Chris," Tommy says. "I'd be moving pianos or substitute teaching or something if not for Ward."

With his young protégés and the veteran Red, Ward's traveling show is once again a true 10-in-1. He bills it as the only one in the United States. Of course, as with all showman claims, it pays to be a little skeptical.

Ward doesn't travel full-time with the show these days and only occasionally works the bally platform. He's turned most of the bally work to Mike, another young protégé. On the road, Tommy manages the behind-the-scene mechanics, as well as performs on stage.

Catching up with Ward isn't easy. He's a celebrity in the show world. He's giving lectures, emceeing other shows around the country, and working on the Hollywood film *Passion Play*, starring Megan Fox, Mickey Rourke, and Bill Murray with appearances by Poobah and Red, the sword swallower.

The 2009 release of *World of Wonders*, a book about his show, has upped his appeal as well. Photographers Jimmy and Den Katz captured stellar images of Ward and the show along with Ward's audacious admission: "I'm a professional liar. I could take a Volkswagen and make you believe it is a Rolls-Royce. If I had another life, I'd like to be a trial lawyer or perhaps an evangelical TV minister."

How could he not be in demand?

### Gibtown, Land of Freak Legends

A carnival season passes before I'm able to sit down with Ward. In the meantime, Showtown U.S.A. beckons. Tommy tells me Gibtown still nostalgically appeals to sideshow fans and performers, even though it's only a ghost of what it once was.

To understand any romance that the gritty backwater community on the east side of Tampa Bay holds, you have to glimpse back, far back, to the time when the Tamiami Trail/U.S. Highway 41 (Gibsonton's main drag) was the primary route to Sarasota and Naples from anywhere north.

In the 1920s, the Ringling Brothers and Barnum and Bailey Circus started wintering in Sarasota. It wasn't much of a town, there was lots of vacant land, the warm winters were easy on the animals, and the circus bigwigs could be bigwigs with wild abandon. John Ringling, for one, lived in high style. He built a Venetian-themed mansion on Sarasota Bay with all the grandiosity and garishness you'd expect of a circus magnate. He gave it a pretentious name, Ca' d'Zan, and built a museum for rare art that he named after himself. This all understandably cemented little Sarasota as a circus town. Other circuses followed. Most all circuses at that time had sideshows.

Sideshow folks were on the fringe of circus life in more ways than one. They entertained audiences in tents outside the Big Top before the circus show. They often didn't even get to eat in the same food tent with circus performers. In Florida they created their own Shangri-La about 50 miles north of Sarasota on the Tamiami Trail, in Gibsonton, a farming community with a few rental fishing cottages. The first sideshow residents discovered it on a fishing trip in the 1920s. They returned and settled. Then their friends came. Sideshow operators and their performers followed. By 1950, Gibtown was the place to winter if you made your living letting people stare at your third eye, pulling rabbits from a hat, or hammering nails up your nose. Sideshow performers literally ran the community. The volunteer fire chief was an 8-foot, 4-inch sideshow giant and the police chief was a dwarf whose head only came up to his cruiser's windowsill. To stop someone, he'd hold up a sign that said "Police, pull over." So many midgets and dwarfs lived in Gibtown that the local post office installed a shorter counter for the "little people."

Most sideshow folks lived in mobile homes. They dined and danced at the private Gibtown Showman's Club on Friday nights. They ate breakfast at Giant's Camp, a diner owned by the "World's Strangest Married Couple," giant Al Tomaini (the fire chief) and his two-foot, six-inch legless wife, Jeanie, once dubbed the "World's Only Living Half Girl." The diner was a hotspot for show folks and their fans for more than a half century. I had the good fortune of eating one of its famous biscuits while the adopted Tomaini children were still running it after their sideshow parents had died. I made the mistake of asking a fellow diner about Lobster Boy. After that, no one would look at me.

Lobster Boy was Gibtown's most infamous resident, and his demise tops anything the most creative writer could dream up. Grady Stiles Jr. was born with ectrodactyly, a genetic deformity that fuses the bones in hands and feet. His fingers were joined to each side, making his hands look like lobster pincers. His legs ended at the knees. He married a sideshow dancer, but they had a tumultuous marriage. Once Maria left him for a dwarf. They later remarried, which turned out to be a fatal mistake.

In 1992, Maria and her stepson, a sideshow blockhead, paid another young sideshow performer $1,500 to murder Grady. Making the story even more surreal, Lobster Boy was shot and killed in his living room while watching the horror movie *Monkey Boy*.

Stiles's wife and family later would claim that Lobster Boy was a vile alcoholic who managed to abuse her even though he walked on his hands. This isn't so far-fetched when you take into consideration that he had managed to shoot his daughter's fiancé. Stiles was convicted of the suitor's murder but escaped prison because of his disability.

Stiles's wife, the blockhead stepson, and the hit man were convicted of murder and manslaughter. Their trials were media carnivals. The Lobster Boy/blockhead murder-for-hire story made headlines around the world and decades later continues to make most every Gibtown documentary. Out-of-town sideshow fanatics still drive by and take photos of the scene of the crime, now a rusty mobile home on an overgrown lot. Locals understandably are a little lobster-weary.

Only 12 miles from the high-rises of downtown Tampa, Gibsonton, on the boggy east side of Tampa Bay at the mouth of the Alafia River, seems far removed. It's a lonely stretch that's scenic only if you own phosphate mines, the area's largest export. The Tamiami Trail/U.S. Highway 41 leads past fertilizer silos, barnacled cargo ships along the Port of Tampa, through stretches of scrubby palm flatland pimpled with gray gypsum stacks.

A small sign amid native palms and scrub marks the turn for the grounds of the International Independent Showmen's Association, formerly called the Gibtown Showmen's Club, site of the world's largest annual carnival tradeshow. More than ten thousand carnies annually converge at the cavernous trade hall for the latest in grab-bars, fried foods, and puke-inducing rides. The club also hosts its own Bike Week extravaganza in February, where motorcycle mania meets carnies in a mélange of Florida fringe worlds. During their off-season, show folks and carnies gather socially at the club's private bar when they come back to roost four or so months out of the year. The season is in swing, and the association doesn't even answer the phones.

Across the mouth of the Alafia River, Gibtown looks like a community whose time has passed. The iconic Giant's Camp diner has been scrapped from the earth and replaced by a tidy green lawn and iron fence. Mosaic, the phosphate and chemical giant, now owns the land. The only reminder of the diner is a steel boot sculpture on a pillar and a white rental cabin that looks far better than it probably ever did. This is as close as Gibsonton gets to a historic district.

Old Gibtown isn't so much a place people move to as one they land in. Almost everyone lives in mobile homes. Mobile homes sit on big empty lots, in trailer parks, jammed up next to weathered cottages, and there are several half-and-halfs, mobile homes with a house built around them. Small dour houses are sprinkled here and there. On the outskirts near Interstate 4, new upper-middle-class subdivisions with stamp-size lots sprout up between trailer parks like flowers rising out of the weeds. Tampa suburbanites have moved in and use the interstate to bypass old Gibtown on their commute. A new Wal-Mart is the local mall.

Despite the griminess, old Gibtown has a bizarre kind of charm. You could probably shoot a gun off in your front yard and the neighbors wouldn't come to their windows. You can do pretty much anything you want on your property including parking an elephant or a Ferris wheel in the backyard. Old-timers proudly claim it's the only area of the country with residential show business zoning allowing such far-out things.

Travelers have little reason to stop unless they're thirsty for a beer or a tank of gas. The main thoroughfare is a string of old bait shops, a used RV and boat lot, a closed thrift store, midcentury motor courts with rotting rental cottages, gas stations, three bars, a small strip club, and a barn-shaped liquor store that you literally drive into for a six-pack.

The post office with the midget-height counters has long since been replaced. The new one shoulders a 4FishStuff store in a sad-looking shopping center.

The only sideshow icon left is the Showtown USA Bar & Grill. Covered on the outside with faded sideshow murals, the bar has been a watering hole for show people since the 1970s. It's lunchtime and the sign out front says it serves the best hamburger in town. Ominously, only a few cars are parked in the sandy lot.

Florida no longer allows smoking around served food. Instead of relegating smokers to congregate outside, Showtown has a wall dividing the grill from the bar, and separate entrances, although they are a little hard to find in the mural. The small grill doesn't look like it's been updated since it opened. No one is in sight. A clatter comes from the kitchen, and the smell of grease hangs in the air. I join the dozen in the bar.

The windowless Showtown has vintage dive bar features, like a black suspended ceiling, a jukebox, U-shaped bar, and an old Budweiser beer light with all the little Clydesdales. But even in its dim and smoky state, you can still see what makes it special. Colorful sideshow artwork and murals cover the walls, the creation of local banner artist Bill Browning, who also painted the ones outside. Spotlights shine on the vivid paintings of oddball performers. If you study long enough, you can find Poobah.

The motley crew of afternoon barflies seem no longer wowed by the decor.

I take a seat among an eclectic assortment of local veterans. There's the chatty Cajun with few teeth who's halfway through a pitcher of beer; Butch, a solemn, mustached retiree in a U.S. Vet ball cap tolerating his Cajun acquaintance; a creepy clean-cut guy in his fifties wearing a Devil Rays cap who won't stop staring at me; and a sharply dressed Bahamian who was raised in London, lived in Los Angeles, and recently retired in nearby Apollo Beach. He just stumbled across the Showtown bar on his way back from being turned away from the local VFW.

They banter about their military service, except for the ogler. None of them work in the carnival business, but Butch says he grew up in Gibtown in the 1950s. His neighbors had a motordrome show—the drive-around-in-a-steel-mesh-ball motorcycle act. Occasionally they'd let him ride around in the ball, too, which of course, is a young boy's dream. Once at the Florida State Fair, they pretended they didn't know him and picked him out of the audience to try it. "I was kind of scared I would mess up, but these two girls were pushing me on." He found that carnival machismo only goes so far with the ladies. When he got off the stage, the girls were gone.

As a teen, Butch bought groceries for the "Half-Girl," Jeanie Tomaini. "She climbed up barstools then hopped around from one to another. She had them all over the kitchen. She was strong as an ox and one of the nicest people you would ever meet." She used to tip him twenty dollars back when a fiver was considered generous.

He paints a romantic image of what the community used to be, which is a little hard to believe given what it is now. He says as a kid he'd walk to the Alafia River and catch fish all day. He'd go swimming at then-undeveloped Apollo Beach, and claims that Tampa Bay was clear enough to see the bottom.

His current neighbor owns fair rides, but Butch says there aren't many carnies around these days. He estimates in the heyday that tent performers and ride operators represented about a fourth of the community; now, maybe 5 percent. "It's just not what it used to be," he says. "I won't even fish in the river anymore it's so polluted."

As he goes off on a tangent about fishing, his friend Bill sidles up to the bar. Another retired veteran, Bill still sports a flat-top and a faded tattoo that looks like he got it in a seaport. With a southern twang he calls out to a passing waitress, "Hey, I've got you down for a slab. Do you want some sides?" She answers, and he scribbles it down on a piece of paper.

Showtown USA Bar & Grill's painted midget door is almost believable, especially when you consider that Gibsonton was once filled with retired sideshow performers.

Bill is from Alabama, too, so we have a brief bonding about southern barbeque, fried catfish, and fresh crappie. Meanwhile Butch tells the female bartender, "We've got you down for a Boston butt. Do you want any sides? We've got baked beans and they are goooood."

These guys are actually selling their home-cooked food inside a restaurant.

When I ask about it, Bill whips out a business card: B&B Barbeque. They smoke pork, cook baked beans, and make coleslaw, all at home on order. It sounds like they'll be smoking a barnyard the next day. "Hey, do you want some ribs or a Boston butt?" Butch asks. "It's the real thing. We smoke it slow and we make our own sauce."

The bartender overhears and adds, "It's good. They've brought me some before."

My stomach growls and I cave to the fantasy of a true southern bar-beque sandwich. He puts me down for a Boston butt. I resist their pitch on the sides. Butch says to call and he'll walk it over to the bar the next night. "I just live down the road, within walking distance."

I drive away wondering why I had just agreed to buy a home-smoked pork roast from a stranger I'd just met in a smoky sideshow bar. Every-one seems to have a pitch in Gibtown.

### Police! Hooves Up!

After leaving phone messages and Facebook e-mails, I get a call back from the King of the Sideshow. "This is Ward Hall," he declares. He's says he's back in town for some speaking engagements, all sounding very official, but graciously agrees to meet with me at his house the next week. He goes on to give incredibly detailed directions, the type people gave before maps. He warns to call an hour before to make sure he's there. I suspect he needs the reminder.

Preparing for our meeting, I discover that while his show may be the only traveling 10-in-1, it's not the only traveling carnival sideshow left in America or Florida. There are various classifications of sideshows, and operators sometimes get in pissing matches over definitions, and who can claim this or that. Regardless, few sideshows exist of any kind. One operator says there are as few as seven and three of those are based in Florida.

Jim Zajicek of Tampa owns Big Circus Sideshow. His is a freak ani-mal show. At fifty, he's still a relative youngster among sideshow op-erators. Like Ward, he's trying to keep the traditional style alive. He's got the classic 80-foot wall of sideshow banners and a carnival shtick so retro he could actually be a time-traveler. He's tall, slim, and wears heavy framed glasses, bowties, and vintage hats. His bally voice is deep and rhythmic in a Rod Serling *Twilight Zone* way. No sequins—Jim's not one for flash.

We meet for dinner near his home in Seminole Heights, a regentri-fied neighborhood in Tampa. He's hitting the road the next morning bound for a Texas State Fair and will bounce from one to another as far away as Utah for the next seven months. Out of costume in a plaid shirt and jeans, Jim blends in with the casually dressed yuppies. Con-trary to his bally persona, offstage he wastes few words.

Jim's show is mainly a museum. He only has a few live deformed animals—a six-legged steer, a five-legged sheep, an albino turtle, a tiny horse, and a two-headed turtle. The others are stuffed or pickled in jars.

A Chicago native, Jim started out in a circus at eighteen. "As soon as they handed me my diploma, I didn't look back," he says. "My dad thought it was just a phase, and I wouldn't stay with it." His first job on a tent crew paid fifty dollars a week. Over the years he took on dozens of other positions. He drove trucks, did electrical work, shoveled animal poop. Along the road he learned acts from performers. He can walk on broken glass, swallow fire, lay on a bed of nails, and pound some up his nose.

In typical showman fashion, Jim bluffed his way into the Big Top. That's how he ended up working with elephants, some of the most dangerous of circus animals. He handled them for nine years, coaching them to stair-stack one another around a ring, bow on one knee, and other things trainers make them do to appear tamed. Jim says the performance is but a small part of the responsibility. "It's a 24-7 job. You always have to be available to take care of them. You clean up after them. You wash them. You start to smell like them because it gets into your skin. I had a waitress one time ask me if I was a pig farmer."

Then he had to deal with animal-rights activists. "You get these people telling you that you are being cruel and questioning your integrity all the time. You start to question it yourself. I miss the elephants, but I don't miss the elephant business," Jim says.

Jim's on the road about nine months a year. He winters in Tampa and houses his live animals near Ocala. But you won't catch his show in Florida, not after what happened at the state fair in Tampa in 2005.

"I was on the bally and I see these deputies coming running up with their guns drawn!"

I repeat what he said to make sure I heard him correctly. "Yes, they had their guns drawn. I do not exaggerate."

The deputies told him it was against the law to display his two-nose cow, dwarf goat, and tiny horse—the farm animals. It so happens that Florida, a state where people can take their orangutan to Hooters, is the only one in America that explicitly prohibits the display of live deformed livestock. They have to be dead—pickled or stuffed.

The law dates back to 1921 and has rarely been enforced. Jim and the Florida State Fair operators didn't know about it, and neither did the Hillsborough County sheriff deputies, until a Tampa radio show host complained about Jim's sideshow.

Jim Zajicek, owner of Big Circus Sideshow. Photo by Lori Ballard.

The law passed at the same time as one banning human freak shows. No one knew about that one either until after sideshows were well established in Gibsonton. Jim says his friend Ward helped get the human one overturned.

Freak animal sideshow operators are a rarity, and Jim doesn't have the money to legally challenge the law by himself. Plus, there's the Florida Cattleman's Association to contend with. The organization squelched attempts to overturn the law, arguing that people might purposefully breed animals to have deformities, you know, because people are itching to build herds of six-legged goats and two-headed cows to exhibit for three dollars a ticket.

"It's just ridiculous," Jim says with disgust. "Ward can tell you more about it and what they went through." Once again, the yellow brick road leads back to Ward. Is there anything he hasn't done in regard to sideshows?

The next week I make the promised call to Ward. He quickly answers, sounding chipper and alert. He's waiting.

### The World of Ward

I miss his street off the Tamiami Trail and turn at the next to get a taste of the neighborhood, which is only one in the loosest sense. The 'hood doesn't have sidewalks. It's filled with old mobiles homes on sandy lots with barely a sprig of grass. Yards, once parking areas for sideshow trailers and carnival trucks, are filled with residents' contractors vans, semis, and old pickups. Children chase one another around a sagging clothesline. A young man in a wife-beater bikes down a thin lane, steering with one hand and holding a can of Busch beer in the other.

By this standard, Ward's corner is a palatial estate. His double-wide sits on an expansive, green grassy corner lot secured by an 8-foot chain-length fence. A crystal-blue swimming pool out front surrounded by a low wall topped with small Grecian statues gives it a budget palazzo feel. An added sunroom with aluminum windows stretches the width of his mobile home. The side yard holds a shuffleboard court. I pull into his looped green concrete drive and park beside an island of Greek colonnades, more statuary and Asian urns filled with dying plants. This is Ward's Ca' d'Zan.

His sunroom door is open, welcoming me inside. The narrow room is busy with drapes framing the wide windows, 1970s metal-framed patio couches, 1960s lamps and a foot-wide Asian-patterned molding along the ceiling, the kind you might see in a Chinese restaurant. It's impeccably neat with shiny clean ashtrays and a fresh pack of matches on every end table. There's no smell of stale cigarette smoke or must, just stagnant air that's sticky hot. The only solid wall is covered in posters of newspaper clippings, photos, letters, and playbills protected behind thin plastic—Ward's wall of wonders.

With one knock, he pops out the front door wearing a tan guayabera shirt, gray polyester slacks, and black-and-white saddle shoes, the kind cheerleaders used to wear in the 1950s. He seems much smaller off-stage, his hair thinner, and his fair skin dappled with age spots. Yet he radiates the energy of a child and shuffles about like a spritely aged leprechaun. His flat lips rarely change shape as he talks, fairly well disguising that he's missing some front teeth.

He says his partner, Chris, is inside on the phone and suggests we talk here. It's obvious that he just wants to docent his museum.

"Now let's start down here," he says, leading me to one of the displays at the end of the room. He reminds me of my spry ninety-year-old grandmother, who had to proudly point out every flower, fruit tree, and vegetable on her farm before letting any visitor inside her house.

Ward's props reinforce his unofficial title as King of the American Sideshow. He's more P. T. Barnum than P. T. Barnum. He points out a playbill for *Phineas*, which he wrote about the infamous eighteenth-century showman's life. Ward and Poobah performed all the roles at the 1995 Circus Fans Association of America convention in Bridgeport, Connecticut, P. T. Barnum's hometown. As if there were any doubt, Ward adds that he played the leading role, P. T.

"Now this is Louise Capps. She was born without arms," he says, pointing to a black-and-white photo of a shapely armless woman in a strapless bodysuit. "She could do anything that anyone else could do but with only her feet. She came to our show at the Texas State Fair in 1979. She married a boy, Bruce Hill, who was a knife thrower on our show. They bought a farm in Oklahoma, and she operates the farm machinery, milks the cows, and she does it all with her feet."

Moving along to a photo of Harold Huge in his full blubbery glory, Ward gives a windy account of how Bruce Snowdon came to be his side-show fat man. He goes over Bruce's college degrees, how he was taking a break from an archaeological dig in the early 1970s when he discovered a photo of a fat man at a local library. Sideshow life sure sounded easier. Specifics flow from Ward as if the fat man had walked into his life only this morning, rather than twenty-six years ago. Sure, Ward's given this tour before and has written about his life. But this man is eighty-one and has the memory of an elephant.

He tells me near the end of Bruce's fat-man career that they billed him as weighing 712 pounds, even though they weren't really sure. "The man literally ate himself to death," he says of Bruce. "He kept gaining more and more weight until he was bedridden and died a year ago." He was fifty-eight.

So, how much did he weigh initially? Ward goes back and studies the photo up close. "I'd say he was about half that size. His goal was he wanted to be that fattest man in the world and so he would get 5 pounds of sugar and put it in a gallon of water and dissolve it and sip on that sugar water all day just to gain more weight."

It's almost inconceivable that someone would purposefully deform themselves to such a fatal extent just to be a sideshow freak; it even suggests a need for some intense psychotherapy. But there's a romantic allure to life on the road, pitching tents in one dusty town after another, no time cards or stress over annual reviews, and never having to worry about fashion faux pas like wearing white after Labor Day. The freedom from conventional life can become addictive.

Take the tattooed lady. Lorett Fulkerson started as a dancer in a hootchie coochie show. She fell so in love with the life that she ensured she would always have a sideshow job by making herself a freak. She attempted to have her entire body inked, but her tattoo artist died after covering 90 percent of her, including the inside of her lower lip. Lorett and her husband, who worked the ticket booth, were with Ward and Chris's show for thirty-two years.

Ward points to a photo of a giant dressed like Aladdin, noting that the costume was one of his creations. He says he likes flamboyant costumes and is quite proud that he made many for his performers, sewing each by hand.

Now comes an homage to Pete Terhurne, a.k.a. Little Pete, a.k.a. Poobah, perhaps the most iconic American circus and sideshow dwarf. His clown face has been on circus posters across the nation. He's had bits parts in multiple movies and made the late-show circuit appearing on Jay Leno's *Tonight Show* and others. He worked and shared a roof with Ward his entire career, some fifty-five years. He juggled while standing on his head, wrestled a python, played a pygmy, played murder victims in a couple of Ward's musicals, and, as previously witnessed, ate fire. Little Pete had never held a job and lived reclusively with his mother when he approached Ward for work on the midway in 1954. Ward became his mentor, coworker, friend, and somewhat caretaker.

I had caught what turned out to be Poobah's final tour at the Florida State Fair. Ward says he's since retired and lives in an assisted-living home in Brandon. "He loves it," Ward says. A brief hint of sadness in his eyes tells he misses his longtime little buddy, but he's in show mode with no time for sentimentality.

Next is Dickie Brisban, whose ankles grew from his hips. "We called him the Penguin Boy because when he walked he waddled like a penguin." Ward says he was playing Jamestown, North Dakota, in 1960 when Dickie showed up looking for work. He was on welfare. He retired twenty-six years later with a nice home in California and a small ranch in Nevada. "I'd say he did pretty good," Ward says with a grin.

That's another thing about freak shows that typically comes up when disability groups cry of their exploitation and cruelty. Sitting in a tent and letting people pay to stare at you was one of the few, if not only, ways for those born without legs, with lobster hands, or covered in thick hair to earn a living before the age of modern surgery. Sideshows offered financial independence. It was also liberating to be with people equally freakish, who saw each other as who they were on the inside instead of judging them for being so profoundly different on the outside. On the road and wintering in Gibtown, they were a family, the only one that some had ever had.

For the hairy woman and scaly man in Ward's next photo, sideshow life was all they ever knew. Percilla, the Monkey Girl, was born in Puerto Rico with a rare genetic abnormality that covered her entire body in thick, black hair. She was way more than a bearded lady. Her father was exhibiting her by the time she was three. After he died she was adopted by a sideshow operator who, Ward says, treated her as his own child and gave her a pet chimpanzee. Yes, the Monkey Girl had her own monkey and even sometimes performed with it. Ward says she fell in love with the Alligator Man, Bennett Bejano, of Punta Gorda, Florida, after he joined her father's show. Bennett had no sweat glands, which gave him scaly skin like a reptile. His early life was amazingly similar to Percilla's. He was put in a sideshow at six and adopted by the sideshow owner after his father died. Monkey Girl and Alligator Man eventually eloped and were billed as the "The World's Most Unusual Couple," not to be confused with "The World's Strangest Married Couple," the Giant and Half-Girl who ran the diner.

Although I'd read some of these tales in Ward's writings, part of his storytelling gift is that he can make you feel that he has never shared the story with anyone else. I'm savoring his craft, but the sunroom's a steam bath and I'm being bled by mosquitoes. I shoo one off his forehead, then wave one away from mine. Ward doesn't seem to notice. He's on full-tilt.

He points out publicity photos from Hollywood movies that he and Chris were involved with—films such as *Carnie* starring Gary Busey and Jodie Foster and *Daredevil* with George Montgomery and Terry Moore. His detailed accounts indicate they were intricately involved with the films and friends with the actors. He throws in a story about Terry Moore's marriage to Howard Hughes. Ward is an encyclopedia of showbiz. As for acting, his most noted cinematic role has always been as himself, a legendary sideshow promoter. He's been in *Gibtown* (2001); the BBC's *Last American Freak Show* (1994); *Showman: The Life and Times of Ward Hall* (2006); *Sideshow: Alive on the Inside* (1999); and several others (all confirmed).

Ward admits he's narcissistic. He confesses this as we look at playbills from his musicals. He says he's written four that were performed at small venues, never making it to Broadway. "I thought because I wrote them they were all going to be big hits. They were all artistically successful and financial flops. I violated the number-one rule in the theater, which is to never invest your own money in the show. I did this because I was so egotistical that these were going to be big hits that why should I share it with anyone. Each time I went broke."

Group photos of wildly costumed performers, snapshots of airbrushed semi-trailer wax museums, film publicity shots, award letters, and newspaper clippings prove just how manic Ward and Chris were in the 1970s and 1980s. Nothing is in chronological order, and Ward jumps from one endeavor to the next with so many tangential details it takes a little on-the-spot calculation and later research to grasp the big picture. In short, they had about fifteen shows going at once across North America: They operated traditional 10-in-1s with only live acts featuring "freaks" from Turtle Man to Artoria the Tattooed Lady, who was inked with works of Raphael and Michelangelo; they owned permanent oddity museums along the Jersey shore; they ran grind shows, which are single-act exhibits featuring marvels such as a giant snake or illusions such as a headless woman; they operated mobile wax museums that featured everyone from Sonny Bono to Jesus and his Apostles at the Last Supper.

Nothing was too grotesque or taboo. Their freak baby grind show featured two-headed fetuses floating in jars. Showmen call them pickled punks. Police eventually confiscated Ward and Chris's freak fetuses, most of which turned out to be rubber dolls.

As with his plays, Ward's blind ambition eventually got the better of him in the sideshow realm. In 1982, he and Chris built the massive production show *Wondercade* with more than forty performers, an orchestra, elephants, chimps, dogs, and birds. It took almost twenty semis to haul it to Las Vegas. The tent seated 2,700. After three weeks, the average daily attendance was 175. "We ran out of money, and I couldn't pay the acts if we had gone on, so I closed the show," Ward says. They blew $1.5 million, most of it borrowed, and were forced to file bankruptcy. He says they worked five years to pay everyone back.

Ever the promoter, Ward's not one to dwell on negatives, and he brings up one of the highlights of his career—the *World of Wonders* exhibition at the Smithsonian in Washington, D.C., in the late 1970s and early 1980s. He proudly points out a formal letter from the hallowed institute and adds the exhibit was written up in the *New York Times*.

He quotes the newspaper's characterizations of him: "When Ward Hall talks, people listen even when they don't want to." We both laugh.

I'm eager to learn more about Ward, not just his accomplishments. Here's a man who made his living by selling others' bizarre deformities and refers to them as "freaks" with impunity when speaking of them professionally. Yet, he clearly respects them and considers many his dear friends. What exactly made Ward Hall, Ward Hall?

Although I think he prefers that we stay in his museum, he notices I've begun to look like I just climbed out of his pool. The sound of a TV news commentator carries through the wall. Chris clearly is no longer on the phone.

The mobile home is fairly new with a slight vault to the ceiling, thick carpet, and faux wood paneling. The living room décor is modest with heavy 1980s furniture—cushiony couches and easy chair, a cluttered computer cabinet and a wooden credenza. A picture of the Last Supper laminated onto wood with scalloped edges hangs over the television. Only a few small photos and awards on a shelf and a wad of promotional T-shirts in a corner hint at their careers. It's clean, comfy, and thankfully, air-conditioned.

Chris turns down the volume on the news and warns Ward that he only has another half hour before he needs to leave to see Little Pete in the assisted-living facility. Ward looks at the clock and says we've got an hour. Chris doesn't argue and sinks back into the couch.

Ward and Chris have been together for more than forty years. Chris is tall in a lumbering, gentle-giant way with thinning wavy brown hair and a quiet reserve, a yin to Ward's yang. He's about twenty years younger than Ward and was a sideshow knife thrower when they met shortly after the death of Ward's longtime partner Harry Leonard "Leonardo," who was also a knife thrower. I'm not sure what that says about Ward's taste in men. His sexuality is one of the few things Ward rarely talks about.

Settling into his easy chair, Ward says he saw his first sideshow for a dime when he nine years old. He only remembers the magic act and that the magician sold little bags of paper magic tricks for a quarter, which Ward couldn't afford. This was during the Great Depression, and Ward lived with his dad in a Denver boardinghouse. A few years later when his dad got a better job, he gave Ward enough change to see another sideshow. This time Ward left with a bag of tricks—spinning paper dolls and folded coin hiders—and plans to create and sell his own. He couldn't afford paper and had to resort to palming it from hotel lobbies. At night he'd cut out copies of the tricks and stow them away for the act he one day hoped to have. At fourteen, he worked in the summer as a circus prop boy. The next spring he took a job as a clown with the Sun Brock's Super Colossal Wild West Show & Hollywood Thrill Circus. "I didn't know anything about being a clown, and when I started, I greased my face with Crisco. The show was really bad," Ward laughs. The circus as a whole had problems and was shut down after only two weeks; the owner was jailed for false advertising and a string of code violations. Someone wasn't happy about the discrepancy between the bally and what they found inside the tent.

Afterward Ward spotted an ad for a circus sideshow magician and a fire-eater in *Billboard* magazine. "I did not have a clue how to do magic tricks, and I did not have a clue how to eat fire," Ward says. He didn't confess this or that he was only fifteen to the circus owner. Not that it would have mattered. America was at war and there was a shortage of able-bodied young men to keep the shows running. The Daily Bros. Circus welcomed him to their winter quarters in Gonzales, Texas.

Ward says he read up on magic tricks and eating fire at the library. "I bought some gasoline and went up on the roof of the boardinghouse to practice about every two to three days because I would burn myself every time and it would take two or three days to heal up," he says.

Saving tips from waiting tables, he bought bus fare to Texas. Then he was off, on his way to join the circus with only two dollars, a steamer trunk filled with handmade paper magic tricks, and a thirty-five-cent fancy jacket he'd picked up at a thrift store.

Fortunately for him, the show's opening was delayed, and he was able to learn enough about magic and fire from other performers to pass come opening day. Even at fifteen, Ward seems to have been more interested in being a salesman. "From the first day I stepped on a sideshow stage, I was in business for myself selling packages of the magic tricks I had made from the stationery in the hotels," he says grinning. He sold the bags for twenty-five cents apiece; as he got better, he started selling them for a dollar. "I really started making some money after that."

A showman was born.

He says he picked up other acts as well from veteran performers. By season's end he knew some ventriloquism, marionettes, and a music act playing a cross saw and whiskey bottles. Harry, who became his friend and partner, taught him knife throwing.

Looking back, Ward says, "I think they probably would have fired me when they took one look at me, but I was willing to do anything that they wanted me to do, and I worked like hell. That year my call was either five in the morning or when the train got in, whichever came first." In addition to performing, he helped put up and take down tents and did whatever backbreaking manual labor was needed. "I worked very hard, but I was doing what I wanted to do. That's the main thing. I was with the circus."

The phone on the kitchen bar rings. Ward answers in his matter-of-fact phone voice. It's clearly a business call, and he's off in less than two minutes. "They want me to emcee a show at Lincoln Center in New York," he tells Chris calmly, as if this is an everyday occurrence.

Chris apologizes to me and reminds Ward again about Little Pete, how the home's workers leave at 4:30 p.m. and there's rush-hour traffic to consider.

Ward ignores him. I'm not sure he even heard Chris. He sits back down and for the first time asks if there's anything I'd like to know.

There is one thing—Florida's anti-freak-show law.

The story he gives says more about showmen's craftiness and their juice in Florida than it does about the law itself.

Ward says none of the showmen knew about the law until it was mentioned in a *St. Petersburg Times* article about various arcane state laws. "When I read it I said, 'we can't have this.' This is where those people live, this is where they have their homes, this is where they pay their taxes. This law would now prevent them from being able to be on exhibit."

Were the law enforced, show operators like Ward would be the ones sent to prison, not the human oddities. The penalty was a thousand-dollar fine and/or a year in the state penitentiary. Ward had good reason to be concerned. Around this time in the 1970s, freak shows faced increasing cries of exploitation by the "do-gooders." Although Florida's law had never been enforced, similar laws in other states had been. Yes, something had to be done, and Ward, also a longtime board member of Florida's Outdoor Amusement Business Association, led the charge.

The legal maneuvering was a sideshow in itself. Ward says that in order to sue, they had to get someone to enforce the law. They hired the former mayor of North Miami Beach as their attorney, and he was a good friend of the chief of police. Voila! The city turned down the World of Wonder's permit application. *World of Wonders*, Poobah, and Sealo the Seal Boy sued.

Conveniently, the Dade County state attorney belonged to the Miami Showman's Association and was an acquaintance of Ward's. He played along and prosecuted. Ward, Poobah, and Sealo's attorney lost the case as planned, and the showmen's group appealed it all the way to the state supreme court.

Winning at the state's highest court level was no sure thing, Ward says. So he and other operators devised an outlandish plan of theatrics should they lose. They would protest and shut down the Miss Universe pageant that year in Miami. It was to be aired live on NBC television. The showmen's lawyers had already drawn up the legal arguments and the time to present it had been set—fifteen minutes before broadcast. Their argument: "We said these people were going to violate the law because the women were malformed because, in our opinion, their mammary glands, their breasts, were larger than the average woman's."

Well played.

The state supreme court overturned the law the week before the pageant.

Yet another instance of Ward Hall saving the Florida sideshow.

The clock shows 3:30 p.m., and Chris speaks up again. "I'm sorry to keep interrupting," he says. "But Mr. Hall could go on until 9:00 o'clock."

Ward doesn't say anything, but pops up out of his chair as if he's just remembered there's some place he needed to be five hours ago. He welcomes me to come again and puts on an enormous pair of black shades that fit over his glasses like a welder's shield. He is out the door so quickly I have to hustle to say good-bye. By the time I catch up, he's climbing into a hulking, bright-red pickup in his black-and-white saddle Oxfords. With a wave and a smile, he backs out and is off to see his dear old friend Little Pete, Poobah.

Showtown's last showman is on the road again.

# CHAPTER 10

# Fringe on Fringe

The website images from the previous year's Butt Naked Biker Bash promise an unusually rowdy weekend. A stark naked biker, grizzly white beard and cue-ball head, and his topless Old Lady rumble through the campground. With the bike still in motion, the woman opens her mouth wide and then bites off the end of a hotdog dangling overhead from a string. The length she bit off will be measured against her competitors, who do the same.

The Bite the Weenie contest ranks with thong pulls and coleslaw wrestling in the catalogue of crude biker entertainment. Throw in nudism, and you have a mutation of Florida fringe in full-throttle glory. You have to ask: Why isn't being a hard-core biker or being just a nudist enough? And of course, the more intimate question: Aren't they worried about burning their most tender body parts on sun-sizzled seats?

The Bash is this weekend, and an employee at the Riverboat Nudist Campground and RV Park says to expect as many as two hundred bikers. This sounds like a grand way to kick off my tour of Florida's nudist communities. I have three on the agenda.

My husband, James, and I load up the SUV with cameras, camping gear, and cooler, tenuously hanging to the possibility of pitching a tent for an around-the-clock immersion into the world of nude bikers. It's clothing-optional. Dressed in shorts and T-shirts, we have no intention of stripping down.

We set out for the heart of nude America, Pasco County, a cow country with strip malls and fourteen nudist communities. Only 20 miles north of Tampa, Pasco has so many residents who prefer daily living in the buff that it's been dubbed the "Nudist Capital of the World" by the American Association for Nude Recreation (AANR), which, interestingly, is headquartered just across the interstate from the Holy Land Experience in Orlando.

There's no official count of how many nudists live in Pasco County, but there are enough that when a group lobbied for a nude polling place, the idea wasn't immediately dismissed by the county elections supervisor. Nudist organizations say it's hard to track their numbers because so many live outside the confines of official nudist communities and a large number are seasonal residents, primarily retirees. There are also countless part-time nudists from the Greater Tampa Bay area who have club memberships or pay by the day.

And then there are the nude tourists. Pasco County tourism officials haven't tracked them, but the county has spent a modest amount of taxpayer dollars to lure them, specifically European nudists; nudist promoters called it the Eurobird campaign. By conservative estimates, 100,000 vacationers a year come to Pasco County for a sunny holiday in the raw.

Residents and guests alike do everything in the buff, and I mean everything. Even things that would seem infinitely more comfortable with a little cloth support here and there. They play tennis wearing only sneakers, run 5K races in nothing more than jogging shoes. They pull weeds from their flowerbeds donning only gloves and a hat, ride bicycles with just a small towel separating them from their vinyl seats. Their only consistent covering is sunscreen.

The communities themselves vary widely. Some appeal to naturists, who shun sexual overtones; others welcome swingers. They range from small hippie campgrounds to massive walled-off upscale neighborhoods with world-class resorts. You can spot children waiting to catch a school bus outside their gates. And if a local nudist development group is successful, seniors will be able to check into a naturist assisted-living facility when the time comes.

I visited two Pasco nudist resorts, the Riverboat Club and Paradise Lakes Resort, on separate assignments for an alternative newspaper more than a decade ago, another lifetime.

Since then, three other upscale nudist communities have taken residence along the now paved road that leads to Riverboat. The shoulders are professionally landscaped with green lawns and stately palms. Stucco homes are protected from prying eyes by sweeping 6-foot walls. Then abruptly, the manicured scenery gives way to the native gangly

Despite its name, the only watercraft you'll find at the Riverboat Nudist RV Club is a derelict sailboat listing in a small pond.

pines and oaks. Pavement turns into a bumpy gravel road. A weathered sign at the end announces the Riverboat Club entrance through a battered wood fence. Some things don't appear to have changed.

There's no one in sight, and only one motorcycle is parked outside a travel trailer that looks like it hasn't been moved since Reconstruction. Not promising. A man wearing only an all-over tan approaches with a clipboard in his hand. He's in his sixties with salt-and-pepper hair, and sags in and around all the natural places.

"Are you part of the swinger group?" he asks.

"No," James shoots back.

He looks at us with a raised eyebrow. "Are you sure?"

Turns out there are so many nude biker events going on this weekend that Riverboat owner Richard "Hyker" LaRiviere canceled the Butt Naked Biker Bash. Even a campground resident who is president of another nude biker club was lured away to a competing nude biker event in Orlando, Hyker says with a sigh.

He booked two swingers groups for the night instead, but it's early and no one has yet shown, he explains. "There's going to be a potluck dinner. Everybody brings a dish." He's referring to food, not partners, and shows us around a bit.

"Then we'll have a foam party. We've got a machine by the stage," Hyker says, pointing to a covered pavilion with strobe lights and a mirrored disco ball hanging from the ceiling. The campground doesn't have a liquor license so alcohol is BYOB, he explains, continuing our quick tour of the recreation area, which is about the size of a school lunchroom.

Following a strange nude man around outdoors is a little bewildering. Since I don't want to stare at his bare ass, I scan the surroundings, which aren't much safer. An older, plump, naked couple suns by the small pool; a man inside the game room leans over the pool table to make a corner shot, giving full view of his droopy genitals.

Straight on, I look only at Hyker's face, ever conscious of not letting my eyes drift downward.

It's true what nudists say about not wearing clothing: You can't tell what a naked person does for a living or how much money they have. Clothes are a uniform that allow us to stereotype one another at first glance.

Nevertheless, given the fact that Hyker lives in a trailer back in the woods, getting as close to nature as Adam and Eve, I assume he's kind of dropped out of society, that he spends most of his time lazing around the tiny, rustic campground and hosting just enough events to allow him that luxury.

However, I am wrong. Hyker has ambitions and interests far beyond running Riverboat. He proudly hands me his business card, which reveals he's a videographer, a filmmaker, and the founder of the Florida Museum of Motion Picture and Television.

His films aren't porn, although a few of his short art flicks do include nude bodies, sometimes that of his adult daughter, XZanthia. It's a rather free-spirited family bond.

XZanthia and other amateur actors, screenwriters, and cameramen work in his production company called Never Nominated Pictures. His studio is in a large metal building at Riverboat, but what's more surprising is what he houses in the other side of the building—more than thirty-five thousand pieces of movie and television memorabilia. His movie-camera collection alone holds the Guinness World Record. Then he has costumes worn by legendary actress Bette Davis and modern-day *King Kong* starlet Naomi Watts; props from *Cleopatra* and *Gangs of New York*, along with spotlights, kid's projectors, and much more. All the collectibles are to be part of the Museum of Motion Picture and Television, which he founded but has yet to find a home for outside the nudist campground.

After selling himself as an auteur, Hyker seems weary of us. We're clearly neither nudists nor swingers. He aims to pass us off to XZanthia, who he says handles all the marketing. We're welcome to look around while he finds her.

The park's been upgraded since my last visit and has a funkier edge. Along with the new covered stage and dance floor, amateur impressionistic paintings rest on tables and along the base of the wall in the community room, giving the suggestion of an artist studio. Mosaics of broken tiles in pathways and half-melted candles around a weathered furniture area send out a hippie vibe. But then a handful of new white mobile homes with tiny bay windows kill any whimsy. It still, of course, has a heap of backwoods Florida—the murky pond remains covered with lily pads, a broken-down sailboat listing at its edge.

XZanthia walks up wearing a short T-shirt and bikini bottoms. A shapely thirty-year-old with long, black dreadlocks and tattoos from ankle to neck, she looks like someone you'd be more likely to see at Nevada's Burning Man experimental-art gathering than at a nudist campground in the middle of Pasco County. She leads us to the office to talk while she readies for an Ybor City art walk.

"I pretty much grew up here," she says. "My parents divorced, and I lived with my mom for a while in California. She sent me back here when I was eleven because things were pretty crazy. It wasn't a good place for a kid."

Makes you wonder how bad it could have been. Especially after she admits that coming of age in a hippie nudist camp wasn't always ideal. "It was hard because my friends weren't allowed to come over." As she developed curves she had to put up with greasy leers from some questionable park visitors. "There were creeps who would stare at me like . . ." She makes googly eyes and hangs her tongue out like a dog. "I'd put something on. That's why I still wear bottoms sometimes by the pool."

As an adult, XZanthia set out for the West, landing in Colorado, where she ran an artist collective for several years. She came back to the Riverboat with big dreams of transforming it into something similar, except with nudity allowed. "I want it to be more talent- than vagina-based," she says.

To that end, she's hosted nude drum circles and glow-in-the-dark parties with go-go dancers in blue wigs, fur boots, and little else. She's managed to make the cult classic *Rocky Horror Picture Show* even more surreal by having young, nude actors interact with the projected film. Imagine naked people doing the "Time Warp."

She grabs me a flier from atop one of the cluttered office desks. It has a large silhouette of a young woman with the word "Party" covering her breasts and "Naked" covering her crotch. The X Bash is advertised as a weekend party with seven bands, six DJs, a foam party, art vendors, and performance artists. In small print along the bottom it says: "Children are welcomed. This is a family event."

I'm wondering if the name X Bash and even XZanthia's name has anything to do with the club drug Ecstasy, which is commonly referred to as *X*. XZanthia seems to read my thoughts. "There are no drugs allowed," she says. "My people are family-oriented. Some of them have kids. I'm a health-food nut, a vegan. I don't do drugs. I don't even drink coffee."

"I want to make X Bash a Florida Burning Man," she says. "People can have themed campsites. I want people to be creative."

It all sounds innocent, artistic, and fanciful with the idealism of youth. Her enthusiasm is so intoxicating that I almost forget we were asked if we were part of a swinger group upon arriving.

So how do her plans jive with the sex parties?

"I want to get away from all that. But hey, when swingers offer to pay thousands of dollars, you can't turn it down. It's what makes the money, pays the bills. Eventually I hope we can rent out enough artist spaces so we won't have to do that stuff."

She stands up and crosses the room, pulling off her T-shirt as she goes, revealing more than just the tattoo that spans her back. She faces us as she picks up another shirt and tugs it down over her large, firm breasts. I look at James, worried he may have passed out. He avoids eye contact, fiddling with the hem of his shirt.

The Butt Naked Biker Bash being a bust, we head out, back to our protective little womb in St. Petersburg. Although disappointed to miss the hotdog-snatching contest, I'll have an opportunity to mingle with other nude bikers next month. The Bare Buns Bikers plan to party all weekend at Caliente Tampa Resort, a more upscale nude environ. In the meantime, nude Florida is worthy of closer inspection.

**Naked in Nature**

Pasco County may have Florida's largest concentration of nude residents, but it's not the only public place in the state where you can walk around in the buff without fear of arrest. In fact, there are twenty-seven American Association for Nude Recreation (AANR) member clubs in Florida, and that doesn't include at least three that haven't joined the association. Some AANR clubs don't have permanent gathering places but instead hold occasional naked soirées at hotels. Then there's Florida's one official nude beach—Haulover Beach in Miami. On typical weekends, the quarter-mile stretch of Atlantic sand is so crowded that nudists have to step over one another to find a place to spread their towels.

Like most Florida lifestyles, nudism originally mushroomed in the state because of the year-round sunshine. Pretty hard to be a full-time nudist where it snows all winter. Pasco County is Grand Central for nudist resorts largely because laws are more lax. Businesses are allowed to sell alcohol around fully naked people. That distinction, however, didn't initially fuel the growth of Pasco's bare-all communal life. The early nudist communities were established when Pasco was truly in the middle of nowhere and no one much cared what you did out there in the sticks.

The Pasco Area Naturist Development Association, also known as PANDAbare.org, by proxy has become the source for the area's nudism history. The group credits a Florida lawyer named Avery Weaver "Bru" Brubacker with founding Pasco's nudism community in the 1940s after he was prescribed "nude time" by his doctor. Bru and his wife started swimming naked in the Gulf of Mexico. Before long they invited friends to join them for skinny dips along the isolated beaches of Gasparilla and Honeymoon Islands. On one of those playful excursions, the crew hatched a wild idea to build a full-time nudist resort. It would be the first of its kind in the United States.

Bru and his wife bought land surrounding a lake in Pasco County and opened the Florida Athletic and Health Association/Lake Como Club in 1941. Membership quickly grew. Hollywood shot an exploitation movie there in the 1950s, aptly titled *The Garden of Eden*. It wasn't the film adaptation of the Ernest Hemingway novel but rather a fiction chronicling the nudist camp's battle for social acceptance.

At its peak in 1972, Lake Como had 3,200 members. Membership has waned since due to intense competition with newer upscale communities and simply because many of the original residents have died and not enough new residents have moved in to replace them.

Lake Como claims to be the oldest naturist community in the United State, and it feels like it. Not that the campground's dilapidated—far from it. But it's a throwback to simpler times when nudism was more about communing with nature than winning a beautiful-body contest. Only a fraction of the camp's 200 acres are developed, and many of the lakeside mobile homes look as if they sprouted up among cypress trees. There are no signs to the bucolic community off U.S. Highway 41; you may need a GPS to find it back in the woods at the end of a long, winding road.

I connect by phone with a member who sets me straight on the difference between nudists and naturists. Lake Como residents are naturists. "A nudist is a person who insists on being nude no matter what. They may be less socially sensitive than we are," says Ted, who preferred not to use his real name. "Naturist is a more encompassing term. They enjoy freedom without clothing. They embrace a lifestyle that is concerned a lot more with being in the environment than a selfish desire to be comfortable with themselves."

You could also call naturists nude purists. They require all members to be totally nude when they step outside their mobile homes and will kick out anyone who leers or makes a sexual display. They are family-oriented and regularly host summer children's camps. Some members were born there.

Like most Pasco residents, Ted is a transplant. He moved to Florida from New York about ten years ago to live full-time as a naturist, something he says he's always been at heart. "I can remember being a kid and playing on the beach and not having a diaper on. Any chance I had to go swimming I took it. Where I grew up in the North, when you went to swim, you swam naked."

Naturally, when he got a little older, he couldn't get away with running naked down a public beach. He was bound by the social conventions of "textiles," the label he and other nudists use for people who wear clothes.

Then came Woodstock. "That's what really got me back into it," Ted says. "It was so much fun being naked in the middle of the crowd." Over the following years, he gradually went nude more and more until eventually he was always nude around his northern home. He wouldn't go to the beach unless he could be naked, and the closest nudist one was forty-five minutes away.

At Lake Como, Ted can walk through the neighborhood completely nude and swim in the pool. He's grown so accustomed to being naked all the time that he hates having to get dressed to go to the grocery store. "I enjoy not having clothing tugging at my tight places," he explains. "I like the freedom of being naked. It's more about the persona than possessions. It's not about body parts. Matter of fact, after a little bit, you don't even see body parts. You see the whole person, what God gave them."

## Boob Art

Caliente Tampa Resort just up the road from Lake Como falls on the extreme opposite end of the nudist-naturist spectrum. It is the nation's largest and, by most accounts, swankiest, nudist resort. More than three thousand nudists live in the 100-acre community, half seasonally. Tens of thousands of other nudists vacation there. It's a private club and requires members to get a background check and pay $1,500 a couple for year-round access to its pools, tennis courts, spa, nightclub, and restaurants. Add to that the day-trippers (any adult with an ID and a pocket of cash can visit for a day), and you have a virtual nude city. About the only things missing are a grocery store and doctors' offices. It even has its own nude travel agency booking tours on nude cruises from the Port of Tampa.

There's been an international buzz about the place since it opened, in part because Paris Hilton worked there for a day as part of her reality TV show *The Simple Life 2*. She later told the *New York Daily News*, "It was the weirdest place I have ever seen." Of course, Paris, being Paris, she also had some snide things to say: "Everyone was naked and old." Cold, but the joke that most people at a nudist resort look better wearing clothes is cliché for good reason.

In the wake of Paris's public put-downs, the resort has labored to draw a younger, hard-body crowd. The resort's website and its ads in the local alternative newspaper show polished photos of perfect, nubile bodies. The resort's nightclub hosts theme parties with sexual undertones and names such as "Eyes Wide Shut" and "Arabian Nights." These titillating promotions to swingers cost the resort its membership with AARN, which promotes wholesome nudism fit for families.

Caliente seems to care less about the loss of AARN's marketing dollars and lobbying power. Swingers tend to be wealthier than old hippie nudists. As Angye Fox, the resort's former spokesperson puts it: "Swingers have pockets, nudists don't."

Angye is my unofficial guide to the resort. She considers herself a "lifestyle nudist," meaning that she's into both swinging and nudism. She was Caliente's spokeswoman from 2008 to 2010 and helped lure the sexually adventurous market. She even promoted the resort at SwingFest.

Her work still revolves around nudism and the swinger lifestyle. She cohosts a weekly alternative-lifestyles radio talk show called *FoXXXy Forum*. Her advertising agency caters to the adult and nudism industries. She runs the FoXXXy Dames website, selling arts and crafts with an erotic flair that she and her friends create. The club's moniker? "We put the 'ass' in class." And this is where it gets really wacky: She occasionally climbs in the bathtub and paints canvases with her breasts. That's right, no hands, just the glands of life.

She calls them Canvas Cleavages, but they don't even remotely look like breasts. "You wouldn't know how they were painted if no one told you," she says. They range from a simple black, breast-blotted Mickey

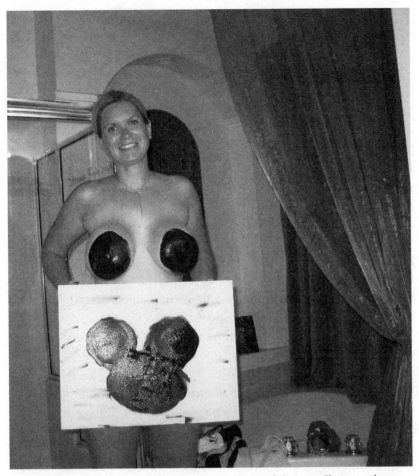

Angye Fox fresh from completing her Disney-inspired Canvass Cleavage that, yes, she painted with her breasts. Artwork comes with an after-photo such as this. Call it a stamp of authenticity. Photo by Angye Fox.

Mouse silhouette to an orange and blue abstract titled *Go Gators*. Of course, what really sells them is the process, or perhaps the imagery of it. She includes a photograph of herself holding the piece, her bare 34F-size breasts still wet with paint.

I connected with Angye through a more reserved friend who plays Bunko with her at their neighborhood clubhouse in a deed-restricted suburb of Tampa, where most every house has a screened pool and three-car garage.

Angye graciously agrees to meet me for dinner at Caliente's gourmet restaurant, Caribe Grill and Bar. This will be a prelude to the following weekend biker event with all-day pool parties.

You might think, given my fringe cred, that going to a nudist resort would be like floating down a calm creek in an inner tube. It's not. I know from visiting Paradise Lakes on an assignment a decade ago that the pressure to bare all is intense, and full nudity is required in the pools. In an ocean of naked bodies, a swimsuit draws stares. Clothing screams, "I'm an outsider!" People tend to be suspicious, perhaps think you're being judgmental or, worse, a voyeur. All of which are the last things a journalist needs for an interview. Disrobing might be inevitable as it was all those years ago. Around a sparsely populated pool, I got over the initial shock and giggles of seeing a bunch of naked people. In the sweltering summer heat, my colleague and I dropped our suits and dove into the water. While we never got the nerve to walk around totally nude, we became so comfortable being topless that we forgot to button our blouses until we were driving home.

Now I'm middle-aged with sags, bulges, and a husband, a husband who's not crazy about the idea of going to a nude nightclub or hanging out with naked bikers.

At least he says he's not as we sit out under the moonlight and commiserate in fear. "You can take your top off and still have your stuff covered," he jokes. "But me, I only have one thing to take off, and I'm definitely not wearing one of those butt-string Speedos."

This brings up the conundrum of what to wear to the nightclub. Angye says I'll want to dress up a little, "maybe a sexy dress," and James, "maybe something like a pair of nice shorts and a Tommy Bahama shirt." It sounds a little strange that people will dress, considering it is a nudist resort. Though relieved, I suspect that the type of sexy dress she's talking about probably isn't one you'd wear to a Junior League party.

## Don't Drop the Knife

The sky is a dreamy mix of orange, gold, and blue as we pull up to Caliente's guard gate. Since it's after 6:00 p.m., the cost is only twenty dollars a couple, as opposed to one hundred dollars for a full day. The streets are quiet in the lull between the daytime nude sunbathing and the nighttime revelry.

We pass a car advertising a "Nude Peekaboo Psychic Spiritual Healer," and I long for a consult with Nellie in Cassadaga. Is the universe trying to tell me something, or does fringe merely attract fringe?

For the most part, the community doesn't look different from any other upscale, gated Florida enclave: modern Mediterranean-style homes and condos; retention ponds spruced up with spewing center fountains; winding, curbed lanes and roundabouts; and strategically planted palms and oaks. Residents are clearly moneyed; even the lower-end modular homes have new Mercedes and BMWs parked outside.

All seems very ordinary until a Range Rover pulls up and a man climbs out totally nude. He disappears through his garage with a McDonald's bag, leaving us to wonder if the locals keep a spare pair of shorts in the glove box in case something goes wrong on a naked drive-thru run.

On the other side of the community, a string of parked cars leads us like breadcrumbs to the actual resort. The two-story club sits atop a Florida hill, meaning, in this part of Florida, that it's man-made and no higher than an interstate off-ramp. Parking lots on both sides overflow, and residents' golf carts sit out front, giving the resort a country-club vibe even though it doesn't have a golf course.

Inside, the resort feels like one you'd find anywhere in America. The doorman wears a doorman uniform sans the hat, the front-desk help, crisp white shirts. There's not a nude body in sight except for the marble Grecian statues by the elevator. To the right, a glass window looks into the Fiesta nightclub. The audience is silhouetted against a brightly lit stage where a clothed comedian throws out one-liners. To the left, casually dressed middle-aged and retired couples sip wine and dine on prime rib and mahi mahi in the gourmet restaurant. In the center, a piano player in Hawaiian shirt and slacks plays Billy Joel classics to clothed couples sitting at high-top tables. A white-shirted bartender pours drinks from behind a polished bar. All seems very mundane until a fat man at the bar spins around. He's naked and his knees are spread.

We spot Angye and her friend from New York between the high tops. She's strikingly statuesque in an elegant, knee-length red dress. Only the fine lines around her blue eyes hint that she's forty. Her waved blond hair frames her patrician features and flows just below her bare shoulders. Her neckline dips only to her clavicle. With mountainous breasts she doesn't need cleavage to ooze sexuality.

Her friend, a producer, has never been to a nudist resort before tonight. "He doesn't have anything like this in his backyard," she says. He scans the crowd and says little. I'm not sure if this is due to personality or awe.

Over dinner, Angye is in PR mode, showing her media savvy by tossing out pop-culture terms and the type of quips that journalists typically circle with stars. "They say what happens in Vegas stays in Vegas. Here, we say what happens in Caliente never happened," she jokes between sips of a dirty martini. Then she plays off of Janet Jackson's "accidental" nipple exposure during a Super Bowl halftime show: "You don't have to worry about wardrobe malfunctions here." Amidst it all, she tells me about the community, its population (half of whom are seasonal), the multiple events, including the attempt and failure at hosting the Lingerie Bowl during Super Bowl XLIII. Having traveled to about seventy-five other nudist resorts and camps around the nation, Angye has a handle on what makes Florida nudists different: a freer, more playful spirit, better bodies, and, of course, deep, all-over tans. She notes nudists in the Midwest tend to be heavier and not as appearance-conscious.

Angye lives at a manic pace. She calls herself a "serial entrepreneur," having started more than thirty businesses from a restaurant to advertising agencies. She says she got her real estate broker's license at nineteen. She's a single mom and says her first priority is her nine-year-old son, who's had an online sports talk show since he was six. ("His voice dropped early.") Her social calendar is filled with charity events, school functions, golf games, and Super Bowls. As she talks about teaching eighth-graders how to write a business plan for America's Teach-In, I have to remind myself that this is a woman who paints with her breasts and has a stripper pole in her bedroom.

She's a little hesitant to talk about her physical transformation since she's been in Florida, perhaps because of her date. But I already know from a *St. Petersburg Times* profile (which she confirmed as accurate) that she hasn't always been a sexpot. In fact, when she moved to Florida from Wisconsin, she didn't wear makeup, dressed in slouchy sweaters, and sported a dishwater-blond mullet. "Business in the front and party in the back" she confesses to me. About ten years, two failed marriages, and a son later, she started changing her appearance—highlighting her hair, working out with a personal trainer, buying new clothes to show off her newly sculpted figure, having surgery to lift her heavy breasts.

She even changed her name from Angela Smits to Angye Fox. Eventually the transformation expanded to her bedroom, which took on a bordello feel with red and black colors, a stripper pole, and the word "Sex" emblazoned across a wall.

If she had stayed in Wisconsin, she doesn't think she could have found the new Angye. To her, Tampa is a "Euro city," a place more accepting of various lifestyles. "There's more tolerance here," she says. "Where I'm from, people tend to keep their blinders on."

Angye got into nudism after a male friend coaxed her into joining him at Paradise Lakes. She would save him money, he argued, since nudist resorts typically charge single men more than couples in order to discourage oglers. "I told him if we get there and there are perverts staring at me and the floor's all sticky, I'm going to leave."

She discovered it wasn't anything like that and found losing her clothes liberating. She became a Caliente regular. In short order, her business mind kicked in, and she set out to give the resort's marketing a makeover. Having her own ad agency, she talked the resort into letting her be their spokesperson. A "lifestyler" as well, she saw the potential for the resort to grow by courting swingers, the ones with pockets.

As we talk, a black-haired young woman in a fishnet bodysuit and platform shoes heads through the lobby toward the nightclub. A hint of what's to come.

Angye says she stopped working for Caliente to pursue her *FoXXXy Forum* Internet radio show, which the resort promotes. Following a Howard Stern–style format, she and her cohost, a licensed sex therapist, cover everything from buying a dildo to getting a tattoo. In one episode, their audio booth is filled with sex toys and they give listeners salient tips on how to introduce a vibrating glove in the bedroom. Angye occasionally rings a bell for emphasis.

Older diners sitting behind us get up to leave. The shirted men, whom we'd assumed were fully dressed, aren't wearing pants. They pass our table exposed from the waist down, flaccid penises and all.

"Did you see that?" Angye's date asks.

Angye laughs. "Once I invited an older couple to dinner and told them not to worry, that people usually dress for dinner. That night, people were nude at every table around us."

Eating naked does have its advantages, I point out. "You don't have to worry about staining your clothes with wine or dropped food."

Being a man with protrusions at risk, Angye's date fires back, "But what if you drop a steak knife?"

James cringes.

### Scaryoke

Before we hit the nightclub, Angye gives us a mini tour, leading us to a balcony overlooking an expanse of pools, hot tubs, bars, and the lakefront beach; it's a mass of man-made water features that tops even the largest area beach resorts. There are five pools in all, the most impressive a massive one with islands and a towering waterfall. Two pools with volleyball nets and a standard-size heated pool that's only waist-deep. They are empty. But on the upper deck where we begin, nude men and women with imperfect middle-aged bodies sit in hot tubs and around an S-shaped pool just wide enough to sit along its outer walls without touching feet in the middle. It's a little tough even for Angye to concentrate on her PR pitch as a heavy woman facing us scissors her legs in the water. "That woman is flashing us," she says, seeming a little embarrassed. I'm not sure if it's because the woman's exposing herself or if it's because she's unattractive. Not the clientele the resort wants to advertise.

Beyond the waterfall pool, a Hank Williams Jr. tune spills from an octagonal tiki bar. A live vocal is muffled by the plastic shades that protect the naked inside from the mild night chill.

Tonight is nude karaoke, or as Angye calls it, "Scaryoke." She's not eager to show us inside, but we insist.

The crowd is sparse but lively. Everyone except us is nude. At the microphone, a man who looks like he could be a retired colonel sings, "Nobody wants to get drunk and get loud." A few in the audience join in as if to prove the lyrics wrong, "all my rowdy friends have settled down."

Singing solo in the nude before a crowd of other naked people has to be a humbling experience, which may explain why everyone in the bar seems to know one another.

Angye is immediately recognized and greeted with warm hugs. One of her acquaintances, Michelle, stops dancing around the room only long enough to be introduced. Michelle's in her thirties, less than 5 feet tall and stocky enough that James later good-heartedly refers to her as a nude gnome. Her escort hangs back, talking and laughing with another man.

Angye introduces us to another friend called Catnip, not because the woman has feline features, but because she wears strange necklaces with chains that clasp each nipple. She's also accessorizing with a short fringe skirt that covers little more than her navel.

Catnip is a 24-7 nudist. She lives in a Caliente condo and makes her living there as well. She creates jewelry and sells it by the pool. She says she has no interest in expanding her business outside the resort.

A slim, cheerful, and deeply tanned woman in her fifties, Catnip says she wasn't always a nudist, and was a little apprehensive about it when her husband introduced her to the culture. After divorcing him, she moved from Chicago to Caliente to live naked full-time. "He didn't think I would stick with it when I left him," she says of her ex-husband. "I love it, and I love living here. I can't imagine living anywhere else. I never have to put my clothes on except to go to the grocery store. I did have to get dressed and go to the dentist office the other day. It felt weird."

We end up getting into a long conversation about jewelry, one of my passions. I quickly forget that she is nude and wearing a strange necklace nipple contraption.

Michelle is still dancing around the bar, belting out lyrics to a Joan Jett song along with a karaoke singer. Then all at once, she bounces over and gives me a chest bump, her naked breasts bouncing into my clothed ones. Like a pinball bouncing from flipper to flipper, she immediately does the same to James, leaving him wide-eyed and speechless.

By all means, it's strange and shocking to get chest-bumped by a nude woman, a stranger at that. But for some reason I find it hilarious rather than offensive. I'm not even threatened that she bare-chest bumped my husband. Perhaps it has a lot to do with her doing it in jest. But I can't help but wonder if I would have felt violated had she been clothed.

While we are still catching our breath, Michelle coaxes Angye up to the microphone for a powerful and sexy rendition of Bonnie Raitt's "Let's Give Them Something to Talk About." They miss a few notes but are smooth enough that it doesn't hurt the ears. They sway close together, Michelle throwing her arms in the air and around Angye, casting an aura of bisexuality.

Angye's date, meanwhile, hangs solemnly by the bar, giving no hint that he's impressed or aroused.

I would be content to spend the rest of the evening among these happy people rather than hit the swinger nightclub inside, but Angye's tour isn't over.

## Nite at the Fiesta

The Fiesta nightclub is packed, and the sexuality crackles like a downed power line. Hundreds of people mingle, drink cocktails, and dance to the fast, heavy beat of techno music. Unlike those in the pool and hot tubs, most of these revelers are under forty with trim bodies that bear more resemblance to the resort's glossy ads.

With few exceptions, the men are fully clothed in shorts or jeans and shirts. Most women wear only enough plumage to sexualize their bodies. Some are in mere string, others topless with slinky skirts short enough to reveal they aren't wearing panties. A few are quite creative: One woman wears only a skirt of long, colorful balloons; another sports a bikini made of Native American dream catchers, the holes circling her nipples and butt crack.

It's a little ironic that people put on clothes to go to a nudist resort's nightclub. Especially since many make an argument that nudism isn't about sex. But even textile nightclubs are hookup spots for singles. So by nature of the venue, everyone wants to look sexy. And if you've seen nude bodies all day, perhaps it takes some degree of clothing, or at least accessories, to remind others what those parts are for.

The hedonistic scene is a lot to take in. A giant screen flashes videos to the heavy beat of the music. A handful of young women dance and grind on the stage. On the dance floor couples in their forties move together, men in clothes and women in stripper wear, a bizarre juxtaposition. Meanwhile, a lone grinning Asian man wearing only fluorescent bands around his wrists and ankles tries his best to dance, his bent arms slightly moving at waist level, feet shuffling side to side. No one gives him a second glance.

On a platform nearby, a woman in a semblance of a dress glides around a stripper pole skillfully enough to make me suspect she's an off-duty Mons Venus dancer. A bare-bottom brunette joins her, and they slither together around the pole like two snakes mating.

Although the degree of skin would only be allowed at a nudist resort, the people, high-energy music, and upscale surroundings are no different than at a nightclub you expect to find in Miami, Las Vegas, or Berlin, but not in semi-rural Pasco County.

Angye coaxes me to talk to an older couple she knows sitting by the dance floor. The gray-haired man is fully clothed while his petite wife works a stripper look. She's wearing a platinum bob wig with bangs, a lacy white push-up bra, string (literally) bikini bottoms, and 7-inch silver platform heels.

As I hover by their table contemplating what to say, he looks over. I smile, but before I can introduce myself, he turns away. They stoically sip their drinks and continue watching the erotic moves on the dance floor.

I tap him on the shoulder.

"I'm a friend of Angye's," I tell him, hoping this will signal that I'm not trying to hit on them.

"She's a good friend to have," he says flatly and turns away.

Then it hits me that using Angye's name wasn't the best calling card for an interview in this environment. She is, after all, a swinger.

I last spotted Angye kissing her date. They've now disappeared.

James and I retreat to a table on the balcony. A young sunburned couple dressed as if they were at a beach bar, plop down at the next table. They've been at Caliente all week, escaping the snow and ice of Minnesota. They aren't nudists and say they would have never visited the resort if not for Brett's dad, who upon retiring revealed himself, literally and figuratively, as a nudist. "Everyone in the family was kind of shocked when he told us he'd bought a condo and was moving to a Florida nudist community."

Brett came to terms with his dad becoming a nudist after coming down for a visit. "Once I saw it, I could kind of get it. I mean, it's really nice. Now we come down twice a year, spring and fall, and hardly leave. There's no need to. Everything is right here, pools, restaurants, bars."

Are they swingers? "No, no, no. But there's plenty of it going on though. All you have to do is go over there," he says tilting his head toward the upper-level conversation pool, site of the earlier scissoring flash.

We pass the unofficial swinging pool on our exit. People are paired up, but there's no way to know who is making out with their own mate and who is with someone else's. Plus, as learned at Swingfest, by some definitions, couples don't have to swap mates to be considered swingers. Merely having sex in the presence of another couple may classify as a soft swap.

Outside the resort, our Honda sits all alone in the distance, facing an outer 6-foot wall. Light poles and various shaped rooftops on the other side indicate another neighborhood. We wonder aloud what it would be like living next door to a nudist community. Wouldn't it be a little bewildering? We stand on a bump of grass and stretch to see over the fence. It looks like any other fancy RV park with paver drives and a small lake. Then a naked gray-haired man steps out of a trailer with a beer. We're peering into another nudist community. Only in Florida.

### When in Pasco

After the erotic environment of the nightclub, James is reticent to re-turn to Caliente for the Bare Buns Bikers party but is not about to let me go alone. To get the full picture of Caliente, it seems imperative to experience it in the full light of day. I know from prior experience at Paradise Lakes that the scene is likely to be more like Scaryoke, sans the bare-breast bumping. Totally nude people around a pool are less in-timidating than ones in butt strings hanging upside down from strip-per poles. But the nudity has to be unanimous. A few dressed people standing around can seem really creepy in a crowd of naked bodies.

Which brings us back to our original dilemma: Can we go au naturel in crowd of strangers?

The tension is punctured as we near the resort on Saturday morn-ing. Less than a mile from Caliente's gate, I stop nervously chattering long enough to notice the AC/DC song playing on the radio. "I've got big balls! . . . And he's got big balls! And she's got big balls!"

Funny and disconcerting at the same time.

At the resort, the music is lighter. A live band plays Tom Petty's "American Girl."

Once again there are hardly any nude or clothed people walking around inside the clubhouse. The view quickly changes as the back bal-cony overlooks a valley of flesh. Naked men and women are spread on most every lounge chair. Herds of them mingle by the pools. Oth-ers play water volleyball, swim, and dance. We have landed on Planet Nude.

Beyond the pools, the Bare Buns Bikers have a shaded booth, and motorcycles fill the adjacent lot. The bikes' chrome gleams in the sun like a beacon. Oddly this seems a spot of sanity. To get there means walking the gauntlet of several hundred naked people in lounge chairs. In jeans shorts and a T-shirt over my bathing suit, I suddenly feel far too clothed. James looks like he wants to run for the car.

People look at us with amusement. One man points as he whispers to another. How many of them are bikers and how many are regulars and vacationers is hard to tell since everyone is nude.

I can only assume that those working the biker booth are Bare Buns Bikers. They aren't just clothed, they also are selling clothing. They have an assortment of T-shirts, all colors and sizes, with the same design on the back: the rear view of a nude couple riding their motorcycles into the sunset.

Kimberly, who's working the booth, helps me choose one. She's slim and wearing a T-shirt and short wrap. She's been riding a motorcycle for fifteen years and has been in the club since it formed about five years ago. She's a breast cancer survivor and is eager to tell me about her motorcycle, which she's had painted pink and white in honor of the cause.

Hidden between the booth and bike trailer, Trudy, a plump woman in a one-piece and sarong sits puffing a cigarette. She hasn't mustered the courage to strip, she says between quick draws. Meanwhile her husband has no such qualms. He's out mingling in the bare crowd.

"We're working on her," Kimberly says. "She's slowly coming out of her shell."

"I did take my top off at the birthday party," Trudy says defensively.

"Briefly," Kimberly concedes.

Bare Buns got its start at the naturist Lake Como and still holds an annual event there. One member managing the cash box says they never, emphasizing "never," have events at the Riverboat campground, where the Butt Naked Bikers have an annual party.

It's clear that the Bare Buns Bikers are not to be confused with the Butt Naked Bikers, the weenie snatchers. This crowd appears tamer and much better groomed. No wires dangling hotdogs are in sight. Not even a nude on a motorcycle, at least not yet.

Kimberly directs me to the club owner, B.G., who's circulating among the crowd, and suggests we check out the bikes. Bikers are immensely proud of their rides, so we take a look.

It's blazing hot in the open grass field. More than fifty motorcycles of all sizes and makes are lined up in rows, their glossy paint jobs looking spit-shined. There are cruisers with fringe hanging from the handlebars, Japanese street racers, even an antique Harley from the 1940s. But nothing like the outrageous choppers and airbrushed trikes at Bike Week.

Kimberly's Harley with flames of pink on the tank is one of the more distinctive. Now nude, she agrees to pose for a photo. She pulls her shirt back on and places a small towel on the bike seat, not just because it is scorching hot. Towels are a hygienic necessity for nudists because no one wants to place their bare bottom down where someone else's has been. Sitting without one is considered very poor form.

B.G. shows up, having gotten word that a journalist wants to talk. She doesn't really look like a biker chick, but then again, she's topless with only a blue sarong tied around her waist and a folded yellow headband around her thick, wavy brown hair. I recognize her from the club's website that shows photos from her recent nudist cruise to Alaska, a rather absurd notion. Why would someone take a naked cruise to a place of snow and icebergs?

I don't get the chance to ask.

B.G. has little time to talk amidst overseeing the event, but she clearly enjoys sharing that the club has grown from one hundred members to around five thousand since she acquired it four years before. "It's the largest nude biker group in the U.S." she says. She lives in Bonita Springs in southwest Florida, but the club has chapters all over America and one in Amsterdam. "We've had 162 events," she adds.

She bristles when I ask if there are 1%ers in Bare Buns and emphatically says no. She goes on to caution me about bringing up such a casual inquiry to other bikers because of the stigma attached to what most consider outlaw clubs. She says she doesn't even like to call Bare Buns a "club." It's an "organization." She points out that 1%er clubs won't allow their members to be in another club. "Besides," she rightly points out, "they can't be nude anyway because they always have to wear their vests."

Obviously bikers can't legally ride naked on public roads, as a drunken one roaring up I-95 found out in 2009. So the opportunities for Bare Buns Bikers to ride in the buff are pretty limited. "We've had a few rides through national parks since there's no law against being nude on federal land. And some ride through a [nudist] community when we're having an event."

Mostly, the Bare Buns bunch rides together clothed and strips down afterward to party. "We are nudists who like to ride motorcycles," B.G. says as we make our way back toward the pool. "Show me one biker who doesn't like to get naked. You won't find many."

She disappears into the crowd of oiled bodies who are downing alcohol like it's ice water.

James looks like he has heartburn. Clearly he's not enjoying himself. "It's the same feeling I had at the swinger convention," he confesses, plopping down on a stool at the far side of the tiki bar, a refuge from the nude. "I'll be OK once I take a break."

Our backs are to the lake, and the nude crowd is comfortably distanced by the bar. Shade and a slight breeze do little to combat the abnormally hot March day. A rock band, whose members appear to be the only other clothed people besides ourselves and the Bare Buns vendors, plays a Lynyrd Skynyrd tune. A Budweiser seems to ease James's mood, or at least makes him tolerant. It doesn't go far enough though for him to jump in the pool. "I'm not going to strip," he says firmly, as if I'm asking if he wants to jump off a ten-story building. "You can if you feel you have to."

Honestly, with a little encouragement, I could. The clear pool water looks inviting. Unlike at the nightclub the weekend before, there are no sexual overtones in the crowd. Despite being naked, people aren't checking one another out. No one is grabbing an ass, rubbing oil on breasts, or kissing. And there's definitely no humping like we saw at the swinger pool scene in Miami. If only for a day in this environment, I could be comfortable dropping my top. Shedding my bottoms, however, is another issue. It's not because I'm worried about exposing flab; although few women here are obese, most couldn't be swimsuit models. And it's not so much because I think people will be staring at my crotch. I've learned that nudists spend more time looking each other in the eye than do clothed people. It's more an ingrained sense of vulnerability, something I'm not sure I can shed.

As I look out over the vast crowd of flesh, hearing their laughter and seeing the ease with which they bare their bodies, I envy their bravery to defy social conventions, their fortitude to unleash their free spirit.

But I'm not ready to reveal this to James, who still seems a little mortified.

He relaxes when a fully clothed retired couple sits down next to me at the bar. They look like tourists you might see taking a breather from a museum tour. The man is wearing shorts, tennis shoes, and a

Kimberly, a Bare Buns Biker, pulled on a shirt for a photo with her bike at Caliente Tampa Resort. Photo by James Harvey.

T-shirt with a smiley face emblazoned with "Life is Good." His slender date sports a quarter-length-sleeve blouse and slacks. They seem like the last people you'd expect to see at a nudist resort, or even riding motorcycles.

They welcome conversation and motion us to move closer. "One of the things I like about nudist resorts is that people are always friendly," he says. "I've been by myself at the pool and had people ask me to come over and join them. I've been at a Ritz-Carlton pool where no one would speak to you."

He gives me his name but asks to go by the pseudonym Robert since he's not ready to announce to the outside world that he's a nudist. He and his date, Carol, rode over on his motorcycle for the Bare Buns bash. "Motorcycles are really my thing. Antique ones especially. At one time I had forty."

He explains they came dressed because he had to pick up Carol at her condo in Paradise Lakes, requiring him to travel on public roads. He jokes, "We just haven't had time to take off our clothes."

Robert is a snowbird, living half the year in one of the fancy modular homes in The Woods—the adjacent nudist RV park that James and I had peered into the previous weekend. I don't mention that little voyeuristic moment.

A retired manufacturing company owner, Robert likes to refer to himself as a naturist because he finds "it's softer, easier for textiles to accept. People look at you like you're some kind of pervert when you tell them you're a nudist."

Sex actually has nothing to do with the nudist lifestyle, he and Carol both say. "One thing I love about it is that you can have a nude woman stand face to face with a nude man and there won't be any sexual overtones," Carol says. "Nudism is actually asexual."

So, what's up with the swingers at Caliente? They assert they aren't swingers, and are not particularly happy that Caliente caters to them, or even allows people to wear clothes. "That's not what the original people wanted," Carol says. "When you came down the balcony to the pool you were supposed to be totally nude. Because of the economy, I think they felt they had to reach out to those in the lifestyle. Do I agree with it? No."

They argue that most nudists aren't swingers and that Caliente's embrace of the lifestyle makes it even harder for textiles to accept nudists. Robert gives the example of a woman he briefly dated before Carol.

"When I told her where I lived, she said, 'Oh, you're one of them.' One of them." He got her to come over for dinner to show her that The Woods is basically like any other upscale RV neighborhood, just that people don't wear clothes. She saw that he wasn't Caligula, but she still couldn't get beyond the fact that he likes living in the nude. "She asked me, 'Would you give this up?' I told her no. This is who I am."

Robert is not just a naturist who also likes to ride motorcycles. He's one of the few in the Bare Buns crew who actually rides in the buff. He often dares to ride naked alone on the open road. Granted, it's just around his neighborhood and the only other developments around are, you guessed it, nudist communities. Even so, he's stealth, cranking up early before most are stirring. "When you get on a cold gas tank," he says, "that will wake you up."

Why go to the trouble? Why expose your genitals to frigid temperatures and your skin to possible road burns? What actually makes one want to ride a motorcycle naked? Robert says it's more than just the rush of air against your bare skin. It goes beyond the naked acceptance of the flawed human body, and it is far more than the exhilaration of riding a rocket with wheels. It's a double dose of freedom. "That's the common denominator between nudism and biking," he says. "It's the pure freedom."

The reflection seems to take Robert far away. His eyes briefly focus on some infinite place in the cloudless sky. "I regret that my children weren't raised this way." He sighs, shakes his head. "Their mother and I divorced when they were small and their mother became a born-again." Now adults, his children have no idea he's a nudist, much less that he lives half the year in a community of them.

The guttural sound of a Harley overtakes the stage music. On the other side of the bar, a bald nude man in sunglasses is navigating his bike through the crowd. His moment of pride is short-lived as motorcycles aren't allowed on the pool deck and he's forced to return to the grass lot.

We leave Robert and Carol to their lunch and check out the vendors, passing again through a throng of nude bodies and once again feeling choking guilt for wearing clothing. Realtors are advertising condos for sale in area nudist communities. A busty one is wearing only a long sarong, and I only recognize her as a realtor because nearby there's a life-size cutout of her in a business suit holding her agency sign.

Next canopy over, Catnip is on the job working from behind a display of smokeless cigarettes, beaded fringe shirts, and her namesake nipple necklaces.

PANDAbare.org, the group that came up with the county's Eurobird nudist tourism campaign, is set up nearby. A woman in her forties with wild red hair and glasses stands stark naked before the group's banner that for some inexplicable reason includes a photo of an actual panda bear.

Marcia, one of the few here with pubic hair, is the group secretary. She considers herself a naturist although accepts that the mainstream generally considers all who live in the buff as nudists. She enthusiastically shares information about her organization. Though they do non-nudist philanthropy such as raising money to feed the poor and help abused women's shelters, their primary efforts promote the business of nudism in Pasco County. Consider them a nudist economic development commission. They attempt to highlight nudists' impact on the local economy by asking the bare set to pay merchants with two-dollar bills. She tells me they are trying to attract a developer to build a nude assisted-living center. As images of doctors wearing only stethoscopes and naked nurses in nerdy white rubber-sole shoes flash through my head, Marcia clarifies that the medical help won't have to bare all. "It's more a place where naturists can go and live out their last days and not have to wear clothes."

The band pauses, and someone announces over the microphone that the Mr. and Miss Bare Buns Biker contest is about to begin. Wondering if there might be hotdogs involved, we make our way to the upper deck for an unobstructed view. The smell of marijuana drifts up from the sandy lake beach where a couple sits under an umbrella showing no interest in the contest or the bikers. The naked Bare Buns crowd in front of the stage clears for a handful of couples of all ages and sizes.

A topless wisp of a woman belts out a shake-and-grind blues tune. Couples start dancing with much less finesse than at the nightclub the week before. A senior citizen in only a 10-gallon hat attempts a Fred Astaire wing move, waving his arms like he's doing a double backstroke as he spreads his feet and legs in sync. A heavy woman sways her hips as her partner does the twisty-shoulder, bent-arms-tucked-at-waist shuffle. A younger athletic couple clearly has them all beat. In the only display of sexuality we've seen all day, they do the front-to-back, booty-to-groin grind, bare-chest-to-bare-breasts sways, and just general dirty-dancing moves. Seems bold in the bright light of day, but when it comes down to it, their dancing isn't any more suggestive than anything you see in any nightclub. There's just no textile between them.

As expected, the crowd cheers loudest for the dirty-dancing couple, cinching their title as Mr. and Miss Bare Buns Bikers. The prize, strangely, is clothing, T-shirts.

The band breaks out into Wild Cherry's "Play That Funky Music," and other couples hit the dance floor. We head to the upstairs bar for the remainder of the party. I've pretty much given up on getting James into the pool. "I'm afraid I'll blind somebody," he says, referring to the whiteness of his private parts.

We watch the band pack up and leave. The crowd below peels away until most lounge chairs are empty. Behind us a scrawny couple in only brown walking shoes racks pool balls for a game. There's something different about them. They have tan lines.

"See, not everyone has an all-over tan," I kid James.

He looks over at them and then gives me a sardonic smile.

"You really want to do this?"

I sense he's cracking. "Well, it is hot," I say, looking longingly down at the massive blue pool with its rushing waterfall. Only a handful of people linger, and they appear too caught up in conversation to notice anyone else. A couple of others swim alone, seemingly in a state of Zen.

We deliberate on the most inconspicuous place to park our towels and clothes. There's really nowhere to escape being seen. I vote against setting up close to the balcony where we are sitting. As hypocritical as it may be, I don't want other clothed people looking directly down on my nude body. We settle on a couple of empty chairs on the far side, close to the pool's edge.

"Are you ready?" I ask of myself as well as James.

"Not really, but let's go."

He chugs his ice water and marches down the stairs, leaving me hustling to keep up. Safely perched on the edge of a lounge chair, I scan the pool deck. Not a head is turned our way.

Leaving no time to chicken out, we tug off our clothes and trot to the water's edge, giggling like mischievous children. No toe-dipping, we plunge into the refreshing blue water, deliciously free.

# Epilogue

While putting this book to bed, I received an e-mail from a man alarmed by an event in south Florida that he thought was training people how to kidnap and torture unsuspecting victims. He provided links to the event's website as proof.

I've been a reporter long enough to be skeptical of sensational claims, especially from a stranger over the Internet. But the alleged acts were serious, so I checked out the links. There among the alleged "torture" and "kidnap" photos was wild-mustached pony-play trainer Foxy dragging a bound Sherifox across a hotel conference room floor.

Despite the dark nature of the photo, I chuckled. Not at the e-mailer's concern, but that I would not only recognize people in the photos, but also know that Foxy and Sherifox were at the Beyond Leather event demonstrating how kinky couples can safely role-play. This moment of awareness was liberating and disconcerting in the same way that I'm astounded by the idea that I can get behind the wheel of a car and drive anywhere I want, but that I can just as easily slam into a tree.

Yes, I see people and Florida differently since completing this project, and no doubt the reverse is true. Knowing the difference between a "hard swap" and a "soft swap" in swinger world tends to raise some eyebrows. My web-browsing history probably put me on some National Security watch list. Not that I visited any sites promoting criminal activity, but my searches would appear obsessively strange to the outside world, or at least outside Florida.

But the lesson from the e-mail is that there is always more to the story; things are not always as they appear.

The agenda of the Beyond Leather event where Foxy and Sherifox shared techniques of their fantasy also reminds me how relatively little of the fringe in the big state of Florida I was able to include in this book. Chronicling all the unusual subcultures and interesting people in the Sunshine State would require an encyclopedia; I selected ones I found iconic in some way.

This book is a snapshot in time, and undoubtedly something stranger or more obscure is just around the corner. The lives of many in this book have changed since I interviewed them.

Ponygroom Tim and Ponygirl Lyndsey adopted a human pet and opened a pony-play training operation. Lyndsey started a web design business specializing in lifestyle websites. Aside from demonstrating their bedroom abduction techniques, Foxy and Sherifox won another international pony-play championship. They, along with Tim and Lyndsey, took their pony-play show to New York and paraded through Central Park.

The furry bottlenose dolphin, his killer whale partner, and their pet dragon moved to Elko, Nevada. The killer whale took a job as an armored car driver.

Monkey Mom returned the following Little League season with yet another baby spider monkey. Florida herpers joined together to build an adoption center in Margate for unwanted Burmese pythons. The project was delayed after they failed to get building permits and the city pointed out the location wasn't zoned for animals.

As this book goes to press, hundreds are searching the Everglades for Burmese pythons. In an effort to eradicate and collect data on the invasive snakes, FFWCC organized the month-long 2013 Python Challenge, offering a total of five thousand dollars in cash prizes to contestants who turned in the longest and the most snakes. Participants only had to pay twenty-five dollars and take a short online course in identifying pythons and humane killing methods (a bolt through the brain). More than one thousand people from across America signed up, including cadres of wannabe reality stars.

Leather & Lace MC formed new chapters in Alabama and Southern California and plans to open a women's retreat in Florida. Bare Bun Bikers plans to open a nude biker resort on the Suwannee River.

King of Trampa Joe Redner was diagnosed with lung cancer and so far has beaten it. Cassadaga Spiritualist Camp opened a history museum with air-conditioning.

Pete Terhurne, a.k.a. Poobah, passed on to the great show in the sky and is greatly missed by his buddy Ward Hall, king of the American sideshow. Showtown USA reduced the food menu and remodeled and ditched the wall between the bar and restaurant in order to win back smoking customers. Sadly, several of the Bill Browning paintings were removed or painted over when the owner flirted with turning the iconic venue into a sports bar.

To the disappointment of swingers far and wide, particularly those who had already paid, Swingfest was cancelled the following year. Under new ownership of a Kentucky "lifestyle" company, the couples-swapping event has since resumed in Florida reportedly drawing even larger crowds. Angye Fox added another business venture to her resume: Owner of the Mile High Fantasy Club, which, as you probably guessed, involves people having sex on planes. And fringe goes on growing and morphing in the sunny state of Florida.

ACKNOWLEDGMENTS

It took far more than a village to make this book possible, more like an entire state of wondrous people who were willing to share their lives with me and many others behind the scenes whose assistance was crucial to this book's completion. The idea for *Fringe Florida* may have remained only that if not for the encouragement of former University Press of Florida editor John Byram and his willingness to help me hone a proposal. Many thanks to Amy Gorelick, John's successor, for not giving up on me as I stumbled along the learning curve of book publishing and battled an unending writer's neurosis.

Lori Ballard, an amazing photographer, was adventurous enough to go along to fetish environs and share her images as well as her friendship. Her wealth of knowledge about the sideshow world was also invaluable.

Thanks to those who shared insight into Florida's unconventional worlds, history, geology, and culture who were not previously mentioned in the book: Fetish Factory co-owner Glenn (who prefers to go by first name only); Jenny Tinnel, Kenny Holmes, and Ernestine Spradley at the Florida Fish & Wildlife Conservation Commission; the Daytona Beach Visitor's Authority; Paul George, an encyclopedia of South Florida history, at the Historical Museum of Southern Florida; Jennifer Haz with the Greater Miami Convention & Visitors Bureau, who shared ideas and her Rolodex; Jessica Taylor with the Fort Lauderdale Visitor's Authority; the folks at the Collier County History Museum; Eric Keaton with Pasco County Tourism; Deb Bowen at Caliente Resort; Carolyn Hawkins with the American Association for Nude Recreation; Vesta at Fetish Con; Jean Villamizar at the Mutiny in Miami; and Kay Rosaire of Kay Rosaire's Big Cat Encounter. My sincere apologies and thanks to others whom I may have overlooked.

Colleagues Craig Pittman of the *Tampa Bay Times*; Trevor Aaronson of the Florida Center for Investigative Reporting; and Lyn Millner, journalism professor at Florida Gulf Coast University, gave precious feedback that helped me take the book to a higher level. Editor Tim Meyer's eagle eye and sense for story provided an additional polish.

Many thanks to attorney Alison Steele for her legal advice. And finally, this book would have never come to fruition without the help and support of my personal editor and best friend, Laura Keane, and my partner in fringe and love, my husband, James Harvey. Laura's tireless commitment, late-night edits, pep talks, tough love, and willingness to call bull on my demons of fear was way beyond what any editor or friend should be expected to provide. All the thanks in the world fall short of my gratitude.

James's unwavering support and willingness to pass me meat on a stick during writing sessions when I was too rabid to approach deserves a clean house and my gourmet, home-cooked meals for the rest of his life. Add to that his willingness to accompany to me to places that made him turn fifty shades of red and my servitude should carry on to another lifetime. Oh, where's Nellie?

In addition to interviews and firsthand experiences, I consumed a voluminous amount of research material—magazine and newspaper articles, books, documentaries, and court and property records. I also lived where modern subcultures thrive, the Internet. I registered with online communities of furries, mudders, and pony players and received e-newsletters of UFO trackers, big-cat lovers, and nude bikers. Message boards, chat rooms, and YouTube.com proved invaluable resources in getting intimate and broader perspectives of fringe in Florida and beyond.

Here are select traditional resources that might be of interest to other fringe junkies. Additional notes follow.

For the overall cultural history of Florida, I recommend:

Mormino, Gary R. *Land of Sunshine, State of Dreams: A Social History of Modern Florida*. Gainesville: University Press of Florida, 2005.

### Chapter 1. Menagerie of Fla-zoons

*Fla-zoon* is my play off the scientific term *neozoon*, meaning animals that live outside their natural habitat. Repeating "Florida exotic animal owner" becomes tedious.

FFWCC's website, www.myfwc.com, is an overwhelming warehouse of information and served as a constant reference to the myriad of rules and regulations involving animals in Florida. FFWCC has several levels of licenses and permits for captive wild animals, but when you cut through the bureaucratic lingo, it comes down to this: Class I consists primarily of animals that can quickly kill you—big cats, baboons, bears, chimpanzees, etc. Class II includes those such as a spider monkey that could merely disfigure you. Class III animals are those that might bite and give you rabies or shake up the ecosystem if allowed into the wild. "Reptiles of Concern" became "Conditional Species" after it became clear that Burmese pythons had invaded parts of the Everglades. These include seven varieties of pythons, the green anaconda, and the Nile monitor.

A note about Gator Ron's near-death experience with the loose black mamba: A *St. Petersburg Times* article reported that it was a green mamba. He told me black. Memories are fallible. Regardless, a bite from either snake is extremely deadly.

Steve Sipek, a.k.a. Spanish Tarzan and former owner of Bobo the tiger, was arrested in 2012 on misdemeanor charges of housing dangerous exotic cats without a USDA permit. FFWCC officers confiscated his two tigers and a leopard. Sipek had previously been cited for not properly feeding or containing the big cats. But the story doesn't end there. He held a fund-raiser at his compound the next month in hopes of raising $8,100 to build new enclosures to meet regulation standards so that he could get his cats back. In a showing of Fla-zoon camaraderie, Dade City's Wild Things loaned him its Leon the Lion, and supporters paid twenty dollars to get their photos taken with Sipek and the borrowed cat. *Palm Beach Post*'s Kimberly Miller reported that event organizers claimed they raised almost $7,000.

As for Carole Baskin's financial state, she says after the legal wrangling over her late husband's estate, she got $300,000 and the multiple investment properties they acquired while married. Charity Star, which tracks non-profits' finances, confirms she doesn't receive a salary from Big Cat Rescue. Her daughter, who acts as president, and her husband, treasurer and chief financial officer, each earns $42,655 annually.

In case you are wondering where one might find monkey diapers, a Marmoset Mom in south Florida sells them and miniature monkey clothing ensembles to monkey owners around the globe. We conversed online, and she shared what led her to run a monkey business: "I enjoy being a monkey mommy. . . . Every morning when I wake up it feels like Christmas morning when I was young but BETTER!"

Bilger, Burkhard. "Swamp Things, Florida's Uninvited Predators." *New Yorker*, April 2, 2009, 80–89.

LaPeter Anton, Leonora. "The Big Cat Fight: Activism, Accusations Lurk behind a Pet Project." *St Petersburg Times*, November 11, 2007.

Laufer, Peter. *Forbidden Creatures: Inside the World of Animal Smuggling and Exotic Pets*. Guilford, Conn.: Lyons Press, 2010.

Lewis, Carole. "How I Began Rescuing Wild Cats." thedailytail.com, October 31, 2010.

Pittman, Craig. "A Florida Crackdown Targets Exotic Reptiles." *St. Petersburg Times*, December 25, 2006.

*Snake Underworld*. Video. Produced by David Clair and Laura Fravel; hosted by Henry Rollins. National Geographic Channel, 2011.

Waddell, Lynn. "Where Is the Cat Man?" *Weekly Planet*, 1999.

## Chapter 2. The King of Trampa

While Joe Redner has been labeled the "father of the lap dance" by Tampa Bay news outlets, the title may be erroneous. Nude dancers at Mitchell Brothers O'Farrell Theatre in San Francisco reportedly were sitting in customers' laps in 1980.

Joe's recollection of dates in some cases varied from those previously reported by local media. However, there were no substantive differences. I checked out his property records and criminal history and confirmed that he's never been arrested for anything more serious than he admitted. Excellent profiles of him by Rory O'Connor in *Tampa* magazine in 1982 and John Guzzo in *Cigar City* in 2010 were particularly helpful.

University of South Florida historian Gary Mormino's interview with the late James Clendinnen, a former *Tampa Tribune* editor, provided colorful insights into Tampa's hellhole-of-the-South era. Scott Deitche, the don of Tampa's Mafia history, and his book *Cigar City Mafia: A Complete History of the Tampa Underworld* were invaluable resources.

Regarding the lap dance trio appearing as a human spider: I'm aware that arachnids have eight legs, but just consider the one at Mons a freak of nature.

Clendinnen, James. Interview by Gary Mormino. August 21, 1980. Hillsborough County Oral History Collection, University of South Florida Digital Collections.
http://ufdc.ufl.edu/UF00006513/00001.

Deitche, Scott. *Cigar City Mafia: A Complete History of the Tampa Underworld.* Fort Lee, N.J.: Barricade, 2004.

Goffard, Christopher. "Tampa's Name Back in Lights." *St. Petersburg Times,* March 9, 2002.

Guzzo, Paul. "Six Feet of Fame: Joe Redner." *Cigar City,* January/February 2010.

Klinkenberg, Jeff. "Joe Redner in the Flesh." *St. Petersburg Times,* January 20, 1991.

Melone, Mary Jo. "Dark Days and Crimes Paid Series: Tampa 1887–1987." *St. Petersburg Times,* June 21, 1987.

O'Connor, Rory. "The Prince of Sleaze." *Tampa Magazine,* February 1982.

Raab, Selwyn. *Five Families: The Rise, Decline, and Resurgence of America's Most Powerful Mafia.* New York: St. Martin's Griffin, 2006.

*Strip Club King: The Story of Joe Redner.* DVD. Directed by Shelby McIntyre. Tampa, Fla.: Aphelion Film, 2008

## Chapter 3. Sisters of Steel

There's much debate about the genesis of the term 1%er. Biker historian William Delaney, a Western Carolina University assistant professor and former Outlaws MC member, dates it and early public perception of bikers as criminals back to the 1949 motorcycle rally in Hollister, California. Following the American Motorcycle Association–sanctioned event, an MC raised hell in the small California town. How much lawlessness actually occurred is unknown, but a staged photograph of a drunken biker at the event appeared in *Life* magazine. Several newspapers reported that the AMA issued a press release following the rally that said 99 percent of bikers were lawful, upstanding citizens. The AMA denies putting out the statement. The term also reflects 1%ers' unwillingness to belong to the AMA, the nation's most recognized motorcycling association.

The U.S. Justice Department's Gang Threat Assessment Report 2009 notes there are twenty thousand 1%ers. The Justice Department goes so far as to categorize the Outlaws and the Mongols motorcycle clubs as "a serious national domestic threat" and says they traffic drugs across the U.S.-Mexican border.

The history of Taco Bowman's rule over Florida motorcycle clubs was compiled from federal court records and interviews. More than thirty articles by the Associated Press, the *Orlando Sentinel, Tampa Tribune, St. Petersburg Times*, and the *Daytona Beach News-Journal* provided additional background. It's worth noting that several Florida leaders and members were convicted of carrying out Bowman's orders.

*Biker Chicks: Leather and Lace.* National Geographic Channel, 2010.

Chachere, Vickie. "Biker Gang Charged with Murder, Extortion." Associated Press. AP.com, August 20, 2003.

———"Bikers Rally Behind Outlaws Leader as Trial Looms in Tampa." *Orlando Sentinel*, March 19, 2001, B-3.

Joans, Barbara. *Bike Lust: Harleys, Women, and American Society*. Madison: University of Wisconsin Press, 2001.

Leusner, Jim. "Bag of Tricks Made Officer a Warlock: Motorcycle Gang Is Undermined by an Undercover Agent." *Orlando Sentinel*, March 4, 1991, A-1.

———. "Warlocks Charge Police Entrapment: A Widow Claims Club Members Were Armed at Her Husband's Funeral Because of a Deputy's Warning." *Orlando Sentinel*, June 19, 1991, B-1.

Osgerby, Bill. *Biker, Truth and Myth: How the Original Cowboy of the Road Became the Easy Rider of the Silver Screen*. Guilford, Conn.: Lyons Press, 2005.

*Outlaw Bikers: Inside the Outlaws.* National Geographic Channel, 2010.

*Outlaw Bikers: Warlock War.* National Geographic Channel, 2010.

## Chapter 4. The Other Wild Kingdom

While I couldn't find any scientific studies on the fur fandom, several unofficial surveys compiled by furries gave me a better sense of the sexual component. Kyle Evans, an Australian fur artist and psychology student, surveyed 276 fellow furries online in 2007. Almost 80 percent said they were turned on to some degree by anthropomorphic characters. The majority (46 percent) classified the turn-on as a minor motivation. Meanwhile, a 2007 University of California-Davis study of 600 furs showed that about half were in relationships, and of those, 76 percent were seeing another furry.

After discovering Dolphin John's online description of his furry partner as a hermaphrodite whale, I wondered how I could have overlooked something so obvious as the Naketa Orcan fursuit having a penis or breasts. I still didn't see any sex organs when I later looked at the fursuit online. Then I realized the attributes are a fantasy much like a piece of John's furotica that I also discovered. The porn art depicted characters from one of his sci-fi universes. The lingerie-clad herm whale not only had human sex organs, but also was involved in a three-way with a bound busty dolphin and a macho dragon-whale hybrid.

Florida Furs typically arrange a field trip to Disney World during the annual Megaplex anthropomorphic convention in Orlando. Much to their disappointment, they aren't allowed to wear their fursuits in the park. Megaplex advertises fursuiter and puppeteer performances for children and adults and an art show (G to furotica, which must be covered). Furry foxes, panthers, puppies, and such also parade through the hotel lobby and generally act silly. What goes on in guest rooms is left to the imagination, but rules posted on the event website imply that like any convention, hooking up is common, albeit furry-style. "Holding hands, hugging, chaste kissing, and the like are fine; anything beyond that is best taken to your hotel room."

For those unfamiliar with Sonic the Hedgehog and Renamon the fox, they are anthropomorphic characters in popular video games. They have been widely fetishized in the fur world.

The underground south Florida glam fetish scene referenced at the Fetish Con after-party relates to the Fetish Factory (FF) store and its Alter Ego events in Fort Lauderdale. FF's co-owner claims theirs is the longest-running monthly fetish party in North America. Their annual four-day bash draws kinksters from as far away as Australia. FF shuns publicity for events and maintains a strict fetish dress code. I was allowed to attend their Halloween party, the only one with laxer costume rules, after I promised not to interview anyone. I nearly suffocated while trying on a conservative latex dress in the FF store, and my husband nearly passed out when he saw the $350 price tag. I opted instead to wear a frumpy witch costume from Target. All said and done, the massive party was no more extreme than Fetish Con's after-parties. See one latex-clad performer pull something from her crotch, you've pretty much seen it all.

Gates, Katharine. *Deviant Desires: Incredibly Strange Sex*. New York: Juno, 1999.

Gurley, George. "The Pleasures of Fur." *Vanity Fair*, March 2001.

Harrell, Ashley. "My Girlfriend Flicka: Giddyup Games Are More Than Childish Fun for Pony Play Fetishists." *Broward/Palm Beach New Times*, June 28, 2007.

Mitchell, Chris. *Cast Member Confidential: A Disneyfied Memoir*. Secaucus, N.J.: Citadel Press, 2009.

Reischel, Julia. "Crush Me, Kill Me: To Understand Florida's Most Bizarre Unsolved Murder, It Helps to Wear Stiletto Heels." *New Times Broward-Palm Beach*, April 20, 2006.

Scott, Paul. *The Fetish Fact Book*. London: Virgin, 2004.

## Chapter 5. Radical Rednecks

Anderson, Zac. "Gone Muddin.'" *Sarasota Herald Tribune*, April 2, 2009.

Kruse, Michael. "From Big Mudding Trucks to Pole Dancing, Redneck Yacht Club Is Down and Dirty." *St. Petersburg Times*, June 12, 2009.

Zuck, Lila. "Swamp Buggy Fever . . . No Antidote!" *ETC*. marconews.com, Naples, October 19, 2008.

### Chapter 6. Spirits, Fairies, and a Blow-Up Mary

I made several attempts to interview Holy Land Experience cast members and employees online as well as in person, but none were willing to talk, at least not to a freelance writer. The park's most popular Jesus actor, Les Cheveldayoff, the Fabio look-alike, did a soft interview on CNN. He also has a Facebook fan page with a profile photo of him as a bloody Jesus carrying a cross.

Details about the Crouches' lifestyle come from the cited *New York Times* article, a lawsuit filed against them by the granddaughter's uncle, and an examination of the ministry's property records. The *Times* article also includes information about the lawsuit and the Crouches' family feud.

Campo-Flores, Arian. "He Calls Himself God," *Newsweek.com*, October 11, 2007. www.thedailybeast.com/newsweek/2007/10/11/he-calls-himself-god.html.

"Florida: Heaven on Earth." *WGCU Presents*, April 21, 2011. http://video.wgcu.org/video/1892746324.

Hopper, Jessica. "Giant African Snails Invade Miami Florida," *ABC News*, September 16, 2011. http://abcnews.go.com/blogs/headlines/2011/09/giant-african-snails-invade-miami-florida.

Stewart, Michael. "Evangelist Arrested on Federal Charges." *Pensacola News Journal*, July 14, 2006, A-1.

Waddell, Lynn, 2010. "Florida's Quran-Burning Pastor." DailyBeast.com, September 9, 2010. www.thedailybeast.com/articles/2010/09/07/terry-jones-pastor-who-want-to-burn-qurans.html.

### Chapter 7. Swing State

Bierman, Noah. "Swingers' Club Patrons Sue BSO over Raids, Arrests in '99." *Miami Herald*, February 18, 2003.

Brinkley-Rogers, Paul. "Trapeze Sex Club Case Takes a Tumble." *Miami Herald*, June 15, 2000. www.miamiherald.com/2000/07/15/625140/june-15-2000-trapeze-sex-club.html#ixzz1g4Aek3n3.

Gardner, Ralph, Jr. "The Unrepentant Voyeur," *Penthouse*, May 1998.

### Chapter 8. Alien Riviera

Don Ware's ouster from the national MUFON board was a painful decision for the board, according to the group's official announcement. However, for two years they had asked Don to stop mailing New Age books on channeling to board members and directors. The final straw was when he brought a channeler to a closed MUFON meeting in 1992, and she shared information she had supposedly received the night before from a spirit guide, "Master Kuthumi." She read it from a computer printout.

Don refused to resign and was voted out of office by roughly three-fifths of the board. The board stated that "Since it has taken 25 years to establish

MUFON's scientific credibility, it seems unwise to allow one individual's unscientific interests to be taken as representative of those of MUFON."

Myers, Craig. *War of the Words: The True but Strange Story of the Gulf Breeze UFO*. Bloomington, Ind.: Xlibris, 2006.

Walters, Ed. *The Gulf Breeze Sightings*. New York: Avon, 1991.

Walters, Ed, and Frances Walters. *UFO Abductions in Gulf Breeze*. New York: Avon, 1994.

## Chapter 9. Showtown's Last Showman

Ward Hall also likes to write about himself. His biographical accounts of life in a sideshow can be found on SideshowWorld.com, a website that's run by sideshow historians and operators who are keeping the past alive, or rather, as their slogan goes, "Preserving the Past and Promoting the Future." The website's various interviews and articles gave context to Ward's oral tales.

I must add that the Boston butt barbecued roast was just as delicious as the bar crowd at Showtown U.S.A. promised it would be.

"Freak Show Ban Unconstitutional." *Lakeland Ledger*, October 12, 1972, A-9.

*Gibtown*. Directed by Melissa Shachat. New York: Decoy Films, 2001.

Hall, Ward. *My Very Unusual Friends*, Tampa: Ward Hall, 1991.

Katz, Jimmy, and Dena Katz. *World of Wonders*. Brooklyn, N.Y.: PowerHouse, 2009.

McIver, Stuart. *Murder in the Tropics*. Sarasota, Fla.: Pineapple Press, 2008, 41–54.

Nickell, Joe. *Secrets of the Sideshows*. Lexington: University Press of Kentucky, 2005.

## Chapter 10. Fringe on Fringe

The Pasco County Office of Tourism Development estimates that the three largest nudist resorts, with about 151 traditional hotel rooms, bring in about $3.3 million in room taxes, or 4.8 percent of the county's overall room tax revenue. This doesn't take into account the condo, home, and modular home rentals of various resorts or what nudists spend in the county.

The first American nudist club was formed by a Baptist minister in Spring Valley, New York, in 1930 with fewer than one hundred members. By 1940, a group was forming in Florida.

Caliente's planned lingerie football event fell through when the network realized the resort couldn't guarantee a nude-free environment. The game was to be aired during halftime of the Super Bowl. Talk about a potential wardrobe malfunction.

As for biking naked on federal land, B.G. of Bare Buns Bikers is correct that there are no federal laws against nudity, but some national parks honor local restrictions. Discretion is advised.

Lenton-Smith. Peter. "Nudists Want to Vote Naked." MyFox Tampa Bay.com, October 31, 2008.

Reeves, Terri Bryce. "Land O'Lakes Collector Attempts Movie Camera Record in Clearwater." *St. Petersburg Times*, November 6, 2009.

Sullivan, Erin. "An Art Buff's Colorful Journey." *St. Petersburg Times*, May 14, 2007.

**LYNN WADDELL** is a freelance journalist whose work has appeared in *Newsweek,* the *New York Times,* the *Wall Street Journal,* the Daily Beast.com, and the *Christian Science Monitor.* She previously worked as a staff writer at the *Weekly Planet* (*Creative Loafing*), the *Las Vegas Sun,* and the *Birmingham News.* She received her master's degree as a Poynter Fellow at the University of South Florida and a bachelor's degree from the University of Alabama. She and her husband, James, live in St. Petersburg, Florida.

The University Press of Florida is the scholarly publishing agency for the State University System of Florida, comprising Florida A&M University, Florida Atlantic University, Florida Gulf Coast University, Florida International University, Florida State University, New College of Florida, University of Central Florida, University of Florida, University of North Florida, University of South Florida, and University of West Florida.